SECURITY
IN A SMALL NATION

Security in a Small Nation

Scotland, Democracy, Politics

Edited by Andrew W. Neal
Centre for Security Research
University of Edinburgh

OpenBook Publishers

https://www.openbookpublishers.com

All external links were active at the time of publication unless otherwise stated and have been archived via the Internet Archive Wayback Machine at https://archive.org/web

Digital material and resources associated with this volume are available at https://www.openbookpublishers.com/product/524#resources

Every effort has been made to identify and contact copyright holders and any omission or error will be corrected if notification is made to the publisher.

Open Reports Series, vol. 4 | ISSN: 2399-6668 (Print); 2399-6676 (Online)

ISBN Paperback: 978-1-78374-268-4
ISBN Hardback: 978-1-78374-269-1
ISBN Digital (PDF): 978-1-78374-270-7
ISBN Digital ebook (epub): 978-1-78374-271-4
ISBN Digital ebook (mobi): 978-1-78374-272-1
DOI: 10.11647/OBP.0078

Cover image: Scottish Parliament (2011) by deargdoom57, CC BY 2.0. Image from Flickr, https://www.flickr.com/photos/deargdoom57/5471878523/

All paper used by Open Book Publishers is SFI (Sustainable Forestry Initiative), PEFC (Programme for the Endorsement of Forest Certification Schemes) and Forest Stewardship Council(r)(FSC(r) certified.

Printed in the United Kingdom, United States, and Australia
by Lightning Source for Open Book Publishers (Cambridge, UK)

Dedicated to the memory of Alyson J. K. Bailes

Contents

Acknowledgements

This book is the product of a seminar series funded by the UK Economic and Social Research Council entitled 'Security in Scotland, with or without constitutional change', which ran from 2013–2015 at the University of Edinburgh (grant reference ES/L00139X/1). The Reports from this seminar series can be found on the title page on the Open Book Publishers website, http://www.openbookpublishers.com/product/524#resources

The editor and principal investigator Andrew W. Neal would like to thank his primary co-investigators, Juliet Kaarbo and Charles Raab, for their wisdom and advice throughout the project. Special thanks to Colin Atkinson for editorial assistance in the early stages of the book project. Thanks also to the many contributors to the seminars, including Stine Bergersen, Didier Bigo, Paul Cairney, Monica den Boer, Francesca Dickson, Faye Donnelly, Gunilla Eriksson, Peter Gill, Jens Christian Svabo Justinussen, Bill Paterson, Paul Rogers, Stephen Tierney, William Vlcek, and others who will remain unnamed due to the political and professional sensitivities of the subject matter.

Notes on Contributors

Colin Atkinson is Lecturer in Criminology and Criminal Justice at the University of the West of Scotland. His research interests focus mainly upon the intersection of crime, policing, intelligence and security, particularly as these issues relate to terrorism and organised crime. Colin has a professional background in intelligence analysis and counter-terrorism. He holds several degrees, most recently achieving an MLitt in terrorism studies (with distinction) from the University of St Andrews and a PhD in sociology from the University of Glasgow. His research has appeared in several peer-reviewed journals. Colin is an associate editor for the journal *Criminology and Criminal Justice*.

Alyson J. K. Bailes was a full-time Visiting Professor at the University of Iceland from 2007 to 2016 and taught at several universities in Europe, including the College of Europe in Bruges, Belgium. She previously served in the British Diplomatic Service for thirty-three years. Bailes was the United Kingdom Ambassador to Finland from 2000 to 2002, Political Director of the Western European Union from 1997 to 2000 and Director of the Stockholm International Peace Research Institute (SIPRI) from 2002 to 2007. Bailes published extensively on European defence, arms control, Arctic security, small states and the Nordic states' foreign policies and edited several books on these subjects. Bailes passed away in April 2016.

Thierry Balzacq is Francqui Research Chair (the most prestigious academic title awarded in Belgium) and Visiting Professor at the London School of Economics and Political Science (LSE). He was the Scientific Director of the Institute for Strategic Research (IRSEM), the French Ministry of Defense's research center (2014–2016). A former Postdoctoral Fellow at Harvard, Balzacq held a Honorary Professorial Fellowship at the University of Edinburgh. In 2015, he was awarded a

Tier 1 Canada Research Chair in Diplomacy and International Security for his world-leading research. He is author/editor of over twelve books in English and French.

Hugh Bochel is Professor of Public Policy at the University of Lincoln. He has wide-ranging interests in British politics and public policy. He is co-author, with Andrew Defty and Jane Kirkpatrick, of *Watching the Watchers: Parliament and the Intelligence Services* (2014).

Nick Brooke is a Teaching Fellow in the Centre for the Study of Terrorism and Political Violence at the University of St Andrews, where he completed his Masters and PhD. Nick teaches at undergraduate and Masters level on topics such as terrorism, nationalism and violence in deeply-divided societies. His research interests include nationalism and terrorism, the relationship between violent and non-violent forms of political protest, the depiction of terrorism and politics in popular culture and the impact of nationalism on British politics.

Andrew Defty is Reader in Politics at the University of Lincoln. He has written widely on parliament and the intelligence services. He is co-author, with Hugh Bochel and Jane Kirkpatrick, of *Watching the Watchers: Parliament and the Intelligence Services* (2014).

Sandy Hardie was a career member of the Diplomatic Service (1973–2001). He later (2005–2012) worked on security sector reform with African and other governments. In the Scottish referendum campaign (2013–2014), he supported Better Together as an adviser on national security issues.

Brian Harris is a criminal psychologist with a background from the policing, military and government sectors of countering terrorism. His experience stems from operations, organisational planning and industry resilience against acts of terrorism. He now conducts research into terrorism and its societal impact, and he specialises on terrorism and the aviation industry. He has over twenty years' operational experience in this field. Brian holds an MBA (distinction) and an Honours Grade BSc in Criminology and Psychology. He is a visiting lecturer at Napier University and is currently finalising his PhD at the University of St Andrews.

Juliet Kaarbo is Professor of International Relations with a Chair in Foreign Policy at the University of Edinburgh. She is founding co-director of Edinburgh's Centre for Security Research. Her research focuses on political psychology, leadership and decision making, group dynamics, foreign policy analysis and theory, parliamentary political systems, and national roles, and her work has appeared in journals such as *International Studies Quarterly*, *European Journal of International Relations*, *International Studies Review*, and *Political Psychology*.

Daniel Kenealy is a Lecturer based at the University of Edinburgh's School of Social and Political Science, where he researches and teaches British government and foreign policy. His work has been published in journals such as *European Security*, *Journal of European Integration*, *West European Politics*, and *Millennium*.

Andrew W. Neal is a Senior Lecturer in Politics and International Relations at the University of Edinburgh and co-director of the Centre for Security Research (CeSeR). He is the author of *Exceptionalism and the Politics of Counter-Terrorism* (2010); co-editor, with Jef Huysmans, Claudia Aradau and Nadine Voelkner, of *Critical Security Methods* (2014); and co-editor, with Michael Dillon, of *Foucault on Politics, Security and War* (2008). He was principal investigator of the ESRC seminar series 'Security in Scotland, with or without constitutional change' (2013–2015), and is currently finalising a monograph on security politics and professional politicians.

Eamonn O'Neill is an Associate Professor in Journalism at Edinburgh Napier University. He is also an internationally and nationally award-winning investigative journalist. He has authored articles and chapters in recent years related to investigative journalism in theory and practice. He is a regular contributor to BBC Scotland.

Charles Raab is Professorial Fellow at the University of Edinburgh and Director of the Centre for Research into Information, Surveillance and Privacy (CRISP). He co-chairs the Independent Digital Ethics Panel for Policing (IDEPP), established by the UK National Police Chiefs' Council. He has conducted research and published extensively on privacy, data protection, surveillance, and security. He gave evidence to UK parliamentary committees (e.g., Intelligence and Security Committee, 2014), and was the Specialist Adviser to the House of Lords Constitution Committee for their inquiry, *Surveillance: Citizens and the State*, HL Paper 18, Session 2008–2009.

Baldur Thorhallsson is Head and Professor at the Faculty of Political Science at the University of Iceland. He is also Jean Monnet Chair in European Studies, and Programme and Research Director at the Centre for Small States at the University of Iceland. He established the Centre for Small State Studies in 2002. His research focus is primarily on small state studies, European integration and Iceland's foreign policy. He has published extensively in international journals, contributed to several academic books and written two books on small states in Europe. He holds a PhD (1999) and MA (1994) in Political Science from the University of Essex in England.

Introduction

Andrew W. Neal

This introduction begins by discussing the meaning and scope of 'security' in the context of the national independence of small states. It then summarises the main points of contention over security in the debate about Scottish independence during the 2014 referendum, including issues of intelligence sharing, border control, policing, resilience planning, cybersecurity, and economic security. It considers the security experiences of some other small European countries, and also the implications of developments since 2014, particularly the Brexit vote. The final section discusses the ESRC seminar series from which this book was produced, and the organisation and content of the chapters.

    https://doi.org/10.11647/OBP.0078.10

Questions about 'security' provide a lens that brings issues of national independence into sharp focus. In the first instance, security concerns the ability of a state to protect its inhabitants from danger. The idea that security is the first responsibility of government has long been a political mantra. But choosing strategies to ensure a country's effective security often entails a tension between the protection of its citizens and their individual freedom. Ensuring that citizens are safe from the excesses of state power, for example through guarantees of privacy and human rights, becomes central to the security debate. Such issues are interwoven with the country's particular style of politics and democracy. Seen in such a light, we must ask what exactly it is that needs to be 'secured'. In the context of national independence, the answer often goes beyond basic survival; it involves values, culture, prosperity, and the place of a state and its people in the world.

The chapters in this book reflect upon the security questions raised by the prospect of Scottish independence from the United Kingdom. Despite a victory for the No side in the 2014 referendum, these questions have not gone away. The vote did not settle the issue of independence for a generation as Unionists hoped it would. The Scottish National Party (SNP) went on to win a landslide of Scottish Westminster seats at the 2015 General Election and remained the governing party of Scotland in the 2016 Scottish Parliament elections. At the time of writing, after the UK's vote to leave the European Union in June 2016, the Scottish First Minister, Nicola Sturgeon, is touting independence as a way to keep Scotland in the EU. There is every chance that Scotland may revisit the question of independence, and thus inevitably the question of Scottish national security, sooner rather than later.

Elsewhere, separatism within other EU member states is still firmly on the agenda, most notably in Spain. And the UK's decision to leave the EU — otherwise known as Brexit — may be the beginning of a major regional, institutional, and geopolitical shakeup. It could have a domino effect, prompting other member states to demand their independence from the EU too. In all cases, independence is not so much an answer but a series of further questions. Independence from what, and to do what? What 'security' would such independence bring? And could a small, newly independent state fare better against forces that even the biggest and most 'secure' states seem unable to control, such as migration, capital flows, and new technologies of communication and social organisation?

There are many current crises that make the true 'independence' of states uncertain. The financial crisis of 2008 has ongoing implications for the financial independence of small states such as Iceland and Greece, as it would for Scotland if it were to become independent, with lingering issues of budgetary deficit and national debt. Terrorist attacks in continental Europe and the Middle East raise questions about the permeability of borders, the effectiveness of international security cooperation, and the intelligence and counter-terrorist capabilities of states, small and large. For example, the police and intelligence services of Belgium — a binational state, the unity of which is consequently sometimes strained — were heavily criticised in the wake of the Brussels airport attack of 22 March 2016.[1] So too were the French services in a high-level review of their responses to the Bataclan attacks.[2]

The issue of security crystallises these questions. Could a newly independent state prevent such challenges from becoming existential crises? What help would it need, and could it expect, from elsewhere? The Scottish independence referendum, its politics and debates, and the successes and failures of its campaigns, bring these issues into sharp relief. Although the experience of the 2014 referendum is now history, the lessons it offers remain current. The debate over Scotland's future continues, and the Scottish experience provides a salient example for other parts of the world that face constitutional challenge and upheaval.

Security in small nations

Security has always been a policy area of special importance, and the events of 11 September 2001 elevated it even higher on government agendas. The perceived threat level in many parts of the world has not since abated. Threats are seen as greater and more numerous in all too many cases.

---

1   Jack Moore, 'Brussels Attacks: Belgian Intelligence Services "Overwhelmed and Outnumbered" by Jihadis', *Newsweek*, 22 March 2016, http://europe.newsweek.com/belgiums-security-services-overwhelmed-and-outnumbered-jihadi-threat-439490

2   Sébastien Pietrasanta, *Au nom de la commission d'enquête relative aux moyens mis en œuvre par l'État pour lutter contre le terrorisme depuis le 7 janvier 2015* (Paris: Assemblée Nationale, 2016), http://www.assemblee-nationale.fr/14/pdf/rap-enq/r3922-t1.pdf

In the intervening decade and a half, the meaning and application of 'security' have not remained the same. Security was traditionally understood as the domain of high politics, commanders-in-chief, militaries, foreign policy, intelligence agencies, and special branches of police. In many countries this legacy has now been supplemented by comprehensive national security strategies; 'whole of government' approaches; national risk assessments encompassing every area of social, political, and economic life; and new forms of security governance covering such diverse areas as cyber, health, environment, energy, and food. The issue of security now encompasses more than the threats a country faces. Security — and the management of *insecurities* — has become an extensive governmental activity involving multiple departments and agencies, both within and across states.[3]

Any examination of state security requires us to consider not only practices of government, but also matters of politics. Liberal democratic governments do not legislate without the public justification of policies and decisions. Ideally, such governments would face constant scrutiny by parliaments, the media, experts, and an engaged public. Historically, however, security has often been shielded from the public eye, confined to the opaque domains of the military and secret intelligence. The wider political class was traditionally kept at arm's length from security governance through mechanisms of official secrecy and limited democratic oversight. Despite increased transparency since the end of the Cold War — for example, the varying degrees of intelligence oversight reform in many countries, including the UK — these obscuring mechanisms still exist. Nevertheless, despite on-going forms of secrecy, the expansion of the meaning and practice of security resulted in broader political examination in recent years. For example, the security of energy supplies, food, health, and the cyber domain do not arouse the same jealous protection of sovereign prerogative as secret intelligence does, and so allows greater scrutiny, deliberation, and contestation.

But exposing security to more political debate and oversight poses problems of ethics and responsibility, which the Scottish referendum

---

3   Didier Bigo, 'Internal and External Aspects of Security', *European Security*, 15, 4
     (2006), 385–404; Didier Bigo, 'Security and Immigration, toward a Critique of the
     Governmentality of Unease', *Alternatives: Global, Local, Political*, 27: 1 (2002), 63–92.

exposed. To what extent should security be politicised? Should its existential importance elevate it above partisanship, as was traditionally the case in the British system?[4] The opportunities for sensationalism that are provided by public security discourse pose a challenge to this tradition. It is difficult for democratic deliberation on security to proceed in an informed, balanced, and rational way when faced with the rhetorical temptations of scaremongering and scapegoating. When dealing with the uncertainties of unknown futures, the politics of fear can be all too effective (as the No campaign in the Scottish referendum showed in a more general sense). Another way to look at this is that it is difficult to oppose policies that claim to increase our security when so much of the necessary information is kept secret by the state. It remains the case that, despite the expansion of the meaning and practice of security, at its core it remains a deeply institutionalised part of state authority, arguably the *raison d'être* of the state itself.

In contrast to these entrenched national security traditions, the politics of national independence are the politics of the new. Proponents call for novel ways of organising social, political, and economic life, free from the structures and constraints of old practices. The Scottish referendum created the opportunity to re-examine the workings of every part of the modern state, including its security apparatus. How much exists for historical path-dependent reasons, rather than by design? Would a new beginning offer the chance to create better ways of doing things? For example, the number and structure of the intelligence agencies in a given country is often the product of historical circumstance. While many small European countries have police and military-based agencies, the UK has separate civilian-based domestic, foreign, and signals (communications and cyberspace) intelligence services (MI5, MI6, and Government Communications Headquarters (GCHQ)).

In its proposals for an independent Scotland, the Scottish Government produced a comparatively radical idea for a single integrated intelligence agency (for further discussion see Chapter 5 in the present volume). If ened, this may have posed problems, such as the concentration of powers of state intrusion in a single agency, but it could also have been a more

---

4   H. Bochel, A. Defty, and J. Kirkpatrick, *Watching the Watchers: Parliament and the Intelligence Services* (Basingstoke: Palgrave Macmillan, 2014), p. 27.

efficient way to tackle security issues in a world where the lines between domestic, foreign, and signals domains are increasingly blurred.

Yet old structures and constraints cannot be made to disappear overnight, even if constitutional relationships change. Embarking on a new path entails a continuing negotiation with the old. Physical geography is fixed, and imbalances in power and resources remain. And while much is fluid in twenty-first century security governance, many of its edifices remain entrenched. Military restructuring, for example, can take decades, especially if new equipment is to be procured or bases are to be moved. These changes can have major implications for local and national economies, and are thoroughly political for the constituencies and interests involved. This was a prominent issue in the politics of Scottish independence, most obviously with the potential relocation of Trident, but also with the future of the Royal Air Force bases on the east coast of Scotland and naval shipbuilding on the Clyde and Forth. The longevity of security apparatuses applies not just to military hardware, but also to security knowledge, authority, and relationships. For example, a newly independent state could indeed create a new intelligence agency, but what depth of experience and knowledge would it have? What sources of intelligence could it access? What cooperative arrangements would it have with allies? And what recognition would it receive domestically and internationally as a credible security authority?

This project

The chapters in this book are the product of a seminar series called 'Security in Scotland, with or without constitutional change', hosted by the University of Edinburgh in partnership with the Universities of St Andrews and Namur, Belgium. The seminars ran from 2013 to 2015 and were funded by the UK Economic and Social Research Council (ESRC) under the umbrella of the wider 'Future of the UK and Scotland' research programme. The seminars began a year before the referendum and concluded a year afterwards. Our main aim was to inform public debate on the security issues posed by Scottish independence. We did this by publishing a number of reports, which went on to feature in the national press.[5] We also aimed to create a new Scotland-based forum for security research and policy dialogue, which we did by creating a new research centre at the University of Edinburgh: the Centre for Security Research or CeSeR. The seminars brought together academic experts, parliamentarians from Westminster and Holyrood, civil servants from the Scottish and UK services, and police, security, and intelligence practitioners, some serving, some retired. The seminars were closed-door events, held under the Chatham House Rule (meaning no public identification of the speakers or attribution of what they said). This rule is never ideal in terms of public dialogue and transparency, but it is often the only basis under which it is possible to have frank discussions with professionals who occupy sensitive or formally impartial positions (for further discussion of the dilemmas of public security discourse, see Chapter 8 in this volume).

The chapters included in this volume represent a core selection of the issues that were covered. Note that we make a distinction between 'security' and 'defence', and although the two are connected, we concentrate primarily on the former. We take security to denote the broadening subject discussed above, while defence relates more to military matters such as troop levels, hardware, bases, broad geostrategic issues, and indeed Trident. Note that the Scottish and UK Governments both made this distinction in their pre-referendum publications, with the Scottish Government White Paper *Scotland's Future* presenting separate chapters on 'International Relations and Defence' and 'Justice, Security and Home Affairs', and the UK Government publishing separate *Scotland Analysis* papers on 'Security' and 'Defence'. We do, however, discuss foreign policy and alliances in our first two chapters. The book aims to reflect on the issues of broadest relevance beyond the immediate demands of the Scottish context, while also being able to inform any future Scottish independence debate. Much was discussed in the seminars that is too specialised or contextual for wider debates about security, such as the internal

---

5   The Reports from this seminar series can be found on the title page on the Open Book Publishers website, http://www.openbookpublishers.com/product/524#resources. They can also be found on the website of the Centre on Constitutional Change, http://www.centreonconstitutionalchange.ac.uk/tags/security-defence

workings of the Scottish police and resilience apparatus (which entails responding to, and recovering from, civil emergencies), or the place of Scotland in the UK National Security Strategy (constitutionally speaking, national security is an area 'reserved' to Westminster, but the broad scope of the security risks and challenges currently envisaged by the UK NSS entails roles and responsibilities for many levels of government, including the Scottish Government). The seminars also covered much that cannot be included for simple reasons of space; for example, we would need another volume to include all the expert analysis we invited from other small countries and territories such as Ireland, the Netherlands, Norway, Sweden, Finland, and the Faroe Islands. This introduction will instead touch on some of this, Chapter 2 discusses Nordic comparisons in depth, and Chapter 5 discusses Norwegian and Belgian intelligence arrangements.

The book focuses on three core themes, presented in three sections, which can be seen as three levels of analysis. They are: (1) small states and security, (2) democratic accountability and oversight, and (3) security, politics, and public debate.

The first concerns the international relations of small states, and the possibilities and limits of independence. The two chapters here discuss the foreign policy of small states (Chapter 1, by Juliet Kaarbo and Daniel Kenealy) and their alliances (Chapter 2, by Baldur Thorhallsson and Alyson J. K. Bailes) through the prism of Scotland.

The second section concerns what are, broadly speaking, constitutional questions of the relationship between democracy, security, and, particularly, intelligence and surveillance. These fraught issues are active and topical in many contexts, including the UK, EU, US, and many small states, particularly since the leaks by Edward Snowden. The first chapter in this section examines the competing meanings and interpretations of security in different national contexts (Chapter 3, by Charles D. Raab); the second considers lessons from Westminster on the reform of parliamentary intelligence oversight (Chapter 4, by Hugh Bochel and Andrew Defty); while the third analyses the politics, practicalities, and implications of the pre-referendum Scottish Government proposals for intelligence oversight in an independent Scotland (Chapter 5, by Colin Atkinson, Nick Brooke and Brian Harris).

The third section concerns micro-level analysis of the political cut-and-thrust of the referendum campaigns, and the ways in which security issues were presented and constructed by the competing sides and the media. The first chapter in this section examines the extent and depth of public debate on intelligence in the campaigns (Chapter 6, by Sandy Hardie); the second assesses how the media handled the issues (Chapter 7, by Eamonn P. O'Neill), while the third considers the ethical dilemmas involved in political debate on security (Chapter 8, by Andrew W. Neal).

The context

The enquiries and discussions in our seminars illuminated much about the modern-day business of security governance. While the temptation in public debate and much of academic scholarship is to look directly at key security decisions made at the highest state level, the practice of security governance is in fact a complex and multi-layered affair. In focusing on Scotland — a partially autonomous region and constituent nation of the United Kingdom with devolved government — it becomes clear that security is not the concern of central government alone, despite national security being a 'reserved area' under the terms of the 1998 Scotland Act.[6] This multi-level complexity is true of developments in security governance in other comparable countries too. One effect of the expansion of the concept of security into a more encompassing risk-based concern is that many more partners and agencies become involved. Beyond the traditional intelligence services, branches of the military, and police forces, security governance increasingly involves local and regional government, private security companies offering personnel and specialised technical services, critical infrastructure providers such as water, power, and transport companies, and local stakeholders such as businesses and community groups.

This kind of complex security governance poses a number of challenges. In the first instance, effective means must be found for agencies to communicate and work together. For example, as mentioned above, a lack of cross-agency coordination and communication in counter-terrorism has attracted criticism in Belgium and France during the last twelve months. Further afield, and with a very different kind of threat, the devastating effect of Hurricane Katrina on New Orleans

---

6   UK Government, *Scotland Act 1998* (London: HMSO, 1998), http://www.legislation.gov.uk/ukpga/1998/46/pdfs/ukpga_19980046_en.pdf

demonstrated the consequences of inept contingency planning and emergency response, and a lack of investment in resilient infrastructure. Addressing these needs can be difficult. For example, many countries have institutional barriers between intelligence agencies and police forces. Sometimes this is by design, in order to prevent the emergence of monolithic centralised security apparatuses (an important concern in countries that have experienced totalitarian forms of government). In other cases the reasons may be more to do with 'turf wars' or historical contingencies; for example, the Nordic countries have more centralised models of policing than the Netherlands or the UK, which have stronger traditions of local autonomy. Despite fears about the growth of security states, there remain many examples of disjointed surveillance, intelligence, and security governance.

In the UK, these multi-level arrangements are not necessarily directly managed from the centre. The Scottish Government has invested much time and effort to pursue its own distinctive way of doing things in certain aspects of security governance, such as with its policing and resilience planning. The 2004 Civil Contingencies Act created a statutory duty for local government to plan and prepare for emergencies and the Scottish Government has taken this a step further. It claims to be 'world leading' in developing a high degree of integration and interoperability between its emergency responders, and has also created its own 'horizon scanning' capabilities.[7] It has created unitary police and fire services for Scotland, which depart from the localised arrangements that existed before and go against a longstanding British tradition of suspicion towards large-scale, centralised, and potentially repressive police forces — a suspicion which can be traced back to the creation of the Metropolitan Police by Sir Robert Peel in the nineteenth century.

Scotland's efforts in security governance, and particularly in resilience planning, have gone well in the sense that there have been few major failures (although problems arising from the implementation of police centralisation led to the resignation of the Police Scotland Chief Constable Sir Stephen House in 2015). Severe winter weather

---

7   Scottish Government, *Preparing Scotland: Scottish Guidance on Resilience, Philosophy, Principles, Structures and Regulatory Duties* (Edinburgh, 2016), http://www.ready scotland.org/media/1166/preparing-scotland-philosophy-principles-structures-and-regulatory-duties-20-july-2016.pdf

caused major traffic disruptions in 2010 and focused government minds on developing resilience capabilities further. Compare this to the Netherlands, where efforts to create a national police force were resisted by local mayors and police unions, and eventually had to be pushed through by the central government.[8] Scotland's efforts in these areas have probably benefited from having a relatively small, non-hierarchical, and centralised form of devolved government.

Beyond this internal focus, multilevel interagency cooperation in the UK-Scotland security relationship has gone well too. For example, the security operation at the 2014 Glasgow Commonwealth Games was widely hailed as a success. It featured complex coordination between Scottish and UK agencies, including multiple police forces, the military, and the security services, as well as several private security providers. This of course raises the question of what would replace the capabilities provided by this cooperation in the event of Scottish independence.

The fact that the SNP Scottish Government has invested in resilience and interagency interoperability is not separable from the politics of independence. Making Scotland more capable and state-like may ease any future transition to independence. It is also performative in the way it makes Scotland *appear* more state-like. A similar example is its foreign aid programme in Africa, which is not normally something that sub-state regional governments do, and which makes the idea of independence less of an imaginative leap. However, the political significance of these investments does not diminish the immediate practical importance of resilience capabilities in Scotland, which has more extreme weather and terrain than the wider UK, and a more unevenly distributed population, both of which pose particular challenges to communities and critical infrastructure. It is notable that these areas of resilience investment are in non-traditional aspects of security governance, where the meaning of 'security' is broader than national security.

In the more traditional areas of national security and intelligence, Scotland is still reliant on the UK. For example, in our seminars it was shown that the specialist crime division of Police Scotland, which lists counter-terrorism among its tasks, depends on support from MI5 on

---

8   Jan Terpstra and Nicholas R. Fyfe, 'Mind the Implementation Gap? Police Reform and Local Policing in the Netherlands and Scotland', *Criminology and Criminal Justice*, 15, 5 (2015), pp. 527–44 (pp. 532–34).

a daily basis. Similarly, in cybersecurity, despite hosting a successful IT sector, Scotland depends on high-level cyber defences provided by GCHQ and the Centre for the Protection of National Infrastructure. Small states can and do provide for their own security in the cyber domain (Finland is a world leader, for example), but these capabilities cannot be created overnight. This is especially important in knowledge-based economies, where industrial espionage and intellectual property theft could dent the attractiveness of a country to businesses and foreign investors. Note that the first objective of the 2011–2015 UK cyber security strategy was to make the UK the 'one of the most secure places in the world to do business online', and it is not clear how an independent Scotland could compete on those terms.[9]

Geography and the legacy of traditional security structures may be difficult to change, but they are not completely hard facts that remove choice and interpretation from government and politics. They represent a context of historical and geographical experience that policymakers and populations can approach in different ways. For example, Finland's international and security outlook has been inseparable from its proximity to Russia. This has shaped its foreign policy, with neutrality in the Cold War followed by a gradual edging towards NATO since the 1990s. Although Finland's geostrategic position may be seen as a constraint, this has also been the source of a strong tradition of security independence and its doctrine of 'total defence'.[10] This is a comprehensive national security model that reaches deep into Finnish social, political, and economic life, featuring, for example, conscription and public/private partnerships for national infrastructure protection.

Similarly, any vision for Scotland's future security would be profoundly shaped by its history in the United Kingdom. This has no doubt produced political differences within Scotland, and between Scotland and the rest of the UK. The politicisation of Trident is the obvious example of cleavage, with a decades-old Scottish hostility to the presence of a nuclear base on the Clyde dovetailing with Scottish

---

9   Cabinet Office, *The UK Cyber Security Strategy Protecting and Promoting the UK in a Digital World* (London, 2011), https://www.gov.uk/government/uploads/system/uploads/attachment_data/file/60961/uk-cyber-security-strategy-final.pdf

10   R. E. J. Penttila, *Finland's Search for Security through Defence, 1944–89* (Basingstoke and New York: Palgrave Macmillan UK, 1991), p. 89.

separatism. The Iraq war also contributed to a sense of alienation from political institutions throughout the UK. Scottish Nationalist politicians have been able to channel this alienation into the idea of an alternative, independent Scottish future. Yet Scotland's history in the UK also shapes aspects of its international outlook. For example, while SNP policy is to remove Trident from Scottish territory, in 2012 the party reversed its thirty-year-old policy of opposition to NATO, which is ultimately a nuclear defence alliance. In contrast, the radical left parts of the pro-independence Yes campaign, which included the Scottish Green Party and the Scottish Socialist Party, remain committed at the time of writing to unilateral nuclear disarmament and Scotland's exit from NATO.[11]

Similarly, the vision of independence produced by the SNP Scottish Government in its 2013 White Paper did not represent a radical break from UK foreign policy traditions. Although it proposed stronger constitutional safeguards on executive war powers and better human rights protections (no doubt a reaction to the politics of the Iraq War and the wider 'war on terror'), it did not suggest a retreat from international affairs, nor anything resembling the post-Cold-War quasi-neutrality of Finland or Ireland. Following the Irish example in particular could have made some sense, given the smallness of the two countries, their connections to the UK, their relatively limited resources, and perhaps even small-scale parallels such as the presence of sectarian divisions and organised crime as internal security priorities. However, the limited 'Irish model' of security and international relations did not even enter the debate. The 'Nordic model' was more often cited, particularly the Danish model of international engagement (Thorhallsson and Bailes discuss small states and alliances in detail in Chapter 2). Despite more radical views on the left of Scottish politics, the SNP remains internationalist, Atlanticist, and Europeanist in outlook. Although its immediate policies depart from the misadventures of UK foreign policy of the past fifteen years, they do not depart from older British traditions of international engagement. The proposals by the Scottish Government in 2013 for an independent Scotland to claim a bigger regional maritime role could even have created greater tension with Russia, particularly

---

11   [N.a.], 'Who We Are', No to NATO Scotland Coalition (2016), http://notonato scotland.org.uk/index.html%3Fpage_id=201.html

given Arctic climate change and the possibility of increased northern shipping and resource extraction.

One major division to emerge between Scotland the rest of the UK concerns the EU and immigration. In the Brexit referendum, the Scottish electorate voted more strongly in favour of remaining in the EU than the rest of the country, with a 62/38 pro-remain split rather than the 48/52 of the UK overall. While at the time of writing it is difficult to envisage how Brexit will play out for the UK and Scotland, the issue has magnified existing political differences. Majority opinion among Scottish politicians has long been against restrictive UK immigration policy, and indeed the 2013 White Paper called for higher levels of immigration in a future independent Scotland.[12] Despite this, Scottish public attitudes to immigration are not so different from those of the wider UK population: a 2015 YouGov poll suggested that 49% of Scots wanted to see less immigration, exactly the same proportion as in the rest of Britain.[13] Based on data from the British Social Attitudes Survey, The Migration Observatory at the University of Oxford states that 'Existing evidence clearly shows high levels of opposition to immigration in the UK'.[14] Yet in the wake of the Brexit referendum, Scottish politicians of all parties have been vocal in trying to reassure resident EU nationals that they remain welcome in Scotland.

How an immigration policy that diverges from that of the remaining UK could work in practice is difficult to imagine. If an independent Scotland remained in the EU while the UK left, this would presumably necessitate some kind of border control to prevent non-UK citizens crossing from Scotland into England via an open border. Given the extent to which freedom of movement in the EU has been politicised and even securitised — for example, former UKIP leader Nigel Farage blamed freedom of movement for the apparent ease with which ISIS militants

---

12 Scottish Government, *Scotland's Future: Your Guide to an Independent Scotland* (Edinburgh: Scottish Government, 2013), http://www.gov.scot/resource/0043/0043 9021.pdf

13 Scott MacNab, 'Immigration: Scots "No More Tolerant Than English"', *Scotsman*, 28 July 2015, http://www.scotsman.com/news/politics/immigration-scots-no-more-tolerant-than-english-1-3714620

14 Scott Blinder and William L. Allen, *UK Public Opinion toward Immigration: Overall Attitudes and Level of Concern* (Oxford: The Migration Observatory, 2016), p. 4, http://www.migrationobservatory.ox.ac.uk/wp-content/uploads/2016/04/Briefing-Public_Opinion_Immigration_Attitudes_Concern.pdf

and weapons made their way to France and Belgium before the attacks in November 2015 and March 2016 — this could prove controversial.[15] More prosaically, because Scotland trades far more with the rest of the UK than with the EU and the rest of the world (perhaps more than twice as much, although the figures are not firm),[16] a hard border would have negative effects on Scotland's economy if it hindered the movement of goods, services and people within Great Britain.

The Brexit vote, and the renewed prospect of Scottish independence as a response, revived some of the thorniest issues from the 2014 referendum, raising questions that would be fundamental to Scottish statehood: what currency would an independent Scotland use? Would it be too risky for the Scottish economy to rely on oil and gas revenues (which have declined significantly since 2014)? At the same time, the Brexit vote has made Scotland appear more state-like, with First Minister Nicola Sturgeon active in 'paradiplomacy' to the EU, looking for a way for Scotland to remain a member or achieve some kind of special status.

In the pre-referendum Brexit debate there was some discussion of the security benefits of EU membership, with prominent former members of the UK intelligence community vocal in their views. Sir John Sawers, former head of MI6, argued that EU systems for sharing information on, for example, the movement of suspect individuals, were an increasingly important part of security governance.[17] Brexit could mean UK exclusion from shaping the development of such systems, although not necessarily from the sharing of information itself. In other areas of EU security the UK had already excluded itself before the EU referendum, playing no formal part in the EU external borders agency Frontex or its successor, the recently approved European Border and Coast Guard Agency. In contrast, the European Arrest Warrant has been used extensively in UK law enforcement. The Quilliam Foundation, a counter-extremism think tank, produced a comprehensive report on this question based on

---

15   Stone, Jon, 'Nigel Farage Says the EU Has Allowed the "Free Movement of Kalashnikov Rifles and Jihadists"', *Independent*, 17 November 2015, http://www.independent.co.uk/news/uk/politics/nigel-farage-says-the-eu-has-allowed-the-free-movement-of-kalashnikov-rifles-and-jihadists-a6737501.html

16   [N.a.], 'Does Scotland Export Twice as Much to England as It Does to the Rest of the World?' (2012), https://fullfact.org/economy/does-scotland-export-twice-much-england-it-does-rest-world; Blinder and Allen (2016).

17   'Row as Ex-Intelligence Chiefs Say EU Membership Protects UK Security', *BBC News*, 8 May 2016, http://www.bbc.co.uk/news/uk-36239741

interviews with twenty high profile security experts including senior British politicians. They concluded that Brexit would not preclude security cooperation between the UK and the EU, and that much of the UK's international security cooperation — particularly intelligence sharing — 'will continue to predominantly take place bilaterally and with the Five Eyes alliance'.[18] Brexit will not affect the UK's place in NATO, and may even increase its commitment to the alliance. In many ways the debate about Brexit and security is inconclusive, in part because there is no EU security 'model' but rather a complex patchwork of agreements and information-sharing arrangements that include EU member states and non-member states.[19]

What Brexit means for the national security of an independent Scotland is therefore not clear either. Given that most UK security governance does not depend on the EU, the UK would appear to be a more important security partner to Scotland than the EU or the rest of its members. Yet there is no guarantee that an independent Scotland either inside or outside the EU would become the 'sixth eye' of the Five Eyes intelligence-sharing arrangement between the UK, US, Canada, Australia and New Zealand. Arguably it would be in the interests of the remaining UK to have close security cooperation with an independent Scotland, as suggested by the Scottish Government White Paper, but there are obstacles here. For example, sharing US intelligence with Scotland would not be in the gift of the UK because of the 'control principle', which prevents intelligence sharing with third parties (for detailed analysis, see Chapters 5 and 7 in this volume). There would also be oversight issues for Holyrood if the UK intelligence services continued to operate in Scotland.

These questions about a future security relationship between an independent Scotland and the rest of the UK are to an extent unanswerable. They depend on future political positions, relationships, and good will that the various 'sides' do not wish to reveal now or cannot know in the present. On the one hand, any concession from Unionists

---

18   Maajid Nawaz and Julia Ebner, 'The EU and Terrorism: Is Britain Safer in or Out?' (London: Quilliam, 2016), http://www.quilliamfoundation.org/press/quilliam-releases-report-on-the-eu-and-terrorism-is-britain-safer-in-or-out/

19   Mapping this field has been a long-running task of Didier Bigo and his colleagues. See D. Bigo and E. Guild, *Europe's 21st Century Challenge: Delivering Liberty* (Farnham and Burlington: Ashgate, 2010).

to the idea of future security cooperation would be a concession to the viability of Scottish independence itself, and so politically unpalatable. On the other hand, the Nationalist interest in projecting reassurance and optimism about security issues might compromise the credibility of their arguments. It is for these reasons that the future of security cooperation between the UK and Scotland in the event of independence is as much a political question as an analytical one, and this is reflected in the focus of this book.

Conclusion

Security in a Small Nation offers a range of expert analysis on these issues. The perspectives of the authors reflect a variety of specialisms, including foreign policy, surveillance and privacy issues, parliamentary intelligence oversight, media, and the politics of security. We hope the analysis presented here will inform the ongoing debate about the future of Scotland, the UK, and the EU, and also shed new light on some deeper questions about security and statehood. The issue of Scottish independence remains a focal point for fundamental questions about the future of nation states and the relationship between democracy and security.

References

[N.a.], 'Does Scotland Export Twice as Much to England as It Does to the Rest of the World?' (2012), https://fullfact.org/economy/does-scotland-export-twice-much-england-it-does-rest-world/

—, 'Security & Defence', Centre on Constitutional Change (Edinburgh, 2016), http://www.centreonconstitutionalchange.ac.uk/tags/security-defence

—, 'Who We Are', No to NATO Scotland Coalition (2016), http://notonatoscotland.org.uk/index.html%3Fpage_id=201.html

—, 'Row as Ex-Intelligence Chiefs Say EU Membership Protects UK Security', *BBC News*, 8 May 2016, http://www.bbc.co.uk/news/uk-36239741

Bigo, Didier, 'Security and Immigration: Toward a Critique of the Governmentality of Unease', *Alternatives: Global, Local, Political*, 27 (2002), 63–92, http://dx.doi.org/10.1177/03043754020270S105

—, 'Internal and External Aspects of Security', *European Security*, 15 (2006), 385–404, http://dx.doi.org/10.1080/09662830701305831

—, and Guild, E., *Europe's 21st Century Challenge: Delivering Liberty* (Farnham and Burlington: Ashgate, 2010).

Blinder, Scott and Allen, William L., *UK Public Opinion toward Immigration: Overall Attitudes and Level of Concern* (Oxford: The Migration Observatory, 2016), http://www.migrationobservatory.ox.ac.uk/wp-content/uploads/2016/04/Briefing-Public_Opinion_Immigration_Attitudes_Concern.pdf

Bochel, H., Defty, A. and Kirkpatrick, J., *Watching the Watchers: Parliament and the Intelligence Services* (Basingstoke: Palgrave Macmillan, 2014).

Cabinet Office, 'The UK Cyber Security Strategy Protecting and Promoting the UK in a Digital World' (London, 2011), https://www.gov.uk/government/uploads/system/uploads/attachment_data/file/60961/uk-cyber-security-strategy-final.pdf

MacNab, Scott, 'Immigration: Scots "No More Tolerant Than English"', *Scotsman*, 28 July 2015, http://www.scotsman.com/news/politics/immigration-scots-no-more-tolerant-than-english-1-3714620

Moore, Jack, 'Brussels Attacks: Belgian Intelligence Services "Overwhelmed and Outnumbered" by Jihadis', *Newsweek*, 22 March 2016, http://europe.newsweek.com/belgiums-security-services-overwhelmed-and-outnumbered-jihadi-threat-439490

Nawaz, Maajid and Ebner, Julia, 'The EU and Terrorism: Is Britain Safer In or Out?' (London: Quilliam, 2016), http://www.quilliamfoundation.org/press/quilliam-releases-report-on-the-eu-and-terrorism-is-britain-safer-in-or-out/

Penttila, R. E. J., *Finland's Search for Security through Defence, 1944–89* (Basingstoke and New York: Palgrave Macmillan, 1991).

Pietrasanta, Sébastien, *Au nom de la commission d'enquête relative aux moyens mis en œuvre par l'État pour lutter contre le terrorisme depuis le 7 janvier 2015* (Paris: Assemblée Nationale, 2016), http://www.assemblee-nationale.fr/14/pdf/rap-enq/r3922-t1.pdf

Scottish Government, 'Scotland's Future: Your Guide to an Independent Scotland' (Edinburgh: Scottish Government, 2013), http://www.gov.scot/resource/0043/00439021.pdf

——, 'Preparing Scotland: Scottish Guidance on Resilience, Philosophy, Principles, Structures and Regulatory Duties' (Edinburgh, 2016), http://www.readyscotland.org/media/1166/preparing-scotland-philosophy-principles-structures-and-regulatory-duties-20-july-2016.pdf

Stone, Jon, 'Nigel Farage Says the EU Has Allowed the "Free Movement of Kalashnikov Rifles and Jihadists"', *Independent*, 17 November 2015, http://www.independent.co.uk/news/uk/politics/nigel-farage-says-the-eu-has-allowed-the-free-movement-of-kalashnivov-rifles-and-jihadists-a6737501.html

Terpstra, Jan and Fyfe, Nicholas R., 'Mind the Implementation Gap? Police Reform and Local Policing in the Netherlands and Scotland', *Criminology and Criminal Justice*, 15 (2015), 527–44, http://dx.doi.org/10.1177/1748895815572162

UK Government, *Scotland Act 1998* (London: HMSO, 1998), http://www.legislation.gov.uk/ukpga/1998/46/pdfs/ukpga_19980046_en.pdf

1. Perspectives on Small State Security in the Scottish Independence Debate[1]

Juliet Kaarbo and Daniel Kenealy

During the Scottish independence referendum campaign, considerable attention was paid, by Scotland's political leaders, its voters, and actors in the international community, to the question of what an independent Scotland's foreign policy might look like. An independent Scotland would quickly find itself in a world that puts many constraints on states' international aspirations. But as a sovereign state, Scotland would have the opportunity to shape the role it would play on the world stage. This chapter examines the debate over an independent Scottish foreign policy during the independence campaign. We describe the type of foreign policy that was projected by the Scottish National Party (SNP) Government in Scotland and the reaction to that projection by actors opposed to independence. We argue that the underlying difference in the two sides was the perspective on small state foreign and security policy and that this difference resonates with long-standing academic debates about small states, and their insecurities, in world politics.

---

1   This paper is a fuller version of J. Kaarbo and D. Kenealy, 'What Kind of International Role and Influence Would an Independent Scotland Have?', in *Scotland's Decision: 16 Questions to Think About for the Referendum on 18 September*, ed. by C. Jeffery and R. Perman (Edinburgh: Birlinn Ltd, 2014), pp. 42–45. In the empirical section on Scotland, this paper draws extensively from R. Beasley, J. Kaarbo, and H. Solomon-Strauss, 'To Be or Not to Be a State? Role Contestation in the Debate over Scottish Independence', in *Domestic Role Contestation, Foreign Policy, and International Relations*, ed. by Cristian Cantir and Juliet Kaarbo (Abingdon and New York: Routledge, 2016), pp. 140–56; R. Beasley and J. Kaarbo, 'Casting for a Sovereign Role: Socialising an Aspirant State in the Scottish Independence Referendum', *European Journal of International Relations* (2017), 1–25.

    https://doi.org/10.11647/OBP.0078.01

On 18 September 2014, voters in Scotland had the opportunity to separate from the United Kingdom and become an independent nation state. During the referendum campaign, considerable attention was paid to the question of what an independent Scotland's foreign policy might look like by Scotland's political leaders, its voters, and actors in the international community. As the world's newest state, what would it want to do, what could it do, and what kind of influence could Scotland have in international relations? In the end these questions were academic, as voters delivered a No vote. Yet the debate was instructive, shedding considerable light on how people think about the security needs and foreign policy potential of small states. With the possibility of a second referendum in the not too distant future, which was made more likely after the June 2016 referendum vote for the UK to leave the EU, these issues have not been left in the past.

Whilst many policy areas (such as health, education, and criminal justice) are already under Scottish authority, independence and sovereignty would bring new responsibilities and opportunities. The leaders of an independent Scotland, and Scottish citizens, would have to design and support a foreign policy for their country, and decide how best to gain influence, secure their interests, and promote Scottish values in the international system. An independent Scotland would quickly find itself in a world that puts many constraints on states' international aspirations, but as a sovereign country, Scotland would have the opportunity to shape the role it would play on the world stage.

This chapter examines the debate over an independent Scottish foreign policy during the independence campaign (dating from the announcement of the Edinburgh Agreement in 2011 to the September 2014 referendum). We describe the type of foreign policy that was projected by the Scottish National Party government in Scotland (the main advocate of independence)[2] and the reaction to that projection by actors opposed to independence within Scotland, and by external actors, including the UK government and international figures. We argue that the underlying difference between the two sides lay in their perspectives

---

2   Although we recognise that there were other actors and non-SNP voters involved
    in the campaign for independence, we focus here on the SNP leadership as the
    main advocate for independence. We also note that not all of the SNP membership
    agreed with all of the foreign policies advocated by SNP leaders.

on small state foreign and security policy, and that this difference resonates with long-standing academic debates about small states, and their insecurities, in world politics. By connecting the empirical debate in the Scottish case to the theoretical debate, we aim to clarify avenues for future research on small states. We also aim to highlight the implications of scholarly research for foreign policy questions faced by small states and sub-state actors aspiring to sovereign statehood in Scotland and elsewhere.

The Yes vision of independent Scottish foreign and security policy

According to evidence of public opinion, issues of foreign policy and security were not the primary concerns of voters during the referendum.[3] Yet the SNP articulated foreign policy based arguments in their effort to persuade voters to support the campaign for independence. The White Paper *Scotland's Future* set out the Scottish Government's vision of an independent Scotland's international role and influence.[4] That vision combines continuity with change. Continuity would be provided by on-going membership in a variety of international organisations, perhaps most prominent amongst them NATO and the EU. But there would also be the possibility of change as an independent Scotland would be free to pursue a set of values and interests somewhat distinct from those of the UK. A neat way of summarising states' visions of their international role is to think of four foreign policy pillars: protection, profits, principles, and pride.[5]

The SNP, articulated in the Scottish Government publication *Scotland's Future*, proposed Scottish membership of NATO and a

---

3   Andrew Black, 'Scottish Independence: What's Going on in Scotland?', *BBC News*, 9 September 2014, http://www.bbc.co.uk/news/uk-scotland-scotland-politics-26550736; Sean Anderson, 'Scottish Independence: Which Issues Have Led the Twitter Debate in 2014?', *Guardian*, 8 July 2014, https://www.theguardian.com/news/datablog/2014/jul/08/scottish-independence-referendum-twitter-analysis-topics-debate-2014

4   Scottish Government, *Scotland's Future: Your Guide to an Independent Scotland* (Edinburgh: Scottish Government, 2013), http://www.gov.scot/resource/0043/0043 9021.pdf

5   We used this formulation previously in Kaarbo and Kenealy (2014).

Scottish defence force as cornerstones of 'protection'.[6] In October 2012, SNP party members at the annual conference voted 426 to 332 to change its 30-year-old opposition to NATO.[7] The approved resolution allowed for an independent Scotland's membership in the alliance, provided that Scotland would not host nuclear weapons. Scotland would earn 'profit' (i.e. secure its prosperity and grow its economy) and thrive in the global political economy, according to the Yes campaign, by adopting liberal, pro-trade foreign economic policies. Central to the 'profit' pillar was continued membership of the EU. The message across these pillars — 'protection' and 'profit' — was, to a large extent, one of continuity. An independent Scotland would continue to be embedded in a range of alliances and institutions geared to provide security and prosperity.

Independence, however, would also allow for change. In the area of 'principles', ethics, and values, the Yes campaign proposed a highly aspirational policy, contrasting with its characterisation of past and present UK foreign policy. The Scottish Government, in *Scotland's Future*, stressed the 'different international priorities' that an independent Scotland would pursue, seen 'most clearly in matters of war and peace and in our relationship with the EU'.[8] The Yes side asserted that if Scotland had been independent, it would not have participated in the unpopular invasion of Iraq in 2003, as the UK did.[9] First Minister Alex Salmond presented an independent Scotland as one that would be less militarised than the UK, and argued that this referendum represented a chance for the Scottish people to change Scotland's international relations. In a union with the UK, he remarked, 'We cannot stop illegal wars. [...] We cannot stop countless billions being wasted on weapons

---

6   NATO represents a sticking point given that the Scottish Greens, who support independence and thus form part of the broader Yes campaign, oppose NATO membership for an independent Scotland. The Radical Independence Campaign, founded during the referendum campaign, were also opposed.

7   [N.a.], 'SNP Members Vote to Ditch the Party's Anti-Nato Policy', *BBC News*, 19 October 2012, http://www.bbc.co.uk/news/uk-scotland-scotland-politics-19993694

8   *Scotland's Future*, p. 209.

9   Bagehot, 'Interviewing Alex Salmond, the Man Who Wants to Break up Britain', *Economist*, 12 January 2012, http://www.economist.com/blogs/bagehot/2012/01/independence-debate-scotland-0

of mass destruction'.[10] The SNP also proposed that an independent Scotland would have a 'triple lock' on military deployments, requiring all military action to be in accordance with the UN Charter, agreed by the Scottish Government, and approved by the Scottish parliament.[11]

The pledge to rid an independent Scotland of nuclear weapons was partly grounded in principle. The SNP's arguments against nuclear weapons were threefold: that they are a useless deterrent against the kind of security threats faced by a modern Scotland; that they are a considerable waste of money that could be better used to support policies that advance Scotland's social values; and that they are immoral weapons of war. According to *Scotland's Future*, 'Trident is an affront to basic decency with its indiscriminate and inhumane destructive power'.[12] Salmond further clarified this anti-nuclear, moral role for an independent Scotland, committing in the much-watched second televised debate to 'a policy that removes nuclear weapons and weapons of mass destruction because they are a phenomenal waste of money as well as being totally morally wrong'.[13]

Scotland's Future described an independent Scotland as a 'champion for international justice and peace', committed to the values of 'international development, human rights, climate change, and climate justice'.[14] Scottish defence forces would be used, in addition to national defence, to support international peacekeeping and humanitarian missions undertaken under the auspices of the UN and in support of international law. Scotland would also contribute in a targeted way to NATO and EU missions. The vision was thus one of Scotland as a good global citizen, a civilian power, with a 'do no harm' principle — especially towards developing countries — firmly embedded in its international role.[15]

Finally, 'pride' has a place in most states' foreign policies. Pride involves the projection of a positive self-image by a country and *Scotland's Future* painted a picture of 'an outward facing nation, exporting goods, people, and ideas around the world [...] [with a]

---

10   C-SPAN, 'Scottish Independence Debate', Washington DC, 25 August 2014, https://www.c-span.org/video/?321045-1/scottish-independence-debate, time point: 3:18.
11   *Scotland's Future*, p. 251.
12   *Ibid.*, p. 232.
13   C-SPAN, 25 August 2014, time point: 1:07:43.
14   *Scotland's Future*, p. 210 and 225.
15   *Ibid.*, p. 231.

proud military tradition'.[16] For a party with 'national' in its name, there was little nationalism or negative xenophobic expressions of pride in the SNP's descriptions of its projected independent foreign policy.

How would an independent Scotland achieve this foreign policy? Nicola Sturgeon, and others campaigning for a Yes vote, argued that small states could 'punch above their weight' and have influence disproportionate to their size.[17] Yes campaigners pointed out that most states in the world are small and that some small states can play an active role in international organisations, often hosting headquarters and offices and placing their citizens in key leadership positions. By adopting 'small but smart' strategies, such as niche diplomacy and economic comparative advantages, small states can be effective and influential. Such notions were reflected in *Scotland's Future*, where small states were presented as lacking large, threatening capabilities and therefore as more credible interlocutors and facilitators.[18] The SNP often invoked wealthy, successful Nordic examples of influential small states and noted that independence 'does not seem to have done Australia any harm'.[19] The SNP leader made similar comparisons to US and Irish independence from Britain.[20]

The No vision of a weak independent Scotland

The No side in the referendum debate — principally the cross-party Better Together campaign — argued that Scotland would be stronger as a part of the UK than it would be on its own. The argument is captured in the phrase, often used in official UK Government analysis, '[a] strong

---

16 *Ibid.*, p. 207.
17 N. Sturgeon evidence to the Foreign Affairs Committee, *Foreign Policy Considerations for the UK and Scotland in the Event of Scotland Becoming an Independent Country, Sixth Report of Session 2012–2013* (London: HMSO, 2013), http://www.publications. parliament.uk/pa/cm201213/cmselect/cmfaff/643/643.pdf
18 *Scotland's Future*, p. 217.
19 Jonathan Pearlman, 'Australians Divided over Scottish Referendum', *Telegraph*, 16 September 2014, http://www.telegraph.co.uk/news/worldnews/australiaand thepacific/australia/11098800/Australians-divided-over-Scottish-referendum.html
20 Alex Salmond, 'Why an Independent Scotland Deserves U.S. Support', *Washington Post*, 7 December 2012, https://www.washingtonpost.com/opinions/why-an-independent-scotland-deserves-us-support/2012/12/07/694ba79a-3a4a-11e2-8a97-363b0f9a0ab3_story.html

voice in the world'.[21] Given that the UK is a permanent member of the UN Security Council, one of the largest members of the EU, and already an experienced participant in other influential international organisations, Scotland's interests, according to those campaigning against independence, are better advanced through these existing channels and institutions and as part of a larger state. Their messages stressed how much larger in terms of sheer numbers and expenditure the UK diplomatic service, economy, armed forces, and intelligence services are in comparison to their hypothetical independent Scottish counterparts.[22]

The No campaign repeatedly pointed out the difficulties and uncertainties that an independent Scotland would face, and the obstacles that could thwart the Yes campaign's foreign policy aspirations. They warned that the EU might not grant the same opt-outs and special terms (for example on the euro, the Schengen area, and the budget rebate) to an independent Scotland as are possessed by the UK.[23] They stressed that the NATO alliance may not accept Scotland as a member if Scotland refuses to house the UK nuclear deterrent on its soil.[24] They questioned SNP assertions about its rights to UK diplomatic assets, such as embassies and consulates.[25] In short, according to the No side, uncertainty was pervasive and risks abounded. Not for nothing was the moniker 'Project Fear' developed for the No campaign. For example, Alistair Darling (the political leader of Better Together) made the argument in the public debates that independence was, fundamentally, a risky decision: 'The

---

21   HM Government, *Scotland Analysis — Cm. 8554: Devolution and the Implications of Scottish Independence* (London: HMSO, 2013), https://www.gov.uk/government/uploads/system/uploads/attachment_data/file/79407/Report_excluding_annexes_Independan...__2_.pdf

22   See, e.g., HM Government, *Scotland Analysis: Cm. 8714: Defence* (London: HMSO, 2013), https://www.gov.uk/government/uploads/system/uploads/attachment_data/file/248654/Scotland_analysis_Defence_paper-FINAL.pdf; HM Government, *Scotland Analysis: Cm. 8741: Security* (London: HMSO, 2013), https://www.gov.uk/government/uploads/system/uploads/attachment_data/file/253500/Scotland_analysis_security.pdf; HM Government, *Scotland Analysis: Cm. 8765: EU and International Issues* (London: HMSO, 2013), https://www.gov.uk/government/uploads/system/uploads/attachment_data/file/271794/2901475_HMG_Scotland_EUandInternational_acc2.pdf

23   HM Government (2013), *Scotland Analysis: Cm. 8765: EU and International Issues*, p. 7.

24   *Ibid.*, p. 62.

25   *Ibid.*, p. 43.

basic difference between Mr. Salmond and me, his priority is to create a separate state, no matter what the risk and what the cost'.[26]

Where the Yes side argued that Scotland deserved its own seat at the table, Better Together argued that independence would not offer Scotland a chance to have its own voice because it would be too small to make a difference. Independence would simply leave Scotland unrepresented.[27] During the televised debates, Darling compared an independent Scotland to Iceland, Ireland and Panama in terms of what it could expect in, and from, the international system.[28]

The UK Government was a key player in the Scottish independence debate, including the discussions over what an independent Scottish foreign policy could do. As noted by Walker,

> The UK government, for its part, instructed each affected department in Whitehall to carry out an assessment of the costs of every kind that would fall on Scotland should it leave the Union. The result was the published series of 'Scotland Analysis Papers' [including papers on EU and international issues, security, and defence]. In addition, various select committees of the UK parliament issued their own reports, [...] emphasising the costs to Scotland and denying or downplaying benefits that might accrue from independence.[29]

For example, the UK Foreign and Commonwealth Office stated that an 'independent Scottish state would have to start afresh in terms of its formal alliances, and links with every other sovereign state'.[30]

The EU was a particularly contentious issue. The Yes campaign, and the Scottish Government, was keen to argue that an independent Scotland would remain a member and play a full and positive role in the Union. In stark contrast, the UK Government published its own legal advice, stating that an independent Scotland would immediately be

26 C-SPAN, 25 August 2014, time point: 50:34.
27 Nicholas Watt, Libby Brooks, and Patrick Wintour, 'Scottish Independence Would Be Disastrous for All UK, Warns John Major', *Guardian*, 10 September 2014, https://www.theguardian.com/politics/2014/sep/10/scottish-independence-referendum-trident-defence-uk-john-major
28 C-SPAN, 25 August 2014, time point: 8:48 and 50:34.
29 William Walker, 'International Reactions to the Scottish Referendum', *International Affairs*, 90, 4 (2014), 743–59 (p. 748). See, for example, Foreign Affairs Committee (2013).
30 HM Government (2013), *Scotland Analysis: Cm. 8765: EU and International Issues*, p. 5. Cited in Walker (2014), p. 749.

outside the EU (and the UN).[31] David Lidington, the UK's Minister for Europe, stated that 'I've been sat around the EU table for the last three years for many discussions about EU enlargement. It is the complexity, the time-consuming nature of those negotiations that the people of Scotland ought to bear in mind. It isn't straightforward'.[32] Once again the implicit message was one of risk and uncertainty.

EU officials and other member states also quickly cast doubt on the automatic nature of Scottish membership, thereby drawing into question the ability of Scotland to define a post-independence role as an actor within the EU for itself.[33] In December 2012 Jose Manuel Barroso, the President of the European Commission, declared that any new state would have to apply for EU membership, despite the SNP's previous claim that an independent Scotland would be able to renegotiate its terms of membership from inside the EU.[34] Spain also used EU membership as a way to cast uncertainty on an independent Scotland's role. On the eve of the vote, the Spanish Foreign Minister reiterated Spain's opinion that EU membership would not be automatic and would require unanimous support from EU member states.[35] 'An independent Scotland would be forced to wait at least five years to join the EU and would then have to sign up to the euro, the Spanish government [...] warned'.[36]

However, not all EU actors shared this perspective. Graham Avery, a former European Commission senior official and a specialist in the area

31   Severin Carrell, 'David Cameron Tries to Put the Brakes on Alex Salmond', *Guardian*, 11 February 2013, https://www.theguardian.com/uk/2013/feb/11/david-cameron-scotland-independence-legal-advice

32   Foreign and Commonwealth Office and The Rt Hon William Hague, 'Prospects of EU Membership for a Newly Independent Scotland', Gov.uk, 16 January 2014, https://www.gov.uk/government/news/prospects-of-eu-membership-for-a-newly-independent-scotland

33   Daniel Kenealy, 'How Do You Solve a Problem Like Scotland? A Proposal Regarding "Internal Enlargement"', *Journal of European Integration*, 36, 6 (2014), 585–600 (pp. 587–89).

34   [N.a.], 'Scottish Independence: EC's Barroso Says New States Need "Apply to Join EU"', *BBC News*, 10 December 2012, http://www.bbc.co.uk/news/uk-scotland-scotland-politics-20664907

35   Martin Roberts, 'Spain Says Scottish Independence Would Be a "Catastrophe"', *Telegraph*, 17 September 2014, http://www.telegraph.co.uk/news/worldnews/europe/spain/11101650/Spain-says-Scottish-independence-would-be-a-catastrophe.html

36   Simon Johnson, 'Spanish Warn Independent Scotland Would Get Euro Not Pound', *Telegraph*, 16 September 2014, http://www.telegraph.co.uk/news/uknews/scottish-independence/11099167/Spanish-warn-independent-Scotland-would-get-euro-not-pound.html

of enlargement, indicated that the UK Government's position — that Scotland could not easily negotiate EU membership — was 'perplexing' and 'absurd', indicating that Scottish voters should dismiss tactics suggesting Scotland would face a challenging process in acquiring EU membership.[37] Barroso and Herman Van Rompuy, the European Council president, asserted that the EU treaties would not apply to newly independent parts of existing member states.[38] Avery described this as 'not the whole truth'.[39] Other EU member states also weighed in, with Czech president Vaclav Klaus and Joelle Garriaud-Maylam, a senior French senator specialising in foreign policy, challenging Barroso's position, stating that such threats 'are not credible' and that an independent Scotland 'would stay in the European Union'.[40]

Beyond the debate about Scotland's ability to join the EU, there were several efforts by the UK Government to portray an independent Scotland as a 'small state' that would suffer economically from its weakness. There were, for example, efforts to highlight Scotland's more limited capacity to exploit its North Sea oil resources than would be the case with support from 'the broad shoulders of one of the top 10 economies in the world [...]', clearly suggesting Scotland required the comparative strength of the UK to effectively manage its most important economic resource.[41]

The question of an independent Scotland's currency, which relates to its foreign economic policy and its ability to provide for its defence, was crucial in the independence debate. There was much debate about whether Scotland would be able to keep the Pound Sterling, as was argued by the SNP.[42] George Osborne, the UK Chancellor of the

---

37 [N.a.], 'Scottish Independence: Scotland Could Join EU in 18 Months, Says Expert', *BBC News*, 30 January 2014, http://www.bbc.co.uk/news/uk-scotland-scotland-politics-25965703

38 *Ibid.*

39 *Ibid.*

40 David Leask, '"Independence Would Not Bar Scotland from EU Membership"', *Herald*, 1 March 2014, http://www.heraldscotland.com/news/13148291._Independ ence_would_not_bar_Scotland_from_EU_membership

41 Stephen Castle and Stanley Reed, 'Scottish Oil and Gas an Issue in Vote on Independence', *New York Times*, 24 February 2014, http://www.nytimes.com/ 2014/02/25/world/europe/scot-oil-and-gas-an-issue-in-vote-on-independence.html

42 This was another bone of contention within the broader Yes campaign. The Scottish Greens were keen to explore new currency options for Scotland, other than the pound or the euro, a view echoed by many on the left wing of the Yes campaign.

Exchequer, indicated that there would essentially be no chance of sharing the pound, with the other major UK political parties (Labour and Liberal Democrats) articulating the same position.[43] This resulted in a back-and-forth with Salmond providing a set of facts countering Osborne's position and accusing the UK Government of 'bullying'.[44]

Other external actors also weighed in on an independent Scotland's foreign policy. NATO, for example, indicated that an independent Scotland would have to apply as a new state and that membership would require unanimous agreement of all twenty-eight states in the alliance.[45] The United States also intervened in this debate. As Walker put it,

> Within the US government, there was concern that its most dependable and influential ally would be diminished by Scotland's departure. In addition, the UK and by extension NATO might be weakened if the referendum resulted in a reduction of military capabilities — including nuclear capabilities—and greater reluctance to deploy military forces abroad.[46]

Uncharacteristically, 'President Barack Obama made an 11th-hour appeal for Scots to vote no, saying he hopes Britain "remains strong, robust and united" and that "The UK is an extraordinary partner for America and a force for good in an unstable world"'.[47]

Other leaders also warned of the dangers of a new small state. *The Scotsman* newspaper reported: 'One of the more controversial moments of the referendum debate saw Australian Prime Minister Tony Abbott

---

43   Andrew Sparrow, 'George Osborne's Speech on Scottish Independence: Politics Live Blog', *Guardian*, 13 February 2014, https://www.theguardian.com/politics/blog/2014/feb/13/george-osbornes-speech-on-scottish-independence-politics-live-blog

44   Andrew Black and Aiden James, 'Scottish Independence: Currency Union Block Could Hurt Firms, Says Alex Salmond', *BBC News*, 17 February 2014, http://www.bbc.co.uk/news/uk-scotland-scotland-politics-26220638

45   Severin Carrell, 'Nato Rejects Alex Salmond Claim over Scottish Membership', *Guardian*, 10 April 2013, https://www.theguardian.com/politics/2013/apr/10/nato-alex-salmond-scottish-membership

46   Walker (2014), p. 747.

47   Raf Sanchez, 'Barack Obama Tells Scotland: Stay United', *Telegraph*, 17 September 2014, http://www.telegraph.co.uk/news/uknews/scottish-independence/11103256/Barack-Obama-tells-Scotland-stay-united.html

state that the world "would not be helped" by Scottish independence'.[48] Abbott also remarked: 'I am a firm friend of the United Kingdom and I want it to remain the United Kingdom, not the disunited Kingdom. It is a matter for Scotland, obviously, but as a friend of the United Kingdom that is my view'.[49] Former Swedish Prime Minister Carl Bildt warned that independence for Scotland could create a 'Balkanisation' of the British Isles and he 'suggested that a Yes vote could have a knock-on effect on Northern Ireland as well as destabilising the UK'.[50] Ireland expressed similar concerns and the head of Shell Oil also warned of the risks and uncertainties of independence.[51]

Small states in world politics: the debate in International Relations scholarship

The debate between the Yes and No campaigns on the influence a small state can have in the world is familiar to scholars of International Relations (IR). Many theoretical perspectives view the international system as dominated by great powers. Weak states are Lilliputians in Gulliver's world[52] and 'the strong do what they can and the weak suffer what they must'.[53] While legally independent, small states, according to these perspectives, are so dependent on others, both in terms of economics and security, that they really cannot pursue an independent foreign policy. Smaller economies are vulnerable to instability in global financial and trade markets and to economic pressures by others. Small states are dependent on military alliances in the face of security

---

48 [N.a.], 'Scottish Independence: Global Reaction', *Scotsman*, 16 September 2014, http://www.scotsman.com/news/politics/scottish-independence-global-reaction-1-3543135

49 [N.a.], 'Scottish Independence: How the World Has Reacted', *Telegraph*, 18 September 2014, http://www.telegraph.co.uk/news/worldnews/11102506/Scottish-independence-How-the-world-has-reacted.html

50 [N.a.], *Scotsman*, 16 September 2014, http://www.scotsman.com/news/politics/independence-may-lead-to-britain-s-balkanisation-1-3432564

51 Severin Carrell, 'Shell Boss Warns against Scottish Independence', *Guardian*, 6 March 2014, https://www.theguardian.com/business/2014/mar/06/shell-chief-warns-against-scottish-independence

52 Robert O. Keohane, 'Lilliputians' Dilemmas: Small States in International Politics', *International Organization*, 23, 2 (1969), pp. 291–310 (pp. 291–310).

53 Thucydides, *History of the Peloponnesian War* (London: Penguin Books Ltd, 1972 [431 BC]), p. 402.

threats and may need to compromise their goals or values in return for protection. The bottom line, for those viewing international politics through the lens of big states making big decisions, is this: small states are rule-takers, not rule-makers.

The two theories that have most dominated IR scholarship — realism and liberalism — both tend to focus on bigger, more powerful states. Realism — both 'classical' and 'neo' — sees international politics as a realm of power. Realism, as a broad approach, is often considered a theory that supports the primacy of great power politics. Whilst Hans Morgenthau, in his classic text *Politics Among Nations*, made space to discuss the strategies that smaller states might adopt, his understanding of the balance of power and his vision of international politics as driven by 'interest defined in terms of power' leaves little room for small states.[54] Employing the analogy of firms in the market, Waltz suggests that when all firms are not of equal size it makes sense to focus on the larger firms or, in this case, larger states.[55] More recent realist scholarship has continued to emphasise that, insofar as the anarchy of international politics can be mitigated, great powers and larger states are responsible for it, with smaller states passively receiving such 'order' as can be attained.[56]

The newest variant of liberalism — associated with scholars such as Andrew Moravcsik — has likewise stressed the importance of power in international politics. Larger states are able to set the agenda, with small states reduced to trying to secure 'side payments' through international

---

54   Hans J. Morgenthau, *Politics Among Nations: The Struggle for Power and Peace*, 6th edn. (New York: Knopf, 1985 [1948]).

55   Kenneth Neal Waltz, *Theory of International Politics* (Reading, MA and London: Addison-Wesley, 1979), Chapter 5.

56   W. Wohlforth, 'Realism', in *The Oxford Handbook of International Relations*, ed. by Christian Reus-Smit and Duncan Snidal (Oxford: Oxford University Press, 2008), pp. 131–49. According to Baldur Thorhallsson and Anders Wivel, 'Small States in the European Union: What Do We Know and What Would We Like to Know?', *Cambridge Review of International Affairs*, 19, 4 (2006), 651–68 (p. 656), which is written from a classical realist perspective, 'Olav Knudsen identifies six key variables that are central to preserving the autonomy of smaller states: strategic significance of geographic location, degree of tension between the leading powers, phase of power cycle for nearest great power, historical record of relations between small state and nearest great power, the policies of other great powers and the existence of multilateral frameworks of security cooperation'.

negotiations and bargaining.[57] Whilst this new liberalism has stressed
the importance of non-state actors, and takes the formation of, and
variation in, state preferences seriously, the predominant focus is on
the bigger powers. For example, in Moravcsik's study of the history of
European integration the emphasis is most heavily placed on France,
West Germany, and Britain as the shapers of the process.[58] One of
the founders of the modern liberal approach to IR, Robert Keohane,
remarked that small states were 'system ineffectual', meaning that they
have to adjust to an international system that is shaped and influenced
by other, larger states.[59]

Other theoretical traditions of IR similarly devote more time and
attention to larger states, or great powers, than they do to small states.
The English School, for example, is concerned with the construction,
maintenance, and erosion of different international societies. The
overarching framework for understanding international society — one
that has continued to animate the English School — gives primacy to the
most powerful states within any given international society, although
Martin Wight, one of the founders of the school, devoted a chapter of his
book *Power Politics* to 'minor powers'.[60] Constructivism shifts the focus
away from material forms of power in order to consider softer forms
of power and ideational power, which has opened up the possibility
of considering how smaller states might be successful in creating and
promoting new norms. Despite this, a constructivist understanding
of how an international system is formed and maintained still places
emphasis on more powerful states.

An opposing view to these traditional IR theoretical perspectives
argues that small states may not be as constrained as structural
approaches imply and, supported by a long-standing and growing body
of research, it demonstrates that they may indeed punch above their
weight.[61] Handel, for example, finds that 'the economic predicament

---

57 See Andrew Moravcsik, 'Negotiating the Single European Act: National Interests
    and Conventional Statecraft in the European Community', *International Organization*,
    45, 1 (1991), 19–56 (pp. 19–57).

58 Andrew Moravcsik, *The Choice for Europe: Social Purpose and State Power from Messina
    to Maastricht* (Ithaca, NY and London: Cornell University Press, 1998).

59 Keohane (1969), pp. 291–310.

60 Martin Wight, *Power Politics* (London: Chatham House, 1978), Chapter 5.

61 An exhaustive presentation of the vast literature on small states is beyond the
    space limits of this chapter. For a review of the small state area of research, see

of the [economically] weak states may not be so severe as traditional economic theory would suggest'.[62] Research on small states challenges the assumption of structural approaches that fewer capabilities (often the operational definition of small states) necessarily translates into less influence. It suggests that the possession of power (capabilities) is not synonymous with the exercise of power (influence).[63] This is true, of course for big states as well: power as capability does not necessarily mean power as influence; not all big states get what they want. Small states may not be able to act autonomously but, in a world characterised increasingly by interdependence, this is often a characteristic of large states too. No states, large or small, are completely self-determining and in control of the effects of their own, and others', actions.

The work on small states problematises the category of 'small state' and challenges static, deterministic, capabilities-based definitions. Small-state scholarship now generally adopts the position that 'rather than continue the search for universal characteristics of small states and their behaviour, the 'small state' concept is best used as a 'focusing device' for highlighting the characteristic security problems and foreign policy dilemmas of the weaker actors in asymmetric power relationships'.[64] Work on small state security, following developments in security studies more generally, has expanded conceptions of security to include survival, economic, societal and environmental security (see Thorhallsson and Bailes, Chapter 2).[65] Small states are no longer seen

---

I. B. Neumann and S. Gstöhl, 'Introduction: Lilliputians in Gulliver's World?', in *Small States in International Relations*, ed. by J. Beyer *et al.* (Seattle: University of Washington Press, 2006), pp. 3–36; Andrew F. Cooper and Timothy M. Shaw, *The Diplomacies of Small States: Between Vulnerability and Resilience* (Basingstoke and New York: Palgrave Macmillan, 2009); Laurent Goetschel, 'Introduction to Special Issue: Bound to Be Peaceful? The Changing Approach of Western European Small States to Peace', *Swiss Political Science Review*, 19, 3 (2013), 259–78. See also the annotated bibliography by J. Beyer, 'Annotated Bibliography', in *Small States in International Relations*, ed. by J. Beyer *et al.* (Seattle: University of Washington Press, 2006), pp. 293–318.

62   See Michael I. Handel, *Weak States in the International System* (London: Frank Cass, 1981); also the summary of Handel's argument in Neumann and Gstöhl (2006).

63   Thorhallsson and Wivel (2006).

64   Clive Archer, Alyson J. K. Bailes, and Anders Wivel, 'Setting the Scene: Small States and International Security', in *Small States and International Security: Europe and Beyond*, ed. by C. Archer, A. J. Bailes, and A. Wivel (Abingdon and New York: Routledge, 2014), pp. 3–25 (p. 9).

65   See, for example, Archer, Bailes, and Wivel (2014).

as dependent; rather they seek shelter in international institutions that they in turn support to create security communities.[66]

Research indicates that small states can also have influence disproportional to their size. Small states can play an active role in international organisations, often hosting headquarters and offices and placing their citizens into key leadership positions. International institutions provide diplomatic space, information networks, and a place to coordinate collective action; leadership allows small states to shape the agenda of regional and global organisations, as norm entrepreneurs, meaning that they can, acting alone or in concert with other small states, challenge existing ideas and understandings that govern international politics and thus ultimately change behaviours and outcomes.[67] Small states can also carve out niche roles, champion specific issues, and broker agreements, as they often enjoy more credibility and neutrality than larger states *because* of their small size. Indeed, 'small states are more efficient as mediators because they can never expect to be successful in pushing their national interests the way large countries can'.[68]

The history of international relations reveals many examples of small states playing important roles (consider Norway's influence in the Arab-Israeli conflict during the 1990s, or Costa Rica's influence in the Central American conflicts of the 1980s). Small states can use their power, and particularly their soft power, in smart ways to advance their interests and exert influence.[69] In economics too, small states can find and then exploit highly profitable niches and smaller economies may be

---

66   Alyson J. K. Bailes, J.-M. Rickli, and Baldur Thorhallsson, 'Small States, Survival, and Strategy', in Archer, Bailes, and Wivel (2014), pp. 26–45; see also Efraim Inbar and Gabriel Sheffer, *The National Security of Small States in a Changing World* (London and Portland: Frank Cass, 1997); and Jean-Marc Rickli, 'European Small States' Military Policies after the Cold War: From Territorial to Niche Strategies', *Cambridge Review of International Affairs*, 21, 3 (2008), 307–25.

67   On norm entrepreneurs, see Christine Ingebritsen, *The Nordic States and European Unity* (Ithaca, NY and London: Cornell University Press, 1998).

68   Thorhallsson and Wivel (2006); Rikard Bengtsson, Ole Elgström, and Jonas Tallberg, 'Silencer or Amplifier? The European Union Presidency and the Nordic Countries', *Scandinavian Political Studies*, 27, 3 (2004), 311–34.

69   On soft power, see, for example, Alan Chong, 'Singapore and the Soft Power Experience', in *The Diplomacies of Small States: Between Vulnerability and Resilience*, ed. by Andrew F. Cooper and Timothy M. Shaw (London: Palgrave Macmillan, 2009), pp. 65–80.

able to adapt more easily to changing economic conditions.[70] There may be other benefits to being small, according to the notion that 'small is beautiful'. Smallness, for example, 'may be a factor that reduces rather than multiplies security headaches. It eliminates the need to make a pretence of self-sufficient defence or even to create military forces it all. It dampens expectations of a significant outgoing contribution to global goods like peacekeeping and, rather, creates a supposition of importing help in natural and accidental emergencies'.[71] Generally, this research indicates that 'small states are neither per se power-brokers nor are they per se political dwarfs in international negotiations'.[72]

This area of research has also identified typical and effective strategies that small states use. These include prioritisation, framing and reframing, attempts to use normative power and soft power, and the use of opportunity structures such as chairing negotiations or serving as president of an international organisation.[73] Some research on small states has concentrated on the effects of size-related obstacles to influence, such as fewer administrative, financial and economic resources and capacities, and on the conditions that affect small-state success and influence.[74] Conditions for success include features of the institutional environment (such as the number of other actors and weighted voting *vs* majority voting), issue types (redistributive *vs* regulative), and policy areas.[75] There is some disagreement on these conditions, however. With regard to policy areas, for example, Thorhallsson and Wivel maintain the more conventional expectation that 'the influence of small states is smaller on security policy than on other policy areas',[76] while in the special issue in the *Cambridge Review of International Affairs*, edited by Diana Panke, the realist expectation that small states will have no influence in security issues was not confirmed across the case studies.[77]

---

70   P. J. Katzenstein, *Small States in World Markets: Industrial Policy in Europe* (Ithaca, NY and London: Cornell University Press, 1985).

71   Archer, Bailes, and Wivel (2014), p. 18.

72   Diana Panke, 'Small States in Multilateral Negotiations. What Have We Learned?', *Cambridge Review of International Affairs*, 25, 3 (2012), pp. 387–98.

73   See, for example, Panke (2012); Thorhallsson and Wivel (2006).

74   See, for example, Panke (2012).

75   See, for example, *ibid.*; Thorhallsson and Wivel (2006).

76   Thorhallsson and Wivel (2006), p. 659.

77   See Panke (2012).

Not surprisingly, when the assumption that capabilities determine influence is relaxed, the explanations of small states' foreign policy look very similar to the explanations of great power and middle power foreign policy. In other words, a vast range of factors, from structural conditions and external threats, to mutually constructed identities, to domestic politics and the psychological aspects of decision making are relevant to understand the foreign policies that small states pursue. Generally, small state research has challenged the more structural explanations and explored other, more agent-based accounts. This is certainly consistent with the turn in international relations theory more generally to incorporate domestic and decision-making factors.[78]

Gstöhl and Ingebritsen, for example, separately argue that, despite an economic interest to be open to regional integration, Scandinavia and other small European countries vary in this respect, and this variance can be explained by domestic political constraints.[79] Other research focuses more on elite beliefs. Keohane argued that state leaders' perceptions of their country's role in the world better account for states' orientations toward international institutions than capabilities, and even more than the perception of need for security protection.[80] Thorhallson points to elite self-perceptions, among other factors, as a key element to explain Iceland's change in foreign policy from a 'system-ineffectual' state to a 'system-affecting' state.[81] Reiter finds that small states 'learn' from past experiences of success and failure and adapt their foreign policies according to these lessons learned, and not to variations in external threat, as realist perspectives would suggest.[82]

---

78   Juliet Kaarbo, 'A Foreign Policy Analysis Perspective on the Domestic Politics Turn in IR Theory', *International Studies Review*, 17, 2 (2015), 189–216.

79   Sieglinde Gstöhl, *Reluctant Europeans: Norway, Sweden, and Switzerland in the Process of Integration* (Boulder and London: Lynne Rienner, 2002); Ingebritsen (1998); and for a domestic political analysis see Miriam Fendius Elman, 'The Foreign Policies of Small States: Challenging Neorealism in its Own Backyard', *British Journal of Political Science*, 25, 02 (1995), 171–217.

80   Keohane (1969).

81   Baldur Thorhallsson, 'Can Small States Choose Their Own Size? The Case of a Nordic State — Iceland', in *The Diplomacies of Small States: Between Vulnerability and Resilience*, ed. by Andrew F. Cooper and Timothy M. Shaw (London: Palgrave Macmillan, 2009), pp. 119–42.

82   Dan Reiter, 'Learning, Realism, and Alliances: The Weight of the Shadow of the Past', *World Politics*, 46, 4 (1994), 490–526.

Overall, the research on small states has come to a position similar to the rest of IR theory. According to Thorhallsson and Wivel, for example, 'only by examining the interaction of materialist and idealist factors at different levels (regional, national and global) will we get a better understanding of the strategy of small states'.[83] They also argue that 'we need to better understand how to combine materialist variables, such as power, with the observation that power affects foreign policy only through the interpretations of policy-makers'.[84] This last point is perfectly consistent with a foreign policy analysis perspective, but still often ignored by other IR theories, even when they incorporate domestic politics and decision-making factors.[85]

The Scottish Government, at the time of the independence referendum, wished to see Scotland become the newest small state in the international system. But, throughout the referendum, Scotland was not a small state. Rather it was a sub-state actor, a constituent part of a sovereign nation state: the United Kingdom. The growing literature on so-called paradiplomacy[86] — that is the diplomacy, or external relations, of sub-states — has generally focused on efforts by sub-state actors to secure economic gain through missions and activities designed to secure foreign trade and investment, or to promote cultural distinctiveness on the global stage (itself also often indirectly economic in nature, designed to boost tourism and exports through enhanced visibility and brand differentiation). Most case studies of sub-state diplomacy are of regions that either do not aspire to be states or are, unlike Scotland in 2014, not on the cusp of becoming a state.

This case study illustrates that, for states that are newly emerging after independence, there exists a set of challenges additional to the general ones faced by small states. Had it become independent, Scotland would have had to negotiate in an environment in which its parent state,

---

83   Thorhallsson and Wivel (2006), p. 665.
84   Thorhallsson and Wivel (2006).
85   Kaarbo (2015).
86   Examples include Samuel Lucas McMillan, *The Involvement of State Governments in US Foreign Relations* (New York: Palgrave Macmillan, 2012); David Criekemans, *Regional Sub-State Diplomacy Today* (Leiden and Boston: Martinus Nijhoff, 2010); Noé Cornago, 'On the Normalization of Sub-State Diplomacy', *The Hague Journal of Diplomacy*, 5, 1–2 (2010), 11–36; A. Lecours, 'Paradiplomacy: Reflections on the Foreign Policy and International Relations of Regions', *International Negotiation*, 7, 1 (2002), 91–114.

the UK, would have been seeking to preserve its standing and prestige in the international system. This adds another layer of complexity and the dynamic that persisted between the emerging state (in this case, Scotland) and the state from which it was emerging (in this case, the UK) would have the potential to curb the ambitions of the new state. This is an issue that scholars of paradiplomacy ought to explore further given the possibility of a second Scottish independence referendum and the ongoing situation in Catalonia.

Conclusion

The two sides of the debate, about how an independent Scotland might fare in the international system given its small size, unfortunately talked over each other. Perhaps this is not surprising in a political campaign, as they often polarise issues and present a black-white picture to voters. It was interesting to note that the two sides would often point to different small states as examples. The Yes campaign, and particularly the SNP leadership, consistently invoked the Nordic states as good examples of small states in the international system.[87] In official publications — such as the UK Government's Scotland Analysis papers — the No side built up arguments about why Scotland would struggle to emulate the Nordic states. However, in more casual settings — such as in television appearances and debates — Iceland was invoked as an example of a state that ended up battered by global economic forces. Similarly, when Alex Salmond suggested that an independent Scotland could use the pound even without the agreement of the UK, the No campaign were quick to liken Scotland, negatively, to Panama, which uses the US dollar in a similar way. It is interesting to note that the SNP shifted the emphasis they placed on specific small states over a number of years. In 2006 Alex Salmond labelled Ireland, Iceland and Norway the 'arc of prosperity', arguing that an independent Scotland could join such an arc.[88] Following the impact of the financial crisis, the references to Iceland and Ireland became less frequent, with Norway, Sweden, and Denmark more commonly invoked.

---

87 *Scotland's Future*, p. 477.
88 [N.a.], 'Salmond Sees Scots in "Arc of Prosperity"', *Scotsman*, 12 August 2006, http://www.scotsman.com/news/salmond-sees-scots-in-arc-of-prosperity-1-1130200

Overall, in the Scottish debate, the No side reflected the long-held perspective in the study of international relations that small states are ineffectual and vulnerable. The Yes side articulated the most positive side of the 'small is beautiful' perspective in small-state research. The truth of how effective and independent Scotland would be probably lies somewhere in the middle. Small states can secure their interests and advance their ideals, but this is not automatic; not all small states are effective in overcoming their disadvantages. The credibility that is key to small states' influence takes time to develop, and is dependent on how others see them. It takes planning, the selection of appropriate policies, the commitment of necessary resources, and the exercise of dynamic leadership for any state, small or large, to deliver a successful foreign policy. The right policies also need the right resources to support them, not only financial resources (a diplomatic network is not cheap) but also human capital. Diplomatic services require the appropriate experience and knowledge and that requires significant and strategic investment. While the foreign policy of democratic states is certainly affected by the public, it is leaders who steer sovereign ships. Leaders that are interested in foreign affairs and skilled at playing a two-level game of domestic and international politics can significantly enhance any state's potential.

References

[N.a.], 'Salmond Sees Scots in "Arc of Prosperity"', *Scotsman*, 12 August 2006, http://www.scotsman.com/news/salmond-sees-scots-in-arc-of-prosperity-1-1130200

—, 'SNP Members Vote to Ditch the Party's Anti-Nato Policy', *BBC News*, 19 October 2012, http://www.bbc.co.uk/news/uk-scotland-scotland-politics-19993694

—, 'Scottish Independence: EC's Barroso Says New States Need "Apply to Join EU"', *BBC News*, 10 December 2012, http://www.bbc.co.uk/news/uk-scotland-scotland-politics-20664907

—, 'Scottish Independence: Scotland Could Join EU in 18 Months, Says Expert', *BBC News*, 30 January 2014, http://www.bbc.co.uk/news/uk-scotland-scotland-politics-25965703

—, 'Scottish Independence: Global Reaction', *Scotsman*, 16 September 2014, http://www.scotsman.com/news/politics/scottish-independence-global-reaction-1-3543135

—, 'Scottish Independence: How the World Has Reacted', *Telegraph*, 18 September 2014, http://www.telegraph.co.uk/news/worldnews/11102506/Scottish-independence-How-the-world-has-reacted.html

Anderson, Sean, 'Scottish Independence: Which Issues Have Led the Twitter Debate in 2014?', *Guardian*, 8 July 2014, https://www.theguardian.com/news/datablog/2014/jul/08/scottish-independence-referendum-twitter-analysis-topics-debate-2014

Archer, Clive, Bailes, Alyson J. K., and Wivel, Anders, 'Setting the Scene: Small States and International Security', in *Small States and International Security: Europe and Beyond*, ed. by C. Archer, A. J. Bailes, and A. Wivel (Abington and New York: Routledge, 2014), pp. 3–25.

Bagehot, 'Interviewing Alex Salmond, the Man Who Wants to Break up Britain', *Economist*, 12 January 2012, http://www.economist.com/blogs/bagehot/2012/01/independence-debate-scotland-0

Bailes, Alyson J. K., Rickli, J.-M., and Thorhallsson, B., 'Small States, Survival, and Strategy', in *Small States and International Security: Europe and Beyond*, ed. by C. Archer, A. J. Bailes, and A. Wivel (Abington and New York: Routledge, 2014), pp. 26–45.

Beasley, R. and Kaarbo, J., 'Casting for a Sovereign Role: Socialising an Aspirant State in the Scottish Independence Referendum', *European Journal of International Relations* (2017), 1–25, https://doi.org/10.1177/1354066116683442

—, and Solomon-Strauss, H., 'To Be or Not to Be a State? Role Contestation in the Debate over Scottish Independence', in *Domestic Role Contestation, Foreign Policy, and International Relations*, ed. by Cristian Cantir, and Juliet Kaarbo (Abingdon and New York: Routledge, 2016), pp. 140–56.

Bengtsson, Rikard, Elgström, Ole, and Tallberg, Jonas, 'Silencer or Amplifier? The European Union Presidency and the Nordic Countries', *Scandinavian Political Studies*, 27 (2004), 311–34, http://dx.doi.org/10.1111/j.1467-9477.2004.00108.x

Beyer, J., 'Annotated Bibliography', in *Small States in International Relations*, ed. by J. Beyer, C. Ingebritsen, S. Gstohl and I. B. Neumann (Seattle: University of Washington Press, 2006), pp. 293–318.

Black, Andrew, 'Scottish Independence: What's Going on in Scotland?', *BBC News*, 9 September 2014, http://www.bbc.co.uk/news/uk-scotland-scotland-politics-26550736

—, and James, Aiden, 'Scottish Independence: Currency Union Block Could Hurt Firms, Says Alex Salmond', *BBC News*, 17 February 2014, http://www.bbc.co.uk/news/uk-scotland-scotland-politics-26220638

C-SPAN, 'Scottish Independence Debate' (Washington DC, 25 August 2014), https://www.c-span.org/video/?321045-1/scottish-independence-debate

Carrell, Severin, 'David Cameron Tries to Put the Brakes on Alex Salmond', *Guardian*, 11 February 2013, https://www.theguardian.com/uk/2013/feb/11/david-cameron-scotland-independence-legal-advice

—, 'Nato Rejects Alex Salmond Claim over Scottish Membership', *Guardian*, 10 April 2013, https://www.theguardian.com/politics/2013/apr/10/nato-alex-salmond-scottish-membership

—, 'Shell Boss Warns against Scottish Independence', *Guardian*, 6 March 2014, https://www.theguardian.com/business/2014/mar/06/shell-chief-warns-against-scottish-independence

Castle, Stephen and Reed, Stanley, 'Scottish Oil and Gas an Issue in Vote on Independence', *New York Times*, 24 February 2014, http://www.nytimes.com/2014/02/25/world/europe/scot-oil-and-gas-an-issue-in-vote-on-independence.html

Chong, Alan, 'Singapore and the Soft Power Experience', in *The Diplomacies of Small States: Between Vulnerability and Resilience*, ed. by Andrew F. Cooper and Timothy M. Shaw (London: Palgrave Macmillan, 2009), pp. 65–80.

Cooper, Andrew F. and Shaw, Timothy M., *The Diplomacies of Small States: Between Vulnerability and Resilience* (Basingstoke and New York: Palgrave Macmillan, 2009).

Cornago, Noé, 'On the Normalization of Sub-State Diplomacy', *The Hague Journal of Diplomacy*, 5 (2010), 11–36, http://dx.doi.org/10.1163/1871191x-05010102

Criekemans, David, *Regional Sub-State Diplomacy Today* (Leiden and Boston: Martinus Nijhoff Publishers, 2010).

Elman, Miriam Fendius, 'The Foreign Policies of Small States: Challenging Neorealism in Its Own Backyard', *British Journal of Political Science*, 25 (1995), 171–217, http://dx.doi.org/10.1017/s0007123400007146

Foreign Affairs Committee, 'Foreign Policy Considerations for the UK and Scotland in the Event of Scotland Becoming an Independent Country, Sixth Report of Session 2012–2013' (London: HMSO, 2013), http://www.publications.parliament.uk/pa/cm201213/cmselect/cmfaff/643/643.pdf

Foreign and Commonwealth Office and The Rt Hon William Hague, 'Prospects of EU Membership for a Newly Independent Scotland', Gov.uk, 16 January 2014, https://www.gov.uk/government/news/prospects-of-eu-membership-for-a-newly-independent-scotland

Goetschel, Laurent, 'Introduction to Special Issue: Bound to Be Peaceful? The Changing Approach of Western European Small States to Peace', *Swiss Political Science Review*, 19 (2013), 259–78, http://dx.doi.org/10.1111/spsr.12047

Gstöhl, Sieglinde, *Reluctant Europeans: Norway, Sweden, and Switzerland in the Process of Integration* (Boulder and London: Lynne Rienner, 2002).

Handel, Michael I., *Weak States in the International System* (London: Frank Cass, 1981).

HM Government, *Scotland Analysis: Cm. 8554: Devolution and the Implications of Scottish Independence* (London: HMSO, 2013), https://www.gov.uk/government/uploads/system/uploads/attachment_data/file/79407/Report_excluding_annexes_Independan..._2_.pdf

—, *Scotland Analysis: Cm. 8714: Defence* (London: HMSO, 2013), https://www.gov.uk/government/uploads/system/uploads/attachment_data/file/248654/Scotland_analysis_Defence_paper-FINAL.pdf

—, *Scotland Analysis: Cm. 8741: Security* (London: HMSO, 2013), https://www.gov.uk/government/uploads/system/uploads/attachment_data/file/253500/Scotland_analysis_security.pdf

—, *Scotland Analysis: Cm. 8765: EU and International Issues* (London: HMSO, 2013), https://www.gov.uk/government/uploads/system/uploads/attachment_data/file/271794/2901475_HMG_Scotland_EUandInternational_acc2.pdf

Inbar, Efraim and Sheffer, Gabriel, *The National Security of Small States in a Changing World* (London and Portland: Frank Cass, 1997).

Ingebritsen, Christine, *The Nordic States and European Unity* (Ithaca, NY and London: Cornell University Press, 1998).

Johnson, Simon, 'Spanish Warn Independent Scotland Would Get Euro Not Pound', *Telegraph*, 16 September 2014, http://www.telegraph.co.uk/news/uknews/scottish-independence/11099167/Spanish-warn-independent-Scotland-would-get-euro-not-pound.html

Kaarbo, Juliet, 'A Foreign Policy Analysis Perspective on the Domestic Politics Turn in IR Theory', *International Studies Review*, 17 (2015), 189–216, http://dx.doi.org/10.1111/misr.12213

—, and Kenealy, D., 'What Kind of International Role and Influence Would an Independent Scotland Have?', in *Scotland's Decision: 16 Questions to Think About for the Referendum on 18 September*, ed. by C. Jeffery, and R. Perman (Edinburgh: Birlinn Ltd, 2014), pp. 42–45.

Katzenstein, P. J., *Small States in World Markets: Industrial Policy in Europe* (Ithaca, NY and London: Cornell University Press, 1985).

Kenealy, Daniel, 'How Do You Solve a Problem Like Scotland? A Proposal Regarding "Internal Enlargement"', *Journal of European Integration*, 36 (2014), 585–600, http://dx.doi.org/10.1080/07036337.2014.902942

Keohane, Robert O., 'Lilliputians' Dilemmas: Small States in Internatinal Politics', *International Organization*, 23 (1969), 291–310, http://dx.doi.org/10.1017/s002081830003160x

Leask, David, '"Independence Would Not Bar Scotland from EU Membership"', *Herald*, 1 March 2014, http://www.heraldscotland.com/news/13148291._Independence_would_not_bar_Scotland_from_EU_membership_/

Lecours, A., 'Paradiplomacy: Reflections on the Foreign Policy and International Relations of Regions', *International Negotiation*, 7 (2002), 91–114, http://dx.doi.org/10.1163/157180602401262456

McMillan, Samuel Lucas, *The Involvement of State Governments in US Foreign Relations* (New York: Palgrave Macmillan, 2012).

Moravcsik, Andrew, 'Negotiating the Single European Act: National Interests and Conventional Statecraft in the European Community', *International Organization*, 45 (1991), 19–56, http://dx.doi.org/10.1017/S0020818300001387

—, *The Choice for Europe: Social Purpose and State Power from Messina to Maastricht* (Ithaca, NY and London: Cornell University Press, 1998).

Morgenthau, Hans J., *Politics Among Nations: The Struggle for Power and Peace*, 6th edn. (New York: Knopf, 1985 [1948]).

Neumann, I. B. and Gstöhl, S., 'Introduction: Lilliputians in Gulliver's World?', in *Small States in International Relations*, ed. by J. Beyer, C. Ingebritsen, S. Gstohl and I. B. Neumann (Seattle: University of Washington Press, 2006), pp. 3–36.

Panke, Diana, 'Small States in Multilateral Negotiations. What Have We Learned?', *Cambridge Review of International Affairs*, 25 (2012), 387–98, http://dx.doi.org/10.1080/09557571.2012.710589

Pearlman, Jonathan, 'Australians Divided over Scottish Referendum', *Telegraph*, 16 September 2014, http://www.telegraph.co.uk/news/worldnews/australiaandthepacific/australia/11098800/Australians-divided-over-Scottish-referendum.html

Reiter, Dan, 'Learning, Realism, and Alliances: The Weight of the Shadow of the Past', *World Politics*, 46 (1994), 490–526, http://dx.doi.org/10.2307/2950716

Rickli, Jean-Marc, 'European Small States' Military Policies after the Cold War: From Territorial to Niche Strategies', *Cambridge Review of International Affairs*, 21 (2008), 307–25, http://dx.doi.org/10.1080/09557570802253435

Roberts, Martin, 'Spain Says Scottish Independence Would Be a "Catastrophe"', *Telegraph*, 17 September 2014, http://www.telegraph.co.uk/news/worldnews/europe/spain/11101650/Spain-says-Scottish-independence-would-be-a-catastrophe.html

Salmond, Alex, 'Why an Independent Scotland Deserves U.S. Support', *Washington Post*, 7 December 2012, https://www.washingtonpost.com/opinions/why-an-independent-scotland-deserves-us-support/2012/12/07/694ba79a-3a4a-11e2-8a97-363b0f9a0ab3_story.html?utm_term=.48fcdb22a76b

Sanchez, Raf, 'Barack Obama Tells Scotland: Stay United', *Telegraph*, 17 September 2014, http://www.telegraph.co.uk/news/uknews/scottish-independence/11103256/Barack-Obama-tells-Scotland-stay-united.html

Scottish Government, *Scotland's Future: Your Guide to an Independent Scotland* (Edinburgh: Scottish Government, 2013), http://www.gov.scot/resource/0043/00439021.pdf

Sparrow, Andrew, 'George Osborne's Speech on Scottish Independence: Politics Live Blog', *Guardian*, 13 February 2014, https://www.theguardian.com/politics/blog/2014/feb/13/george-osbornes-speech-on-scottish-independence-politics-live-blog

Thorhallsson, Baldur, 'Can Small States Choose Their Own Size? The Case of a Nordic State—Iceland', in *The Diplomacies of Small States: Between Vulnerability and Resilience*, ed. by Andrew F. Cooper and Timothy M. Shaw (London: Palgrave Macmillan UK, 2009), pp. 119–42.

—, and Wivel, Anders, 'Small States in the European Union: What Do We Know and What Would We Like to Know?', *Cambridge Review of International Affairs*, 19 (2006), 651–68, http://dx.doi.org/10.1080/09557570601003502

Thucydides, *History of the Peloponnesian War* (London: Penguin Books Ltd, 1972 [431BC]).

Walker, William, 'International Reactions to the Scottish Referendum', *International Affairs*, 90 (2014), 743–59, http://dx.doi.org/10.1111/1468-2346.12138

Waltz, Kenneth Neal, *Theory of International Politics* (Reading, MA and London: Addison-Wesley, 1979).

Watt, Nicholas, Brooks, Libby, and Wintour, Patrick, 'Scottish Independence Would Be Disastrous for All UK, Warns John Major', *Guardian*, 10 September 2014, https://www.theguardian.com/politics/2014/sep/10/scottish-independence-referendum-trident-defence-uk-john-major

Wight, Martin, *Power Politics* (London: Chatham House, 1978).

Wohlforth, W, 'Realism', in *The Oxford Handbook of International Relations*, ed. by Christian Reus-Smit and Duncan Snidal (Oxford: Oxford University Press, 2008), pp. 131–49.

2. Do Small States Need 'Alliance Shelter'? Scotland and the Nordic Nations

Baldur Thorhallsson and Alyson J. K. Bailes[1]

The aim of this chapter is to examine how Scotland as a potential independent state would prosper based on the existing small state literature and lessons of the Nordic states. The chapter argues that, as any other small entity, Scotland, as an independent small state, would need external shelter in multiple dimensions. We have found that four entities — NATO, the EU, the remnant UK, and the US — are best suited to meeting Scotland's needs for economic, societal, and political shelter including hard and soft security. However, these solutions would incur costs different from, and not necessarily lesser than, those carried by Scotland within the present union. An independent Scotland would have to weigh the cost/benefit balance of full shelter provided by these four entities and consider important opt-outs secured by the Nordic states. The Nordic states themselves cannot provide an alternative for any key dimension of shelter but the lessons of varied Nordic experience, and softer kinds of shelter to be found within Nordic cooperation, could provide valuable lubrication for the transitional process and a supportive pillar for Scotland's accommodation to independent existence in the world.

---

1   We are grateful to Sverrir Steinsson for his exceptional research assistance and comments. The chapter draws extensively on Alyson J. K. Bailes, Baldur Thorhallsson, and Rachael Lorna Johnstone, 'Scotland as an Independent Small State: Where Would It Seek Shelter?', *Icelandic Review of Politics and Administration*, 9, 1 (2013), 1–20; Alyson J. K. Bailes, 'Small States and Security: Does Size Still Matter?', in *Small States in the Modern World: Vulnerabilities and Opportunities*, ed. by H. Baldersheim and M. Keating (Cheltenham and Northampton, MA: Edward Elgar Publishing, Inc., 2015), pp. 23–41.

How do small states survive and prosper in the international system? This is a debate that resurfaced with the Scottish independence referendum of 2014. For some, an independent Scotland would be too small to remain viable as a prosperous state. Others argued that an independent Scotland could be prosperous but that it would need to stay in, or join, the EU.[2] Nordic models and experiences were frequently mentioned in this debate[3] and used to demonstrate that small societies can be prosperous on their own.[4] However, with important exceptions,[5] the discourse on Scotland's smallness has not yet received much attention in the small-state literature. This chapter seeks to draw lessons from the academic research on small states, and particularly research on the Nordic states, which may be applied to an independent Scotland. How Scotland compares with the Nordics in some key indicators is shown in Table 1.

Based on the existing literature and the lessons from the Nordic states, we argue that Scotland as an independent small state would need external shelter in multiple dimensions. We identify four entities — NATO, the EU, the US, and rUK — that seem most suited to meeting Scotland's needs for economic, societal, and political shelter. However, these solutions would incur costs different from, and not necessarily lesser than, those carried by the Scottish people within their present union. Costs associated with memberships (or full shelter

2   Jo E. Murkens, *Scotland's Place in Europe* (London: Constitution Unit, University College London, 2001); Scottish National Party, 'Senior EU Official Backs Benefits of Small States', 2012, https://web.archive.org/web/20141202110524/http://www.snp.org/media-centre/news/2012/dec/senior-eu-official-backs-benefits-small-states [last saved to the Wayback Machine 2 December 2014].

3   E.g. P. Hanlon and F. U. Karki, 'Health, Culture and Society: A Scottish-Nordic Conversation', in *Radical Scotland: Arguments for Self-Determination*, ed. by Gerry Hassan and Rosie Ilett (Edinburgh: Luath Press Ltd, 2011), pp. 85–101.

4   A. Salmond, 'Scotland's Place in the World. Hugo Young Memorial Lecture', London, 25 January 2012, http://www.guardian.co.uk/politics/2012/jan/25/alex-salmond-hugo-young-lecture

5   E.g. Michael Keating, 'The Political Economy of Self-Determination', in *Radical Scotland: Arguments for Self-Determination*, ed. by G. Hassan and R. Ilett (Edinburgh: Luath Press Ltd, 2011), pp. 40–48; D. Donald and A. Hutton, 'Economic Self-Determination: Towards a Political Economy of Scottish Citizenship', in *Radical Scotland: Arguments for Self-Determination*, ed. by G. Hassan and R. Ilett (Edinburgh: Luath Press Ltd, 2011), pp. 49–62.

in the terminology of the literature) of the EU and NATO have led to important opt-outs by the Nordic states, and an independent Scotland would have to weigh the cost/benefit balance no less carefully. Here we shall look at the main shelter options and their likely price tags, while also asking what the Nordic nations themselves might be able to offer.

Table 1. Scotland and Nordic nations: comparison of key 'size' variables[6]

	Population (thousands)	Territory (sq. km.)	GDP per capita ($)	Military Capacity		
				Military Spending (% of GDP)	Armed Force Personnel	
					Active	Reserves
Sweden	9690	450,295	42,874	1.2	15,300	200,000
Denmark	5640	43,094	43,094	1.3	17,200	53,500
Finland	5464	338,145	39,160	1.4	22,200	354,000
Scotland	5254	78,772	39,642	(UK 2.2)	(UK 169,150)	(UK 78,100)
Norway	5136	323,802	66,135	1.4	25,800	45,940
Iceland	328	103,000	36,483	*None*	*None*	*None*
Greenland	56	2,166,086	-	*None*	*None*	*None*
Faroe Islands	48	1393	-	*None*	*None*	*None*

Alliance shelter theory

Generally, the International Relations (IR) literature argues that small states need a protecting power. Realists, with their emphasis on 'hard' power competition, usually find that small states survive by relying on the mercy of powerful states or by joining military alliances. A small state can either align itself with the most powerful state in its environment

---

6   Population information from World Bank, 'Countries and Economies' (2015), http://data.worldbank.org/country; territory from [N.a.], *CIA World Factbook* (CIA, 2015), https://www.cia.gov/library/publications/the-world-factbook/ GDP information from 2012 (in International Dollars) from the Scottish Government (GDP includes a proportionate allocation of UK oil/gas revenues); military expenditure from SIPRI, 'Military Expenditure Database' (2015), http://www.sipri.org/research/armaments/milex/milex_database; armed forces from the International Institute of Strategic Studies (IISS), *The Military Balance 2015* (London: Taylor & Francis, 2015).

(bandwagoning) or join coalitions against that state (balancing).[7] Liberal international relations scholars, who emphasise cooperation especially in economic affairs, likewise argue that small states depend on a larger power. They need access to large markets, and must find ways to constrain more powerful states peacefully. Small states consequently cherish regional and international organisations as means for restraining powerful states through norms and rules, while promoting peace and trade.[8] Constructivist scholars have also emphasised small states' need for social status, which implies recognition by great powers.[9] There is not much disagreement among IR scholars about small states' dependence on large states, international organisations and international norms for their survival and prosperity.

Building on these insights, we propose a framework that takes account of the different dimensions of small states' vulnerabilities, and the different solutions available for small states seeking to alleviate them. We may initially conceptualise these vulnerabilities as being political, economic, and societal.[10]

i) *Political Shelter*. The framework divides political shelter into three distinct categories. First, the most obvious way in which small

---

7   G. Liska, *Nations in Alliance: The Limits of Interdependance* (Baltimore: Johns Hopkins University Press, 1962); R. E. Osgood, *Alliances and American Foreign Policy* (Baltimore: Johns Hopkins Press, 1968); P. W. Schroeder, 'Alliances, 1815–1945: Weapons of Power and Tools of Management', in *Historical Dimensions of National Security Problems*, ed. by K. E. Knorr (Lawrence: University Press of Kansas, 1976), pp. 227–62; Stephen M. Walt, *The Origins of Alliance* (Ithaca, NY: Cornell University Press, 1987); G. H. Snyder, *Alliance Politics* (Ithaca, NY: Cornell University Press, 1997).

8   R. O. Keohane, *After Hegemony: Cooperation and Discord in the World Political Economy* (Princeton: Princeton University Press, 1984); Robert O. Keohane and Lisa L. Martin, 'The Promise of Institutionalist Theory', *International Security*, 20, 1 (1995), 39–51; G. J. Ikenberry, *After Victory: Institutions, Strategic Restraint, and the Rebuilding of Order after Major Wars* (Princeton: Princeton University Press, 2001); Baldur Thorhallsson and Anders Wivel, 'Small States in the European Union: What Do We Know and What Would We Like to Know?', *Cambridge Review of International Affairs*, 19, 4 (2006), 651–68; D. Panke, *Small States in the European Union: Coping with Structural Disadvantages* (Farnham and Burlington: Ashgate, 2010).

9   Carsten Holbraad, 'The Role of Middle Powers', *Cooperation and Conflict*, 6, 2 (1971), 77–90; B. de Carvalho and I. B. Neumann, *Small State Status Seeking: Norway's Quest for International Standing* (New York: Taylor & Francis, 2014).

10 Baldur Thorhallsson, 'Domestic Buffer Versus External Shelter: Viability of Small States in the New Globalised Economy', *European Political Science*, 10, 3 (2011), 324–36; Baldur Thorhallsson, 'Iceland's External Affairs in the Middle Ages: The Shelter of Norwegian Sea Power', *Icelandic Review of Politics & Administration*, 8, 1 (2012), 5–37.

states are vulnerable is in their lack of hard power. With smaller populations, less absolute wealth and less territory, small states lack the self-sufficiency, resources and strategic depth needed to defend themselves, including the maintenance of adequate armed forces. Second, small states are also vulnerable when it comes to diplomatic power. With a smaller base for taxation, small states lack administrative capacity.[11] A smaller civil service makes it harder for small states to run their societies effectively, and a smaller diplomatic corps makes it more difficult for them to engage in bilateral and multilateral negotiations. Third, small states can be sheltered by the norms and rules of the international system. To summarise, small states consequently depend on larger states or organisations for both military and diplomatic backing. International organisations have particular benefits in reducing inequality between states, providing information and cutting the transaction costs of diplomacy.

ii) *Economic Shelter.* Small domestic markets and concentrated production make small states acutely dependent on international trade. With relatively few, or no, natural resources and without the economies of scale to produce a wide range of goods, small states rely on importing vital goods and exporting the few products in which they have comparative advantages. This external dependence also means that small state economies fluctuate more than larger economies, as prices for commodities rise and fall, and international economic crises hit them harder than many other states.[12] Small states consequently depend on open trading relationships with larger economies, and promote free trade and economic integration for the goods and services in which they have comparative advantage.[13] In this setting, economic shelter may come from a state and/or an organisation in the form of direct economic assistance and investment, a currency union, beneficial loans, favourable market access, a common market and so forth.

---

11 Baldur Thorhallsson, 'The Size of States in the European Union: Theoretical and Conceptual Perspectives', *European Integration*, 28, 1 (2006), 7–31 (p. 19).

12 Handel (1981); P. J. Katzenstein, *Corporatism and Change: Austria, Switzerland, and the Politics of Industry* (Ithaca, NY and London: Cornell University Press, 1984); Katzenstein (1985).

13 A. Alesina and E. Spolaore, *The Size of Nations* (Cambridge: MIT Press, 2003).

iii) *Societal Shelter*. Innovation and ideas are usually associated with
large populations and free exchanges. Small states risk cultural,
educational and technological stagnation without the free flow
of people, goods and ideas.[14] Isolation prevents states, especially
when small, from keeping pace with development and adopting
best practices. Individuals from small states also cherish the
ability to tap into broader cultural and ideological currents. Small
states, like any others, are not solely concerned with material
well-being but seek ontological security for their sense of self
and identity; they rely especially on predictability and order to
ensure this.[15] They want to feel good about their position in the
world and have their standing recognised by others.[16]

We may consequently expect that small states will seek economic,
political and societal shelter, and that their prosperity will be strongly
linked to the nature and depth of shelter they can find. Such shelter
does not, of course, come without costs. Shelter providers may impose
conditions on smaller states in exchange for the shelter, reducing the
small partner's freedom of manoeuvre and choice.[17] The need to align
with undesirable large states or organisations may be costly in normative
terms, as the minor partner ends by acting in ways inconsistent with
its national identity and preferred image. Participation in regional
and international organisations may also stretch the administrative
resources of small states.[18] Nonetheless, there is plenty of important and
inexpensive shelter available for small states — at least in Europe.

---

14   S. Rokkan, D. W. Urwin, and European Consortium for Political Research, *Economy,
     Territory, Identity: Politics of West European Peripheries* (London: Sage, 1983).
15   Ted Hopf, 'The Promise of Constructivism in International Relations Theory',
     International Security, 23, 1 (1998), 171–200; Jennifer Mitzen, 'Ontological Security
     in World Politics: State Identity and the Security Dilemma', *European Journal
     of International Relations*, 12, 3 (2006), 341–70; B. J. Steele, *Ontological Security in
     International Relations: Self-Identity and the IR State* (Abingdon and London: Taylor &
     Francis, 2008); Ayşe Zarakol, 'Ontological (in)Security and State Denial of Historical
     Crimes: Turkey and Japan', *International Relations*, 24, 1 (2010), 3–23.
16   de Carvalho and Neumann (2014).
17   D. Vital, *The Inequality of States: A Study of the Small Power in International Relations*
     (Oxford: Clarendon Press, 1967), p. 5.
18   Alyson J. K. Bailes and Baldur Thorhallsson, 'Instrumentalizing the European
     Union in Small State Strategies', *Journal of European Integration*, 35, 2 (2013), 99–115.

Nordic states' shelter

The five Nordic states all have populations smaller than 10 million (see Table 1), and similar political (democratic), social (welfare-oriented, egalitarian) and cultural (secular, open and liberal) systems. Historically violent, the Nordics have built a new image as a non-aggressive, high-minded family of states whose troops go abroad only for peace missions. Despite many similarities between them, the Nordic states have opted for different forms of shelter, as shown in Table 2. Economic shelter is typically found in European integration, but the level of participation differs between the Nordic states. Political shelter is found in NATO and the European project, the former providing 'hard' and the latter 'soft' security. Also, the US offers the Nordic nations political cover directly or indirectly. Societal shelter is mainly sought via Nordic cooperation.

Table 2. Present economic, political, societal and security shelter of the Nordic nations and Scotland

Shelter Type	Economy	Currency union	Political	Societal	Hard security	Soft security
Sweden	EU	*No*	EU	EU/NC[a]	*No*	EU/Schengen
Denmark	EU	DKK(EU)[b]	EU/NATO	EU/NC	NATO	EU/Schengen
Finland	EU	EU	EU	EU/NC	*No*	EU/Schengen
Scotland	UK/EU	UK	UK/EU/NATO	UK/EU	UK/NATO	UK/EU
Norway	EEA/ EFTA[c]	*No*	NATO	EEA/NC	NATO	Schengen
Iceland	EEA/EFTA	*No*	NATO	EEA/NC/ WNC[d]	NATO/US	Schengen
Greenland	DK[e]	DK	DK/US/NATO	DK/NC/WNC	DK/US/NATO	DK/Schengen
Faroe Islands	DK	DK	DK/NATO	DK/NC/WNC	DK/NATO	DK/Schengen

[a] Nordic Cooperation.
[b] Danish krone (DKK) pegged to the euro.
[c] European Economic Area/European Free Trade Association.
[d] West Nordic Cooperation.
[e] Denmark.

Shelter in NATO and the US

Unable to deter or defeat Russian threats with their own small forces, the Nordics after World War Two had to balance the logic of seeking big-power protection against that of avoiding provocation and distancing themselves from the military actuality of confrontation between East and West. Finland continued as a buffer state, opting for neutrality and friendly relations with both East and West. Plans for a four-member Scandinavian Defence Union containing Sweden, Norway, Denmark and Iceland fell apart over differences between Norway and Sweden over NATO guarantees.[19] These four states then jumped different ways in 1949: Iceland, Norway and Denmark becoming founding members of NATO, and Sweden settling for neutral status — as shown in Table 2. The choices of the four states reflected their threat perceptions and history. As one simplified explanation suggests, neutrality had failed in World War Two for the three prospective NATO members whereas the Swedish policy of neutrality had paid off.

NATO membership was, however, not without controversy for these formerly neutral states. Norway and Denmark insisted on no stationing of foreign troops or nuclear objects on their soils during peacetime, with the exception of Greenland.[20] Iceland entered into a basing agreement with the US in 1951 after painful internal debates, driven by the growing perception of global instability in the wake of the Korean War, its own lack of armed forces, and fears that NATO membership alone was not a sufficient deterrent to Soviet aggression or a Socialist coup.[21] Iceland's NATO membership and the US basing agreement would remain highly divisive issues in Icelandic politics until the late 1970s.[22]

With the end of the Cold War, the strategic salience of all parts of Europe for US planners began to wane, but as Russian forces evacuated former Warsaw Pact territories and NATO expanded, the remaining concentration of Russia's strength along its Northern coastlines actually

---

19 G. Lundestad, *The United States and Western Europe since 1945: From 'Empire' by Invitation to Transatlantic Drift* (Oxford: Oxford University Press, 2003), pp. 51–52; Tony Insall and Patrick Salmon, 'Preface to the Nordic Countries: From War to Cold War, 1944–1951', *Scandinavian Journal of History*, 37, 2 (2012), 136–55.

20 Lundestad (2003), p. 57.

21 Valur Ingimundarson, *The Rebellious Ally: Iceland, the United States, and the Politics of Empire 1945–2006* (Dordrecht: Republic of Letters, 2011).

22 Ingimundarson (2011).

increased the relative importance of Nordic stability. Since 2008–2009, strategic interest has been attracted back to the area by speculations on the opening up of the Arctic,[23] as well as the evidence of Russian aggression in Georgia (2008) and Ukraine (2014). Under its new Strategic Concept of 2010,[24] NATO has offered Nordic and Baltic member states enhanced contingency planning for possible attacks, and in 2014 — in reaction to Ukrainian events — both Sweden and Finland signed up for closer territorial defence cooperation with NATO.[25]

For the two most easterly, non-allied Nordics, the indirect and informal nature of Western strategic cover after 1949 made other potential shelters more interesting. After joining the EU in 1995, Finland and Sweden played an influential role in the development of the Union's military arm, now the Common Security and Defence Policy (CSDP).[26] While keen to avoid the EU's competing with NATO or provoking Russia, they valued whatever 'soft' protection might come from equal involvement in a militarily active European family. Both embraced the new language in the EU's Treaty of Lisbon (entering into force on 1 December 2009) committing EU members — albeit with strictly limited practical effect — to help each other in case of military attack, regardless of alliance status.

If Nordics must sacrifice their precious sovereignty and free choice in defence, they will do so for partners who really can protect them, not for each other. Thus, when in 2011 they adopted a mutual 'solidarity' declaration,[27] it explicitly excluded cases of warlike attack. Aside from the sphere of peacekeeping, Nordic regional defence cooperation has been a relatively late-blooming flower, currently coordinated through

---

23   Christian Le Mière and Jeffrey Mazo, *Arctic Opening: Insecurity and Opportunity* (Abingdon and New York: Routledge, 2014).

24   NATO, 'Strategic Concept' (2010), http://www.nato.int/lisbon2010/strategic-concept-2010-eng.pdf

25   A. Klus, 'The Nordic Dimension of the Ukrainian Crisis', New Eastern Europe (2014), http://www.neweasterneurope.eu/interviews/1242-the-nordic-dimension-of-the-ukrainian-crisis

26   M. Strömvik, 'Starting to "Think Big": The Nordic Countries and EU Peace-Building', in *The Nordic Countries and the European Security and Defence Policy*, ed. by Alyson J. K. Bailes, Gunilla Herolf and Bengt Sundelius (Oxford: Oxford University Press, 2006), pp. 199–214.

27   Nordic Ministers, 'Declaration of Solidarity' (2011), http://www.utanrikisraduneyti.is/media/nordurlandaskrifstofa/Norraen-samstoduyfirlysing-ENG.pdf

the framework of the Nordic Defence Cooperation (NORDEFCO).[28] Reactions to the Russia-Ukraine crisis have spurred new talk of, notably, a Finnish-Swedish axis; but a Swedish independent policy review in 2014 (the *Bertelman Report*) warned that no degree of cooperation, with anyone, can release Sweden from the quandary caused by its own defence cuts.[29] At best, intra-Nordic defence work can be seen as embroidery upon the still overwhelmingly trans-Atlantic nature of the region's 'hard' shelter umbrella.

Shelter in the EU

Through European integration, the Nordic states find numerous types of shelter, primarily economic. They also enjoy considerable political cover (soft security shelter) from membership of Schengen and enormous societal shelter, for example from the EU's research and development projects (see Table 2). In 1973 Denmark became the first Nordic state to join the EU, with Sweden and Finland ultimately joining after the end of the Cold War. From 1994, Iceland and Norway have been members of the European Economic Area (EEA) and thus of the EU's Single Market, deeming it sufficient economic shelter for the time being. They have all taken part in Schengen from the beginning and cooperate with the agencies EUROPOL and EUROJUST.

At the same time, Nordic relations with the EU have been diverse and often idiosyncratic. Collectively the Nordics are relative newcomers to the European project. Absent at the signing of the Treaty of Rome, the Nordic states opted for limited trade partnerships with the EU, such as the European Free Trade Association (EFTA). In 1994, Norway negotiated terms for entry for the second time but its people voted No again. Iceland applied for membership in 2009 following its economic crash, but froze the application in 2013. Since spring 2015 its government

---

28 H. Ojanen, 'Nordic Defence Cooperation — Inspiration for the EU or a Lesson in Matching Expectations?', TEPSA Policy Paper (2014), http://www.tepsa.eu/tepsa-policy-paper-by-hanna-ojanen-nordic-defence-cooperation-inspiration-for-the-eu-or-a-lesson-in-matching-expectations; Tuomas Forsberg, 'The Rise of Nordic Defence Cooperation: A Return to Regionalism?', *International Affairs*, 89, 5 (2013), 1161–81.

29 Government of Sweden, 'International Defence Cooperation: Efficiency, Solidarity, Sovereignty' (2014), http://www.icds.ee/fileadmin/media/icds.ee/failid/Bertelman2014.pdf

no longer considers Iceland an applicant state — though it has not formally withdrawn the membership application. Greenland is the only entity to have left the EU, by a referendum in 1985 after it had been obliged to join with Denmark. Britain is on course to follow Greenland in the next few years. The Faroe Islands, another autonomous Danish territory, were allowed their own choice at the time of Danish entry and opted not to join, entering into a *sui generis* relationship with Brussels. The three Nordic members of the Union each have a distinct status, with only Finland participating fully in all EU policies including Economic and Monetary Union (EMU). In 2003 Sweden's people voted against participating in the Eurozone. Denmark gained four opt-outs in 1993 at the time of ratifying the Maastricht Treaty: from EMU, EU defence, European citizenship, and justice and home affairs.

The choice of economic shelter for the Nordic states consequently varies, reflecting not only national levels of Euroscepticism but also objective features of their economic structure. All Nordic states are similar in having lofty economic and welfare standards combined with relatively large state sectors, requiring the private sector to produce high added value. Norway, Iceland, the Faroe Islands and Greenland, however, profit mostly from natural resources (fish, oil, gas, other power sources and tourism); and this, as well as political culture and geography, may help explain why they have not seen strong enough protective benefits in the EU to be willing to cede sovereignty.[30] For Sweden and Denmark with their more continental orientation and greater agricultural and industrial exports, the appeal of the EU market has been stronger.[31] Finland's motives for EU entry and its commitment to EMU are the most clearly security-related: the EU helped to compensate for the collapse of former Soviet trade, and sealed the Western character of the Finnish land and people.[32] Just as with defence, however, some of these national solutions appear more easily sustainable than others. While Norway hardly wavered with the economic crash of 2008, Iceland suffered abject failure in the attempt to

---

30   Ingebritsen (1998); Baldur Thorhallsson, *Iceland and European Integration: On the Edge* (London: Routledge, 2004).
31   Ingebritsen (1998).
32   [N.a.], 'Finland and Europe: In and Happy', *Economist*, 9 October 1997, http://www.economist.com/node/102291

diversify its narrow economic base by building up banking services — a classic small-state ploy. Another volatile industry, tourism, has now 'replaced' the financial sector as a 'saviour' from the reliance on fisheries and energy supplies to the aluminium industry.

Shelter in Nordic cooperation

Despite never achieving (or perhaps wanting) full regional integration, the Nordics have nevertheless supplied each other with significant elements of shelter: most obviously societal (see Table 2), but also supplementing the primary economic, diplomatic and soft security shelter derived from the EU, NATO and the US. Nordic cooperation is formalised in the Nordic Council, a parliamentary cooperation body supplemented since 1971 by the Nordic Council of Ministers (NCM). These institutions deal with a wide range of issues such as culture, media, the economy, business, working life, education, research, environment, legislation, justice, welfare, and gender equality, and have more recently expanded their coverage to at least the 'softer' security fields.

Achievements of Nordic cooperation include the Nordic Passport Union, established by four of the nations in 1958 (Iceland joined in 1965), which waives the obligation for citizens of the Nordic States to travel with passports between Nordic states.[33] The Nordic Convention on Social Assistance and Social Services and the Nordic Convention on Social Security allow migrant Nordic citizens to claim social security on the same basis as the nationals of the state in which they live.[34] The common Nordic labour market, first agreed to in 1954 (agreement renewed in 1982), reflects a 'fundamental right for nationals of the Nordic countries to be able freely to take up employment and settle in another Nordic country'.[35]

---

33 Nordic Council, 'The Nordic Passport Convention' (2015), http://www.norden. org/en/om-samarbejdet-1/nordic-agreements/treaties-and-agreements/passport-issues-citizenship-and-national-registration/the-nordic-passport-convention

34 Nordic Council, 'Nordic Convention on Social Assistance and Social Services' (2015), http://www.norden.org/en/om-samarbejdet-1/nordic-agreements/treaties-and-agreements/social-and-health-care/nordic-convention-on-social-assistance-and-social-services

35 Nordic Council, 'Agreement Concerning a Common Nordic Labour Market' (2015), http://www.norden.org/en/om-samarbejdet-1/nordic-agreements/treaties-and-agreements/labour-market/agreement-concerning-a-common-nordic-labour-market

Intra-Nordic trade is extensive: 19% of Nordic exports go to other Nordic countries and 22% of Nordic imports come from other Nordic countries. Greenland (86.6%), Faroe Islands (62.6%) and Iceland (27.9%) import the most from other Nordic states whereas Greenland (93.7%), Sweden (24.7%) and Denmark (23.0%) export the most to their co-Nordics.[36]

Nordic states have a reputation for diplomatic cooperation in international bodies. Nowhere is this plainer than in the United Nations, where the Nordic states overcome their small size by taking joint positions and initiatives, and supporting each other in bids for elections of non-permanent Security Council members. This Nordic unity has survived Finland's and Sweden's EU entry which also commits them to EU group efforts at the UN.[37] Nordic cooperation also results in more influence in bargaining within the EU. Since the 1990s the Nordic Heads of Government have pre-consulted before major EU meetings, either streamlining their views or finding non-damaging ways to agree to differ. The Nordics have concocted joint inputs to high-profile EU policies, such as the Nordic Battle Group (though excluding Denmark) for EU military missions, and more recently, a proposed joint rescue module for civil emergencies.[38] According to Panke, the Nordic states can, through such systematic cooperation, 'increase their collective bargaining leverage and shape EU policies more effectively than through unilateral action'.[39]

The Nordic states have cooperated among themselves in 'soft' security since the 1950s, notably through networks of police and rescue organisations. In 2009 a programme to boost mutual learning and collaboration when dealing with civil emergencies was launched as the 'Haga process'. The Haga system has by now reviewed many specific

---

36   Nordic Council of Ministers, *Nordic Statistical Yearbook 2014* (Copenhagen: Nordic Council of Ministers, 2014), p. 111.

37   Katie Verlin Laatikainen, 'Norden's Eclipse the Impact of the European Union's Common Foreign and Security Policy on the Nordic Group in the United Nations', *Cooperation and Conflict*, 38, 4 (2003), 409–41.

38   Alyson J. K. Bailes and C. Sandö, *Nordic Cooperation on Civil Security: The Haga Process 2009–14, Occasional Paper*, Institute of International Affairs and Centre for Small State Studies (Reykjavík 2014), http://www.ams.hi.is/wp-content/uploads/2014/04/The-Haga-Process-PDF.pdf

39   Diana Panke, 'Small States in the European Union: Structural Disadvantages in EU Policy-Making and Counter-Strategies', *Journal of European Public Policy*, 17, 6 (2010), 799–817.

issues and operational areas, albeit with sparse visible results.[40] Its latest studies, notably on host nation support for cross-border civil operations, have highlighted the considerable variations in national structures and laws regarding non-military security. Cultural differences over central-local burden-sharing, over how far to trust the military, and over public-private relations, further complicate the picture. Haga's limitations are, however, to some extent compensated by other advances being made e.g. in Nordic cyber-security cooperation and cooperative research into societal security.[41]

Scottish shelter options

As seen in Table 3, four entities — NATO, the EU, the US, and the rUK itself — appear best suited to meeting Scotland's needs for economic, societal, and political shelter (including hard and soft security). In its given, north-west European and 'strong state' context, Scotland's independence — should it ever happen — would be more of a 'velvet divorce' than a violent (conflict-driven) breakaway or radical régime change. The new country's strategy might thus be expected to lean towards continuity at least in relation to its international alliances. Further, Scotland's peripheral geographical site and its shortage of neighbours mean that it has few, if any, truly new options for any dimension of shelter. In fact, the SNP have made clear that Scotland has a vital interest in staying in the EU and would also wish to remain a full member of NATO. Controversy during the referendum debate hinged on the conditions on which this might happen and especially, whether Scotland would have a residual right to membership (as a former part of the UK) or would need to apply afresh.

Table 3. Hypothetical shelter solutions for Scotland after independence

Economy	Currency union	Political	Societal	Hard Security	Soft security
EU/rUK	rUK	EU/NATO/NC	rUK/EU/NC	rUK/US/NATO	rUK/EU

---

40   Bailes and Sandö (2014).
41   *Ibid.*

What is clear is that the Scottish situation lacks direct European precedent, as no member state has split up after previously joining NATO and/or the EU. This leaves room for widely diverging hypotheses, as was seen in the referendum campaign. To an outside observer, however, it seems hard to build realistic scenarios where London would wish or be able to treat Scotland in a zero-sum, purely hostile and vengeful way — at least on strategic points — when facing a peaceful split. After all, Scotland would remain physically attached to the rUK, as its strategic hinterland and main buffer against the traditional line of perceived threat from Russia. It would fall to London to try to reassure NATO about the impact of the split on defence readiness in, and contributions from, the British Isles.

Shelter in NATO, the US and the remnant UK

The logic of Scotland's seeking its 'hard' strategic shelter from NATO is both external and internal. No other organisation offers the collective military strength to deter possible assailants (from any quarter), while also following democratic practices that give a voice to its smallest members. Some Scots may appreciate being part of a trans-Atlantic political community based on democratic values. Others might simply find it a reassuring element of continuity.

From an internal viewpoint, being a small member of NATO gives scope to reduce national defence spending and avoid building a full range of force capabilities. Small members that deviate from this pattern normally have special reasons for threat-consciousness, such as Estonia, on the Russian border.[42] During the crisis sparked by Russian action in Ukraine, NATO has renewed its appeal for all Allies to meet a norm for 2% of GDP spent on defence,[43] but it continues to send mixed signals to its smaller members by stressing specialisation and offering them designated reinforcements. Also, its recent 'Smart Defence' concept

---

42 Alyson J. K. Bailes and Örvar Þ. Rafnsson, 'Iceland and the EU's Common Security and Defence Policy: Challenge or Opportunity?', *Icelandic Review of Politics & Administration*, 8, 1 (2012), 109–31.

43 NATO, 'Wales Summit Declaration', 5 September 2014, http://www.nato.int/cps/en/natohq/official_texts_112964.htm (A declaration issued by the Heads of State and Government participating in the meeting of the North Atlantic Council in Wales.)

positively encouraged members to give up capabilities too limited to be viable.[44]

NATO's collective budget is very small and not a significant cost for a nation like Scotland. Like the Nordic neighbours, the Scots would more probably have to 'pay' by continuing to contribute to NATO-led (as well as EU- or UN-led) military missions abroad; even small states can meet niche requirements in this context, while their presence conveys political solidarity. In the independence debate, the SNP said they would wish Scotland to join in such tasks when backed by a clear international-legal mandate — i.e. not Iraq-style coalitions.[45] One study at the time claimed that intervention forces as well as basic territorial defence could be provided for little more than half the money Scottish taxpayers currently contribute to UK defence.[46] The SNP itself proposed to save GBP one billion annually on the latter figure.[47] Much would, of course depend on the division of former UK forces; on whether Scotland tried to sustain independently viable naval and air arms, with their high equipment costs (the SNP suggested sharing air and sea bases with the UK which would open up an extra dimension of cover); and other possible changes in force structure, such as a revised active/reservist balance.

Would NATO itself want to keep Scotland, as a small 'security importer' with reduced defence spending and capacity, where — moreover — the dominant political movement proposes to declare itself a non-nuclear state and remove the present Trident nuclear submarine base at Faslane?[48] The major headaches this poses for the UK Government should not obscure the fact that very few NATO states now have other people's nuclear forces on their territory, and Scotland's nearest neighbours — Norway and Denmark — co-founded NATO while rejecting any such presence. (Iceland joined this position in the 1980s.) Viewed logically, NATO should care about maintaining an effective UK deterrent, and about handling the delicate London-Edinburgh

---

44   NATO, 'Smart Defence', 1 September 2015, http://www.nato.int/cps/en/SID-34AEED99-772DF4E3/natolive/topics_84268.htm

45   E.g. Scottish Government, *Your Scotland, Your Voice: A National Conversation* (Edinburgh: Scottish Executive, 2009), p. 119.

46   Stuart Crawford and Richard Marsh, *A' the Blue Bonnets: Defending an Independent Scotland* (London: Royal United Service Institute, 2012).

47   [N.a.], 'In Full: SNP Resolution on Nato', *Scotsman*, 16 July 2012, http://www.scotsman.com/news/politics/in-full-snp-resolution-on-nato-1-2414919

48   Scottish Government (2009).

negotiations sensibly, rather than about exactly where the British assets ended up. It would be hard for it to reject Scottish accession on the grounds of military spending or force size, when other recent entrants' performance has varied considerably and Iceland, a founder ally, has no forces at all. What would probably dominate, ultimately also in London's view, would be the case for maintaining unbroken NATO coverage (with its scope for coherent US reinforcement) across the Nordic/North Atlantic space, and having Scotland as a modest contributor rather than a detached free-rider.

The United States does not want an independent Scotland and has made that clear. It does not want to lose access to Scottish facilities and have a strategic black hole north of the rUK. This would be a serious setback for US defence leaders who envisage a gradual strategic 'pivot' away from Europe to Asia. Should this nevertheless happen, while protective of the rUK's interests, Washington could be expected to urge London to reduce the risks by building a good defence understanding with its new northern neighbour. Edinburgh would come under equally strong US pressure to cooperate and would have good cause to do so. Its territory's ultimate shelter would be US nuclear and conventional might, as is the case for all the present Nordic (and Baltic) nations. Further, 'the USA is Scotland's largest [overseas] export market and the leading source of inward investment into Scotland'[49] — investments that would be least disrupted if Scotland's present EU status was preserved. Scottish cultural and societal links with North America are strong, as in Ireland. Overall, one might imagine Washington not only strategically underwriting Scottish/British solutions but actively brokering them, as it has done between London and Dublin at crucial turning points — a classic aspect of political shelter.

The analysis thus far makes plain that good 'shelter' solutions for Scotland depend, not least, on coming to terms with the rUK as shown in Table 3. In reality, the latter would be Scotland's primary shelter even after independence: in strategic, economic, and soft-security terms, and also societally and culturally insofar as cross-border agreement would reduce disruption and distress for ordinary citizens. The SNP has

---

49   Scottish Development International, 'North America Briefing' (2013), http:// www.scottish-enterprise.presscentre.com/International-activity/North-America-briefing-445.aspx [accessed 6 February 2013].

stated that an independent Scotland would wish to retain the Queen as monarch (to keep close societal links with the UK) and the pound sterling as currency (implying backing from the Bank of England), so an independent Scotland is highly likely to, at least, seek such shelter at a minimum.

Shelter in the EU

As Norway's and Iceland's cases show, the European Union does not automatically appeal to Northern European small states as a shelter. Scotland, however, has already experienced and on balance profited from it for forty years (see Table 2). Anti-EU feeling is less dominant than in the UK. Brussels may even seem a more palatable source of authority than London. Continued presence in the EU would thus be an obvious solution for Scotland's shelter needs in the areas of the economy, 'soft' security, and societal (as regards concrete functions like communication and infrastructure) and some political dimensions, as shown in Table 3.

Recent Irish experience of EU support during the debt crisis underpins this case, but also highlights the price to be paid.[50] How the overall 'costs' of EU shelter for an independent Scotland might change is a complex question that is only starting to be probed in public debate. How would Scotland's independently assessed contribution and its receipts from EU funds compare with what it experiences as part of a much larger net-contributing nation? If Scotland had to make a new membership application as many (including the President of the European Commission) believe,[51] could it stay outside the Schengen system and maintain a ceiling on its budget contribution as earlier negotiated for the UK? These are important questions, but such material concerns have not deterred other recent small applicants to the EU, who reasoned rather in terms of the vulnerabilities they would feel outside the Union, the even less attractive prospect of trusting a national

---

50   Peadar Kirby and Baldur Thorhallsson, 'Financial Crises in Iceland and Ireland: Does European Union and Euro Membership Matter?', *JCMS: Journal of Common Market Studies*, 50, 5 (2012), 801–18.

51   Severin Carrol, 'Barroso Casts Doubt on Independent Scotland's EU Membership Rights', *Guardian*, 21 September 2012, https://www.theguardian.com/politics/2012/sep/12/barroso-doubt-scotland-eu-membership

protector, and the support and discipline of a political community grounded in the world's most peaceful values.

Scotland's calculation may be even easier because it faces ceding no sovereignty to Brussels beyond what it is already accustomed to. Only joining the Euro would change that, and the SNP have no such plans at present — though the calculus might change after Brexit. Granted EU membership, Scotland would have far fewer representatives and votes and a much smaller voice at the EU table than the UK has at present. But that would be offset by the freedom to promote its own distinct European interests — which Scottish representatives, unlike genuinely new entrants, could do with skills honed for decades. They could freely seek new political/tactical alliances with member states both small and large.

Shelter in the Nordic family

Enough has been said already to show that the Nordic states as such cannot offer Scotland sufficient shelter in any vital dimension, given their own limitations and strategic dependence. They all rely openly or *de facto* on the US and NATO, while Iceland and Greenland have special bilateral defence arrangements with Washington. Further, all are deeply involved in the European integration process as full members or as part of the Common Market through the EEA. Greenland and the Faroe Islands, though not formally in the EU, have fisheries agreements with Brussels and draw indirect economic benefits through Denmark. All enjoy a wide range of political and societal protection from the Union's diplomatic strength and its extensive regional, research, educational and cultural programmes. All derive soft security benefits — not currently available elsewhere — from European cooperation in fields such as environmental and energy security, disease control and migration management: all of which would be equally pressing concerns for Scotland.[52]

Iceland's case as the Nordic state with the most acute shelter needs may illustrate the point. The other Nordics could neither fill the whole gap left in Iceland's military security after US forces withdrew in 2006, nor rescue the Icelanders from their exceptionally severe economic

---

52   Bailes and Thorhallsson (2013).

crash in 2008. Yet, to balance this, Nordic cooperation offers Iceland crucial political and societal links with an otherwise remote European mainland; provides a multiplier effect for its policies on key issues like the Arctic; and draws it into joint positions on many European and international issues where it shares in the undoubted appeal of the Nordic 'brand'. Such Nordic practices offer a powerful example for other small states of how to exert influence despite smallness, and they would *prima facie* provide a very desirable added element for Scotland's hypothetical shelter-building as well. The SNP for its part has explicitly stated that it wishes to follow the Nordic model and its norms and values. With such a new partner, the Nordic states could continue to lead by example[53] and encourage others to adopt their 'good' practices.

Specifically, the Nordic states could support Scotland's negotiation of good bargains with the US and rUK, inside and outside multilateral institutions, and would have powerful motives for doing so, given their own stake in North European stability. They could provide political inspiration and cover for distinctive characteristics the Scots might want to stress in fields like peace promotion, arms control, humanitarian initiatives and the anti-nuclear stance (as well as social-liberal values at home). Both these roles would provide 'political' shelter for Scotland's willed identity change. Concrete economic, soft security, and societal benefits could be sought through closer Scottish-Nordic cooperation, including common approaches to the growing Arctic challenge. Scotland's reduced military resources could be optimised by studying Nordic lessons and joining Nordic initiatives like NORDEFCO, the current framework for five-nation defence cooperation.[54]

Might this mutually sheltering relationship take institutional form? Scotland could *prima facie* try to join both Nordic Cooperation (in its parliamentary and governmental dimensions) and the West Nordic Cooperation (WNC) of Iceland, the Faroes, Greenland and coastal Norway. Nordic political and public attitudes would surely be sympathetic, but the precedent involved in granting NC membership might give pause since the Baltic States were earlier denied it.

---

53 C. Ingebritsen, *Scandinavia in World Politics* (Lanham and Oxford: Rowman & Littlefield, 2006).

54 Håkon Lunde Saxi, *Nordic Defence Cooperation after the Cold War* (Oslo: Norwegian Institute of Defence Studies, 2011).

Admitting Scotland to the WNC might be less contentious given its close geographical presence — including Shetland and Orkney — and common issues such as oil/gas exploitation. Alternative forms of association, or new 'Nordic-plus' cooperation frameworks, could doubtless be invented.

Scotland needs to find like-minded states in order to receive backup in international negotiations. The Nordic nations seem like ideal partners but if they are not willing to support Scottish negotiation positions, and, for example, would rather remain silent in order to keep cordial relations with the US and the rUK, Scotland has to look for other partners or move closer to the US and/or the rUK positions.

Conclusion

The five Nordic states have lived for decades with the same strategic asymmetry that would face an independent Scotland. They have found many-sided shelters while maintaining strong national idiosyncrasies. The diversity in the types of shelter pursued by the Nordic states reflects each state's unique challenges and the costs associated with different shelter options. Norway, Denmark and Iceland found military shelter in NATO, whereas Finland and Sweden were best served by neutrality. An equally wide range of Nordic national solutions applies to relations with the EU. In each other, the Nordic states find many types of shelter, primarily societal. In other dimensions, the shelter of Nordic cooperation basically supplements that provided by European integration, NATO and/or the US.

In extending the general small state analysis and lessons of the Nordic model to a potential independent Scotland, we have found four entities — NATO, the US, the rUK itself, and the EU — *prima facie* best suited to meeting Scotland's needs for economic, societal, and political shelter including hard and soft security. As any other small entity, a Scotland moving towards independence would need to weigh carefully the benefits and costs of these shelter options and how they compare to the benefits and costs of its current arrangements within the UK. In doing so it would need to dismiss at the outset any notion that Nordic neighbours could either provide an alternative for any key dimension of shelter, or invent solutions offering escape from the sometime very tough choices to be made and prices to be paid. With that once clear, however, both the lessons of (varied) Nordic experience, and the comradeship and softer kinds of shelter to be found within the Nordic family, could provide valuable lubrication for the transitional process and a supportive pillar for Scotland's accommodation to independent existence in the world.

References

[N.a.], 'Finland and Europe: In and Happy', *The Economist*, 9 October 1997, http://www.economist.com/node/102291

——, 'In Full: SNP Resolution on Nato', *Scotsman*, 16 July 2012, http://www.scotsman.com/news/politics/in-full-snp-resolution-on-nato-1-2414919

——, *CIA World Factbook* (CIA, 2015), https://www.cia.gov/library/publications/the-world-factbook/

Alesina, A. and Spolaore, E., *The Size of Nations* (Cambridge: MIT Press, 2003).

Bailes, Alyson J. K., 'Small States and Security: Does Size Still Matter?', in *Small States in the Modern World: Vulnerabilities and Opportunities*, ed. by H. Baldersheim and M. Keating (Cheltenham and Northampton, MA: Edward Elgar Publishing, Inc., 2015), pp. 23–41.

——, and Rafnsson, Örvar Þ., 'Iceland and the EU's Common Security and Defence Policy: Challenge or Opportunity?', *Icelandic Review of Politics & Administration*, 8 (2012), 109–31.

——, and Thorhallsson, Baldur, 'Instrumentalizing the European Union in Small State Strategies', *Journal of European Integration*, 35 (2013), 99–115, 10, http://dx.doi.org/10.1080/07036337.2012.689828

——, and Johnstone, Rachael Lorna, 'Scotland as an Independent Small State: Where Would It Seek Shelter?', *Icelandic Review of Politics and Administration*, 9 (2013), 1–20, http://dx.doi.org/10.13177/irpa.a.2013.9.1.1

——, and Sandö, C., *Nordic Cooperation on Civil Security: The Haga Process 2009–14, Occasional Paper*, Institute of International Affairs and Centre for Small State Studies (Reykjavík, 2014), http://www.ams.hi.is/wp-content/uploads/2014/04/The-Haga-Process-PDF.pdf

Carrol, Severin, 'Barroso Casts Doubt on Independent Scotland's EU Membership Rights', *Guardian*, 21 September 2012, https://www.theguardian.com/politics/2012/sep/12/barroso-doubt-scotland-eu-membership

Crawford, Stuart and Marsh, Richard, *A 'the Blue Bonnets Defending an Independent Scotland* (London: Royal United Service Institute, 2012).

de Carvalho, B. and Neumann, I. B., *Small State Status Seeking: Norway's Quest for International Standing* (New York: Taylor & Francis, 2014).

Donald, D. and Hutton, A., 'Economic Self-Determination: Towards a Political Economy of Scottish Citizenship', in *Radical Scotland: Arguments for Self-Determination*, ed. by G. Hassan and R. Ilett (Edinburgh: Luath Press Ltd, 2011), pp. 49–62.

Forsberg, Tuomas, 'The Rise of Nordic Defence Cooperation: A Return to Regionalism?', *International Affairs*, 89 (2013), 1161–81, http://dx.doi.org/10.1111/1468-2346.12065

Government of Sweden, 'International Defence Cooperation: Efficiency, Solidarity, Sovereignty' (2014), http://www.icds.ee/fileadmin/media/icds.ee/failid/Bertelman2014.pdf

Handel, Michael I., *Weak States in the International System* (London: Frank Cass, 1981).

Hanlon, P. and Karki, F. U., 'Health, Culture and Society: A Scottish-Nordic Conversation', in *Radical Scotland: Arguments for Self-Determination*, ed. by Gerry Hassan and Rosie Ilett (Edinburgh: Luath Press Ltd, 2011), pp. 85–101.

Holbraad, Carsten, 'The Role of Middle Powers', *Cooperation and Conflict*, 6 (1971), 77–90, http://dx.doi.org/10.1177/001083677100600108

Hopf, Ted, 'The Promise of Constructivism in International Relations Theory', *International Security*, 23 (1998), 171–200, http://dx.doi.org/10.2307/2539267

Ikenberry, G. J., *After Victory: Institutions, Strategic Restraint, and the Rebuilding of Order after Major Wars* (Princeton: Princeton University Press, 2001).

Ingebritsen, Christine, *The Nordic States and European Unity* (Ithaca, NY and London: Cornell University Press, 1998).

—, *Scandinavia in World Politics* (Lanham and Oxford: Rowman & Littlefield, 2006).

Ingimundarson, Valur, *The Rebellious Ally: Iceland, the United States, and the Politics of Empire 1945–2006* (Dordrecht: Republic of Letters, 2011).

Insall, Tony and Salmon, Patrick, 'Preface to the Nordic Countries: From War to Cold War, 1944–1951', *Scandinavian Journal of History*, 37 (2012), 136–55, http://dx.doi.org/10.1080/03468755.2012.666643

International Institute of Strategic Studies (IISS), *The Military Balance 2015* (London: Taylor & Francis, 2015).

Katzenstein, P. J., *Corporatism and Change: Austria, Switzerland, and the Politics of Industry* (Ithaca, NY and London: Cornell University Press, 1984).

—, *Small States in World Markets: Industrial Policy in Europe* (Ithaca, NY and London: Cornell University Press, 1985).

Keating, Michael, 'The Political Economy of Self-Determination', in *Radical Scotland: Arguments for Self-Determination*, ed. by G. Hassan, and R. Ilett (Edinburgh: Luath Press Ltd, 2011), pp. 40–48.

Keohane, Robert O., *After Hegemony: Cooperation and Discord in the World Political Economy* (Princeton: Princeton University Press, 1984).

—, and Martin, Lisa L., 'The Promise of Institutionalist Theory', *International Security*, 20 (1995), 39–51, http://dx.doi.org/10.2307/2539214

Kirby, Peadar and Thorhallsson, Baldur, 'Financial Crises in Iceland and Ireland: Does European Union and Euro Membership Matter?', *JCMS: Journal of Common Market Studies*, 50 (2012), 801–18, http://dx.doi.org/10.1111/j.1468-5965.2012.02258.x

Klus, A., 'The Nordic Dimension of the Ukrainian Crisis', New Eastern Europe (2014), http://www.neweasterneurope.eu/interviews/1242-the-nordic-dimension-of-the-ukrainian-crisis

Laatikainen, Katie Verlin, 'Norden's Eclipse the Impact of the European Union's Common Foreign and Security Policy on the Nordic Group in the United Nations', *Cooperation and Conflict*, 38 (2003), 409–41, http://dx.doi.org/10.1177/0010836703384004

Le Mière, Christian and Mazo, Jeffrey, *Arctic Opening: Insecurity and Opportunity, Iiss Adelphi Series* (Abingdon and New York: Routledge, 2014).

Liska, G., *Nations in Alliance: The Limits of Interdependance* (Baltimore: Johns Hopkins University Press, 1962).

Lundestad, G., *The United States and Western Europe since 1945: From 'Empire' by Invitation to Transatlantic Drift* (Oxford: Oxford University Press, 2003).

Mitzen, Jennifer, 'Ontological Security in World Politics: State Identity and the Security Dilemma', *European Journal of International Relations*, 12 (2006), 341–70, http://dx.doi.org/10.1177/1354066106067346

Murkens, Jo E., *Scotland's Place in Europe* (London: Constitution Unit, University College London, 2001).

NATO, 'Strategic Concept' (2010), http://www.nato.int/lisbon2010/strategic-concept-2010-eng.pdf

—, 'Wales Summit Declaration', 5 September 2014, http://www.nato.int/cps/en/natohq/official_texts_112964.htm

—, 'Smart Defence', 1 September 2015, http://www.nato.int/cps/en/SID-34AEED99-772DF4E3/natolive/topics_84268.htm

Nordic Council, 'Agreement Concerning a Common Nordic Labour Market' (2015), http://www.norden.org/en/om-samarbejdet-1/nordic-agreements/treaties-and-agreements/labour-market/agreement-concerning-a-common-nordic-labour-market

—, 'Nordic Convention on Social Assistance and Social Services' (2015), http://www.norden.org/en/om-samarbejdet-1/nordic-agreements/treaties-and-agreements/social-and-health-care/nordic-convention-on-social-assistance-and-social-services

—, 'The Nordic Passport Convention' (2015), http://www.norden.org/en/om-samarbejdet-1/nordic-agreements/treaties-and-agreements/passport-issues-citizenship-and-national-registration/the-nordic-passport-convention

Nordic Council of Ministers, *Nordic Statistical Yearbook 2014* (Copenhagen: Nordic Council of Ministers, 2014).

Nordic Ministers, 'Declaration of Solidarity' (2011), http://www.utanrikisradu neyti.is/media/nordurlandaskrifstofa/Norraen-samstoduyfirlysing-ENG.pdf

Ojanen, H., 'Nordic Defence Cooperation — Inspiration for the EU or a Lesson in Matching Expectations?', TEPSA Policy Paper (2014), http://www.tepsa.eu/tepsa-policy-paper-by-hanna-ojanen-nordic-defence-cooperation-inspiration-for-the-eu-or-a-lesson-in-matching-expectations

Osgood, R. E., *Alliances and American Foreign Policy* (Baltimore: Johns Hopkins Press, 1968).

Panke, Diana, *Small States in the European Union: Coping with Structural Disadvantages* (Farnham and Burlington: Ashgate, 2010).

—, 'Small States in the European Union: Structural Disadvantages in EU Policy-Making and Counter-Strategies', *Journal of European Public Policy*, 17 (2010), 799–817, Pii 925180850, http://dx.doi.org/10.1080/13501763.2010.486980

Rokkan, S., Urwin, D. W., and Research, European Consortium for Political, *Economy, Territory, Identity: Politics of West European Peripheries* (London: Sage, 1983).

Salmond, A., 'Scotland's Place in the World. Hugo Young Memorial Lecture' (London, 25 January 2012), http://www.guardian.co.uk/politics/2012/jan/25/alex-salmond-hugo-young-lecture

Saxi, Håkon Lunde, *Nordic Defence Cooperation after the Cold War, Oslo Files on Defence and Security* (Oslo: Norwegian Institute of Defence Studies., 2011).

Schroeder, P. W., 'Alliances, 1815–1945: Weapons of Power and Tools of Management', in *Historical Dimensions of National Security Problems*, ed. by K. E. Knorr (Lawrence: University Press of Kansas, 1976), pp. 227–62.

Scottish Development International, 'North America Briefing' (2013), http://www.scottish-enterprise.presscentre.com/International-activity/North-America-briefing-445.aspx [accessed 6 February 2013].

Scottish Government, *Your Scotland, Your Voice: A National Conversation* (Edinburgh: Scottish Executive, 2009).

Scottish National Party, 'Senior EU Official Backs Benefits of Small States' (2012), https://web.archive.org/web/20141202110524/http://www.snp.org/media-centre/news/2012/dec/senior-eu-official-backs-benefits-small-states   [last saved to the Wayback Machine 2 December 2014].

SIPRI, 'Military Expenditure Database' (2015), http://www.sipri.org/research/armaments/milex/milex_database

Snyder, G. H., *Alliance Politics* (Ithaca, NY: Cornell University Press, 1997).

Steele, B. J., *Ontological Security in International Relations: Self-Identity and the IR State* (Abingdon and London: Taylor & Francis, 2008).

Strömvik, M., 'Starting to 'Think Big': The Nordic Countries and EU Peace-Building', in *The Nordic Countries and the European Security and Defence Policy*, ed. by Alyson J. K. Bailes, Gunilla Herolf and Bengt Sundelius (Oxford: Oxford University Press, 2006), pp. 199–214.

Thorhallsson, Baldur, *Iceland and European Integration: On the Edge* (London: Routledge, 2004).

—, 'The Size of States in the European Union: Theoretical and Conceptual Perspectives', *European Integration,* 28 (2006), 7–31, http://dx.doi.org/10.1080/07036330500480490

—, 'Domestic Buffer Versus External Shelter: Viability of Small States in the New Globalised Economy', *European Political Science,* 10 (2011), 324–36, http://dx.doi.org/10.1057/eps.2011.29

—, 'Iceland's External Affairs in the Middle Ages: The Shelter of Norwegian Sea Power', *Icelandic Review of Politics & Administration,* 8 (2012), 5–37, http://dx.doi.org/10.13177/irpa.a.2012.8.1.1

—, and Wivel, Anders, 'Small States in the European Union: What Do We Know and What Would We Like to Know?', *Cambridge Review of International Affairs,* 19 (2006), 651–68, http://dx.doi.org/10.1080/09557570601003502

Vital, D., *The Inequality of States: A Study of the Small Power in International Relations* (Oxford: Clarendon Press, 1967).

Walt, Stephen M., *The Origins of Alliance* (Ithaca, NY: Cornell University Press, 1987).

World Bank, 'Countries and Economies' (2015), http://data.worldbank.org/country

Zarakol, Ayşe, 'Ontological (In)security and State Denial of Historical Crimes: Turkey and Japan', *International Relations,* 24 (2010), 3–23, http://dx.doi.org/10.1177/0047117809359040

3. Security, Privacy and Oversight

Charles D. Raab

This chapter looks at conceptual and practical issues concerning 'privacy' and 'security' as they affect the oversight of security and intelligence services. It considers these issues in the light of three recent seminal reports in the UK and one in the US. Taking a critical view of the conventional wisdom surrounding the concepts of 'privacy' and 'security' and of the way the values they represent are thought to be reconcilable, this contribution argues that a better grasp of the relationship between these two areas in theory and practice is an important component of satisfactory oversight of intelligence activities. In addition, the extent to which overseers and other policy actors can keep abreast of technological developments is identified as a problem for the effectiveness of legislation and oversight, requiring changes to existing procedures.

https://doi.org/10.11647/OBP.0078.03

The long-awaited British debate on the extent to which the security and intelligence services are — and how they could be — effectively kept within the bounds of the rule of law and the workings of a healthy democracy gathered pace in 2015. Among the most prominent events in this period were the publication of three reports from a range of weighty participants and commentators: the Intelligence and Security Committee of Parliament (ISC); David Anderson QC, the Independent Reviewer of Terrorism Legislation (IPR); and the Royal United Services Institute (RUSI).[1] A controversial Draft Investigatory Powers Bill was introduced into Parliament in November 2015. It drew considerably upon Anderson's report especially, and travelled on a somewhat potholed pathway until it reached the statute book in November 2016.

In these post-Snowden times, the three reports have attracted much comment and criticism, but also — and to different extents — some praise for having moved the issue further into the public arena, and for having raised a range of questions for public and political debate. They also provide an insight into the way the issues are considered in the counsels of the state, and into the perceptions and (mis)conceptions that colour any attempt to deliberate on the problems and to move towards a better system of oversight of surveillance and intelligence activities. The reports bring a mixture of both stale and fresh air to one of the most crucial contemporary issues affecting the relationship between citizens and the state.[2] This chapter does not attempt to review in detail or to appraise the reports' recommendations and the commentary that they have spawned in traditional and social media, among interested parties, and in academia.

---

1   Intelligence and Security Committee of Parliament, *Privacy and Security: A Modern and Transparent Legal Framework* (London: HMSO, 2015), https://b1cba9b3-a-5e6631fd-s-sites.googlegroups.com/a/independent.gov.uk/isc/files/20150312_ISC_P%2BS%2BRpt(web).pdf; David Anderson, *A Question of Trust: Report of the Investigatory Powers Review* (London: HMSO, 2015), https://www.gov.uk/government/uploads/system/uploads/attachment_data/file/434399/IPR-Report-Web-Accessible1.pdf; Royal United Services Institute for Defence and Security Studies, *A Democratic Licence to Operate: Report of the Independent Surveillance Review* (London: Royal United Services Institute for Defence and Security Studies, 2015).

2   See an earlier investigation into this subject: House of Lords Select Committee on the Constitution, *Surveillance: Citizens and the State, 2nd Report of Session 2008–09, Hl Paper 18-I* (London: HMSO, 2009), http://www.publications.parliament.uk/pa/ld200809/ldselect/ldconst/18/1802.htm. This did not, however, deal centrally with national security and intelligence.

Others have described and assessed the ISC and other oversight bodies in terms of their historical origins, and the remits, expectations, and positions within the constitutional orders of their political systems. Their strengths, but especially their deficiencies, in providing satisfactory oversight and in holding intelligence services to account have been at the forefront of scholarly attention.[3] Somewhat less discussed is the relationship between intelligence, oversight, and human rights, although this has also been critically explored in recent years with regard to the UK.[4] The chapter therefore focuses on these areas that need deeper consideration and re-thinking, and looks across the Atlantic for some of the illumination of practices and concepts that is required if oversight is to be improved in the country. In particular, it brings into view some underlying conceptual issues that have been overlooked both by commentators and oversight practitioners. The way in which under-specified notions of privacy, security, and balance might be more fully and soundly articulated is central to this discussion. These matters bear upon the processes and institutions of oversight, and on the rights-related assumptions that are entailed when intelligence agencies and overseers consider the necessity of limiting surveillance.

Although this chapter does not examine or comment on the Investigatory Powers Act, the latter applies to Scotland with, it appears, mainly *mutatis mutandis* variations that take account of Scottish institutional and jurisdictional dimensions, such as the implementation of interception warrants and other differences.[5] It should be pointed out

---

3   See, for example, Mark Phythian, 'The British Experience with Intelligence Accountability', *Intelligence and National Security*, 22, 1 (2007), 75–99; Andrew Defty, 'Educating Parliamentarians About Intelligence: The Role of the British Intelligence and Security Committee', *Parliamentary Affairs*, 61, 4 (2008), 621–41; L. E. Halchin and F. Kaiser, *Congressional Oversight of Intelligence: Current Structure and Alternatives* (Washington, DC: Congressional Research Service, 2012); Samuel J. Rascoff, 'Presidential Intelligence', *Harvard Law Review*, 129, 3 (2016), 633–717.

4   See, for example, Peter Gill, 'The Intelligence and Security Committee and the Challenge of Security Networks', *Review of International Studies*, 35, 4 (2009), 929–41; Peter Gill, 'Intelligence, Threat, Risk and the Challenge of Oversight', *Intelligence and National Security*, 27, 2 (2012), 206–22; Ian Leigh, 'Rebalancing Rights and National Security: Reforming UK Intelligence Oversight a Decade after 9/11', *Intelligence and National Security*, 27, 5 (2012), 722–38; Peter Gill, 'Evaluating Intelligence Oversight Committees: The UK Intelligence and Security Committee and the "War on Terror"', *Intelligence and National Security*, 22, 1 (2007), 14–37.

5   See, for example, sections 21, 22, 30, 39, 117, 118 and 125 of the Act. Note that members of the Scottish Government, and not only Scottish Ministers in the UK Government, may be involved in warrantry processes.

that most statutory law in this area covers the UK as a whole, although Scotland has a separate Regulation of Investigatory Powers Act, and the machinery of oversight is likewise unified. Similarly, in terms of the focus of this chapter on concepts of privacy and security, there is currently no significant Scottish angle that would affect the intelligence matters under consideration, at least in terms of the way data protection (which is not the same as privacy, but is closely related to it) is enshrined in law and implemented through regulatory machinery.[6] In areas that are perhaps parallel to the data protection regime but arguably not directly relevant to the proposed investigatory powers legislation, there are some Scottish differences that have at times come into the limelight: for instance, a shorter period for the retention of DNA data in law enforcement.[7] Possibly more significantly for future challenges brought on transparency grounds, Scotland has a separate Freedom of Information Act that has its own Commissioner and judicial regime capable of deciding matters differently. Whilst it is not clear that these variations will have a bearing on any oversight and adjudication of the Act, future constitutional scenarios for the UK could entertain questions about whether an independent Scotland, for example, might have the scope to develop a different understanding of security and privacy to underpin different legislative provisions for security, and for oversight arrangements.

The question of oversight

In addition to conceptual issues, the performance of oversight requires further inquiry, partly in terms of the outlooks that shape it, but also in terms of machinery and process. Institutions, processes, and incisive interrogation are intertwined aspects of oversight. Effectiveness has partly to do with the structures and mechanisms that are put in place to hold the intelligence and security services accountable. The degree of independence of this machinery might well shape the ability of overseers

---

6   As will be mentioned in a later section, data protection concerns the privacy of personal data, but there are many other domains in which privacy might be at stake.
7   This was regarded favourably in the European Court of Human Rights decision in the case of *S. and Marper v. The United Kingdom* (Applications nos. 30562/04 and 30566/04), 4 December 2008.

to ask the right questions, and hence put limits to the effectiveness of their oversight. The capacity to ask the right questions is also related to the conceptions, assumptions and thinking that underlie them; and this, in turn, owes much to the individuals, personalities, and backgrounds that are represented in these structures. This intertwining is not quite circular, but tendencies to closure in the oversight 'club' are strong, given — for all its internal diversity and scope for dissensus — the tightly-knit nature of the security, intelligence, defence, and foreign-policy community that presides over the channels of oversight and accountability, and thus arbitrates the intellectual basis of oversight (see Chapter 7 for a discussion of this community and its relationship to the wider field of politics). Schattschneider long ago observed famously that '[s]ome issues are organized into politics while others are organized out': an institutional 'mobilization of bias' that leaves many issues and alternative perspectives out of account, or suppresses them.[8] The understandable need for opacity and the near-closure of the oversight process abets this bias, and also militates against the prospects for wider and better-informed debate about national security throughout society and the political system. In the absence of dramatic events (e.g., the Snowden revelations) triggering convulsions of public and political opinion, leading to some embarrassment in the intelligence and oversight community, demands for greater transparency are easily defeated, ostensibly for good reasons, thus further deepening public scepticism and lack of trust in government and politics.[9] This is a predicament for which there are no clear solutions, especially at a time when such scepticism and even revulsion is at a high level.

The intelligence and security services are bound by a sense of mission: our continued safety and security is the paramount rationale for their role and their claim on the material and governmental resources of the country. *How* safe and secure we, and the country, need to be kept is never explained or debated: 'safety' and 'security' enjoy the status of ineffability.

---

8   Elmer E. Schattschneider, *The Semisovereign People: A Realist's View of Democracy in America* (New York: Holt, Rinehart and Winston, 1960), p. 71; This can be seen as an exercise of power, see Steven Lukes, *Power: A Radical View* (Basingstoke and New York: Palgrave Macmillan, 2004).

9   On scepticism, see Mark Phythian, 'Still a Matter of Trust: Post–9/11 British Intelligence and Political Culture', *International Journal of Intelligence and CounterIntelligence*, 18, 4 (2005), 653–81.

In fulfilling their mission, the services are circumscribed by the rule of law and by specific regulations that include certain practices and exclude others, and they are bound to respect privacy and other rights. Whether the rule of law is maintained in the intelligence and security process has to do in part with the way in which these services understand the effects of their performance upon individuals and society, with respect to the values of security (or safety), privacy, and the exercise of freedoms, and bring this understanding to bear on their operations.

The oversight machinery's enquiry into these matters is therefore aimed at ensuring not only the effectiveness of these services but also their adherence to constitutional and legal circumscription. As agents in an accountability process, overseers should be able to require that the services give accounts — stories about the performance of their role — but should also be able and willing to interrogate those accounts, probing them for evidence and explanation, and perhaps challenging them with alternative constructions of the stories and different ways of thinking about the values that are served by security activity.[10] By itself, the statutory framework for oversight of the services cannot tell one about the effectiveness of oversight in practice, which — as already been indicated — has a great deal to do with the way oversight roles and powers are exercised and the way the machinery of oversight is constituted and populated. These latter factors, in turn, affect the way in which overseers think about what they are doing, and upon their understanding of the values at stake when the intelligence and security services perform their work. Oversight depends upon the enquiry to which the intelligence and security services are, or will be, subject when they undergo scrutiny, by the way the questions are shaped by conceptual understandings and frameworks, and by the parameters that are set in the oversight process.

There is a second and consequential step in this process. Overseers are intermediaries who act on behalf of the general public or its parliamentary representatives, but oversight bodies are themselves

---

10   In a related field, see C. Raab, 'The Meaning of "Accountability" in the Information Privacy Context', in D. Guagnin, L. Hempel, C. Ilten, I. Kroener, D. Neyland and H. Postigo (eds.), *Managing Privacy through Accountability* (London: Palgrave Macmillan, 2012), pp. 15–32.

accountable to the latter for their performance of this role, and thus for the way they have held the intelligence and security services to account. Here, too, there are dilemmas about transparency, and a necessary element of trust that the public or Parliament must have in the veracity of the accounts that these intermediaries give, and in their effective performance of the oversight stewardship role. How the public or Parliament is able to interrogate the *overseers'* accounts, or to challenge them, is a conundrum that mirrors, at this level, that of the intermediaries' primary relationship to the intelligence and security services. Regarding both the security or intelligence services and the oversight bodies, this is not precisely the problem indicated by the frequently asked question, *quis custodiet ipsos custodes?* (who watches the watchmen?), for the buck does stop somewhere in the constitutional and practical make-up of parliamentary democracy (see Bochel and Defty in Chapter 3 for further discussion). It rather concerns how the guardians at both levels do their work, and how they frame and act out their 'take' on the values that underpin the work they carry out.

There are many dimensions of the vexed question of how, in a democracy, security and intelligence organisations, including law-enforcement agencies, can be subject to effective and transparent oversight procedures. The three reports mentioned above all cast light upon the current state of the art, and make many recommendations across a very wide range. There is no space here to look at any of these in depth; however, some important facets can be highlighted, upon which the conceptual, ethical and legal aspects of this chapter have some bearing. Oversight should be independent of the agencies and of the government. The importance of this autonomy, and the importance of the separate assessment of technologies, and of legal and ethical compliance, lies, in part, in the ability of independent overseers and assessors to ask questions that would probably not be asked from within the culture that prevails among security and intelligence officials. It is also necessary that the overseers should have sufficient technical knowledge to be able to relate those facts to values. Some of those questions might not only be about privacy and civil liberties, but also about the means and ends of security; and they might even enable fresh perspectives to be taken on just what constitutes privacy, security, risk and harm.

Understanding security and privacy

One of the main high-profile public issues in the work of intelligence and security services — and indeed in policing as well — is the extent to which their operations pay due regard to the liberties and rights of individuals and groups who may be affected by the covert or overt collection and use of personal information in the course of performing security-related intelligence work. This is not a question of malevolence or turning a blind eye to soft values by a hard-boiled professional culture, but one of cognition: how the services understand the wider world beyond the operation or tasks that they are called upon to perform, and how they bring to bear criteria of success or effectiveness that lie further afield than the achievement of specific objectives. Liberties, rights and the nature of security are topics and ideals that are difficult enough for philosophers, lawyers and other academic specialists to grapple with, let alone those who have to take them into consideration in the heat of their working day, and then to give an account of how they brought this thorny bundle to bear upon their activities. But the same goes for the overseers, who evaluate what is done by the overseen. For the participants in both parts of the oversight 'two-step', how the ostensibly competing imperatives — security, and rights and liberties — are to be reconciled is a perennial dilemma. It cannot be answered by formulaic methods or rhetoric, but must be considered in each instance, or class of instances, in which such competition is felt to arise, in the light of a more general clarification of the underlying principles that guide the application of these values in practice.

A relevant illustrative case in point where this reconciliation and a search for new approaches is attempted is the investigation that the ISC, the Intelligence and Security Committee of Parliament, launched into security and privacy with a call for evidence in December 2013. This was only a few months after the Snowden revelations of the mass surveillance activities of the US's National Security Agency (NSA) and the UK's Government Communications Headquarters (GCHQ) had caused considerable reaction in political circles, in the media, and among concerned interest groups in the UK, the US, and around the world. The ISC announced that it was 'broadening its inquiry into the laws which govern the intelligence agencies' ability to intercept private communication. In addition to considering whether the current statutory framework governing access to private communications remains adequate, the Committee is also considering the appropriate balance between our individual right to privacy and our collective right to security'.[11] The ISC's subsequent report held fast to this framing of the way it saw privacy and security. It did not elaborate upon what 'security' might mean. It never considered that the privacy of the individual, and the value of privacy, might be about more than just the individual and the value to her of the right of privacy, and it did not question the nature of the process of achieving 'balance'.

For the Government's part, Philip Hammond, the then UK Foreign Secretary, echoed the ISC's outlook in saying:

> We are after all, all of us in our private lives, individuals who seek privacy for ourselves and our families, as well as citizens who demand protection by our government from those who would harm us. So we are right to question the powers required by our agencies — and particularly by GCHQ — to monitor private communications in order to do their job. But we should not lose sight of the vital balancing act between the privacy we desire and the security we need.[12]

Note that it is as 'individuals' that we are said to seek privacy, but as 'citizens' we demand protection from harm; it is 'the privacy we desire' *versus* 'the security we need'. The rhetorical effect of these associations and contrasts would be quite different if they were reversed in each part of the statement; moreover, a 'balancing act' is asserted in describing the relationship.

We might be able to escape these deep-seated ritual constructions in our search for the best way to frame the guiding principles underpinning the work of oversight and accountability. If the ISC, and ministers or other government actors in their oversight roles, are to exercise their functions, they need to examine the assumptions that underpin these functions, and they need sometimes to ask awkward questions. How well equipped they are to do this, by virtue of their constitutional

---

11   Intelligence and Security Committee of Parliament, 'Privacy and Security Inquiry — Call for Evidence' (11 December 2013), https://b1cba9b3-a-5e6631fd-s-sites.googlegroups.com/a/independent.gov.uk/isc/files/20131211_ISC_Call_for_papers-Privacy.pdf

12   Foreign and Commonwealth Office and The Rt Hon Philip Hammond, 'Foreign Secretary Intelligence and Security Speech', Gov.uk, 15 March 2015, https://www.gov.uk/government/speeches/foreign-secretary-intelligence-and-security-speech

position, composition (in the case of agencies), resources and remit, is at issue. Moreover, the assumptions that form their mindset need to be articulated and subject to public discourse and debate.

Let us look at these issues. The first one lies in the way 'security' is construed. There are many ways of understanding 'security' — or its fellow, 'public safety'[13] — and whatever right is considered to pertain to it, as well as its relationship to other rights.[14] Leaving aside the question of individual or personal security, one issue is that 'collective' security could refer to security at a variety of levels: for example, international, national, local, neighbourhood, or social group. Directly or indirectly, the intelligence and security services' activities involve all of these. How the demands for security at each of these levels might be promoted in the presence of the right to privacy (itself of diverse meanings), and thus the nature of any reconciliation, will vary. Another issue is whether *objective* security, involving probabilities of risk, and/or *subjective* security, involving feelings of insecurity, should be at the focus of attention in security activities and in their oversight (for example, in judging necessity and proportionality), and how these two perspectives can be reconciled.[15]

---

13   The distinction between 'security' and 'safety' is blurred, and their usage often interchangeable. Philip Hammond used the words 'safe' and 'safety' eleven times and 'security' eighteen times in his RUSI speech of 10 March 2015 on Intelligence and Security; Foreign and Commonwealth Office and The Rt Hon Philip Hammond (2015). Both the UK Conservative Party and Labour Party 2015 election manifestoes used 'safe', 'secure', and derivative words profusely and indiscriminately in relation to an enormous variety of issues: banking, borders, children, communities, the country, cyber activity, cycling, the economy, the elderly, energy supplies, families, farming, the Green Belt, health care, hospitals, jobs, the Middle East, neighbourhoods, religious practice, retirement, work, etc.

14   See Lucia Zedner, 'The Concept of Security: An Agenda for Comparative Analysis', *Legal Studies*, 23, 1 (2003), 153–75; Lucia Zedner, 'Seeking Security by Eroding Human Rights: The Side-Stepping of Due Process', in *Security and Human Rights*, ed. by Benjamin J. Goold and Liora Lazarus (Oxford: Hart, 2007), pp. 257–77; Lucia Zedner, *Security: Key Ideas in Criminology Series* (London and New York: Routledge 2009); S. Fredman, 'The Positive Right to Security', in *Security and Human Rights*, ed. by B. J. Goold and Liora Lazarus (Oxford: Hart, 2007), pp. 307–24; L. Lazarus, 'Mapping the Right to Security', in *Security and Human Rights*, ed. by B. J. Goold and Liora Lazarus (Oxford: Hart, 2007), pp. 325–46.

15   Jennifer Chandler, 'Privacy Versus National Security: Clarifying the Trade-Off', in *Lessons from the Identity Trail: Anonymity, Privacy and Identity in a Networked Society*, ed. by I. R. Kerr, V. M. Steeves, and C. Lucock (Oxford: Oxford University Press, 2009), pp. 121–38.

The second issue is the way in which 'privacy' is construed. Privacy as a fundamental but not absolute right is enshrined in prominent national and international legal instruments. However, privacy's importance goes beyond that of the individual: it is a crucial underpinning of interpersonal relationships, of society itself and its groups and categories of persons, and of the workings of democratic political systems. Although defining 'privacy' has long been highly contentious,[16] the trans-individual meaning and its implications for rights and freedoms is gaining ground in academic commentary[17] and is appreciated in constitutional argument and judicial decision as well as in some prominent reports. To consider privacy only as an individual right — or as a mere 'desire' — is to slight its fuller significance in theory and practice. When individual privacy is protected, the fabric of society, as well as the functioning of political processes and the exercise of important freedoms, are thereby protected. When it is eroded, society and the polity are also harmed. It is in the public interest, and not only in the interest of the individual, to have privacy protected as a 'constitutive public good': a societal good, understood as an integral and essential element of society itself.[18] In that sense, we *need* privacy as *citizens*, and not just as customers or consumers of goods and services in the commercial marketplace.

---

16   See Ferdinand David Schoeman, *Philosophical Dimensions of Privacy: An Anthology* (Cambridge University Press, 1984), p. 444.

17   Sources include Daniel J. Solove, *Understanding Privacy* (Cambridge, MA: Harvard University Press, 2008); Priscilla M. Regan, *Legislating Privacy: Technology, Social Values, and Public Policy* (Chapel Hill: University of North Carolina Press, 1995); Helen Nissenbaum, *Privacy in Context: Technology, Policy, and the Integrity of Social Life* (Stanford: Stanford University Press, 2009); Benjamin J. Goold, 'Surveillance and the Political Value of Privacy', *Amsterdam Law Forum*, 1 (2008), 3–6; Julie E. Cohen, *Configuring the Networked Self: Law, Code, and the Play of Everyday Practice* (Yale: Yale University Press, 2012); Ferdinand David Schoeman, *Privacy and Social Freedom* (Cambridge: Cambridge University Press, 1992); V. Steeves, 'Reclaiming the Social Value of Privacy', in *Lessons from the Identity Trail: Anonymity, Privacy and Identity in a Networked Society*, ed. by I. R. Kerr, V. M. Steeves, and C. Lucock (New York: Oxford University Press, 2009); Colin Bennett and Charles Raab, *The Governance of Privacy: Policy Instruments in Global Perspective* (Cambridge, MA: MIT Press, 2006), Chapter 2; Charles Raab, 'Privacy, Social Values and the Public Interest', in *Politik Und Die Regulierung Von Information*, ed. by A. Busch and J. Hofmann (Baden-Baden: Nomos, 2012), pp. 129–51.

18   Ian Loader and Neil Walker, *Civilizing Security* (Cambridge: Cambridge University Press, 2007), p. 145.

In stark contrast, there is the assertion that 'the provision of basic security is the paramount human good, upon which all other political goods depend'.[19] Whilst the individual's right may be set aside for legal and legitimate reasons, such as the overriding importance of other rights and interests, including security, the claims of the latter to prevail must be argued — as it certainly can be, in given instances — and not merely asserted. However, they must not be permanently accepted by default, and may ultimately be a matter for the courts to determine in terms of necessity and proportionality. Insofar as these claims may be made on behalf of organisations whose legitimacy lies in their acting in support of 'collective' interests, to ignore the perception that privacy is *also* a collective citizen interest is to put a thumb on the 'balancing' scale. It is also powerfully to shape the public understanding of what is at stake by relegating the social and political value of privacy to the status of a claim that need not be seriously respected. Moreover — although this point cannot be discussed further here[20] — just as there are many dimensions and levels of security, *information* privacy, which was prominently at stake in mass surveillance of the kind illuminated by the Snowden revelations that instigated the inquiries and reports, is only one kind of privacy; privacy (e.g., of the body or of space) is often invaded even if information is not collected and processed further, including its communication through myriad channels.

The third issue concerns the relationship between security and privacy, and their reconciliation or 'balancing'. The ISC's view of the 'balance' or trade-off between individual privacy — and, indeed, other individual rights and liberties — and national security was neither inescapable nor unbiased in terms of what the implicit outcome should

---

19   Amitai Etzioni, *Security First: For a Muscular, Moral Foreign Policy* (Yale: Yale University Press, 2008), p. xviii.

20   See Rachel L. Finn, David Wright, and Michael Friedewald, 'Seven Types of Privacy', in *European Data Protection: Coming of Age*, ed. by Serge Gutwirth *et al.* (Dordrecht: Springer Netherlands, 2013), pp. 3–32; David Wright and Charles Raab, 'Privacy Principles, Risks and Harms', *International Review of Law, Computers & Technology*, 28, 3 (2014), 277–98; The latter article points to a further issue requiring exploration: the non-privacy effects of surveillance on individuals, groups and categories, which could be very important in the context of intelligence and oversight. See the discussion of harms of intelligence collection to 'vital interests' in Ross Bellaby, 'What's the Harm? The Ethics of Intelligence Collection', *Intelligence and National Security*, 27, 1 (2012), 93–117.

be.[21] In contrast, in another context — that of cyber security — the President of Estonia said: 'freedom and security need not contradict each other: secure online interactions, enabled by a secure online identity, is a precondition for full internet freedom'.[22] This is the beginning of a departure from conventional wisdom. The report by RUSI clearly staked out the ground for a fresh departure by casting doubt on the existing terms of public debate:

> The most striking characteristic of public discussions on surveillance to date is the perceived dichotomy between the rights or values of collective security and privacy. A common and repeated assumption made by politicians, the media and the general public is that these values are opposed, and that the issue is one of 'national security' versus 'personal privacy'. The subsequent assumption is that a trade-off can be made between the two: Is the right balance being struck between national security and civil liberties, or between collective security on the one side and individual freedoms and personal security on the other?[23]

Another step, perhaps more paradoxically, is to reflect on whether privacy and civil liberties (or freedoms) should not themselves be regarded, at least in some respects, as valuable because of the security and safety — not least, of personal data — they provide for individuals, groups and societies. As do national security strategies, they can involve protective, precautionary, defensive and risk-averse measures taken in the face of technologically assisted policy initiatives. In societies driven

---

21 See analogously Jeremy Waldron, 'Security and Liberty: The Image of Balance', *Journal of Political Philosophy*, 11, 2 (2003), 191–210; Chandler (2009); Charles Raab, 'From Balancing to Steering: New Directions for Data Protection', in *Visions of Privacy: Policy Choices for the Digital Age*, ed. by C. Bennett and R. Grant (Toronto: University of Toronto Press, 1999), pp. 68–93; Relevant arguments on privacy and security in the context of democracy are developed in Annabelle Lever, *Democracy, Privacy and Security* (Rochester: Social Science Research Network, 2015).

22 Toomas Hendrik Ilves, '"Rebooting Trust? Freedom *vs* Security in Cyberspace" Opening Address at Munich Security Conference Cyber', Office of the President, Republic of Estonia (Munich, 31 January 2014), https://vp2006-2016.president. ee/en/official-duties/speeches/9796-qrebooting-trust-freedom-vs-security-in-cyberspaceq. Office of the President, Republic of Estonia (Munich, 31 January 2014

23 Royal United Services Institute for Defence and Security Studies (2015), p. 216. These remarks underline points made in the author's evidence to the ISC inquiry and to Anderson. See Independent Reviewer of Terrorism Legislation, *Investigatory Powers Review Written Submissions (H-V)* (London: Independent Reviewer of Terrorism Legislation, 2015), https://terrorismlegislationreviewer.independent.gov. uk/wp-content/uploads/2015/06/Submissions-H-Z.pdf

by counter-terrorism, law enforcement, and a preoccupation with personal safety, ever-increasing volumes and granularity of personal data are collected, mined, shared and stored in the name of security and safety. In those circumstances, privacy can provide a secure refuge for individuals and groups against the prying eyes of the state or private companies, whether that refuge serves inward-looking individual purposes or the possibility of external sociality and participation. To be secure in our homes is, at the same time, to inhabit a protected private space: one of the meanings of privacy. If so, the overlapping or even isomorphic relationship between privacy and security is far more subtle than might be imagined, and cannot be glossed over by a rhetoric of the 'opposed' rights or values of security and privacy.[24] The unfortunate example of societies under totalitarian or authoritarian governments, in which surveillance affords neither privacy nor personal security at the level of persons and groups, serves as a reminder of the importance of this point.

The affinity between privacy and security has begun to be appreciated in various quarters, such as the US, where the Review Group on Intelligence and Communications Technologies, appointed by President Obama, reported in December 2013.[25] In a section on Principles, the Review Group Report included the following:

1. The United States Government must protect, at once, two different forms of security: national security and personal privacy.

In the American tradition, the word 'security' has had multiple meanings. In contemporary parlance, it often refers to national security or homeland security. One of the government's most fundamental responsibilities is to protect this form of security, broadly understood. At the same time, the idea of security refers to a quite different and equally fundamental value, captured in the Fourth Amendment to the United States Constitution: 'The right of the people to be secure in their persons, houses, papers, and effects, against unreasonable searches and seizures, shall not be violated [...]'. Both forms of security must be protected.[26]

24 Charles Raab, 'Privacy as a Security Value', in *Jon Bing: En Hyllest/A Tribute*, ed. by D. W. Schartum, L. Bygrave, and A. G. B. Bekken (Oslo: Gyldendal, 2014), pp. 39–58.
25 The President's Review Group on Intelligence and Communications Technologies, *The NSA Report: Liberty and Security in a Changing World* (Princeton and Oxford: Princeton University Press, 2014).
26 *The NSA Report*, pp. 14–15.

In seeing that privacy itself has security value,[27] the Review Group Report subtly shifted the terms of policy and debate in a way that is available to other policy deliberations outside the specifically American constitutional context. This construction, of course, does not by itself necessarily undermine the idea that conflict may occur between collective and individual meanings of security. But by considering afresh the connection between privacy and security, it throws into question — on both the level of policy discourse and rhetoric, and on the legal level — the implicitly unequal weighting between these two desirable values. This inequality would most likely be reflected in the outcome of any attempt to 'balance' the two in a construction that pits the national interest against that of the individual. This may especially be the case in the climate of fear and vulnerability brought about by terrorism and other real or perceived attacks.[28] Individual rights have historically been set aside, albeit temporarily, in favour of collective ones or in favour of collective anxieties that construe national sovereignty and territorial integrity to be severely threatened. The Review Group Report was indeed explicit and sceptical about the question of 'balancing':

> 3. The idea of 'balancing' has an important element of truth, but it is also inadequate and misleading. It is tempting to suggest that the underlying goal is to achieve the right 'balance' between the two forms of security. The suggestion has an important element of truth. But some safeguards are not subject to balancing at all. In a free society, public officials should never engage in surveillance in order to punish their political enemies; to restrict freedom of speech or religion; to suppress legitimate criticism and dissent; to help their preferred companies or industries; to provide domestic companies with an unfair competitive advantage; or to benefit or burden members of groups defined in terms of religion, ethnicity, race, and gender.[29]

---

27 See Raab (2014).

28 Gill observes: 'The pressures on intelligence agencies to "deliver results" and on parliamentary and other oversight bodies to relax oversight are greatest when security fears and uncertainties are at their height. This is the danger of the oft-quoted need to "balance" security and rights; the need for oversight is actually greater at times such as this in order to promote effectiveness and prevent abuses of human rights' (Gill (2009), p. 221). He also asserts that 'intelligence can advance human security but the role of oversight remains to ensure that intelligence is conducted proportionately, not to seek some mythical "balance" between rights and security' (*ibid*, p. 218).

29 *The NSA Report*, p. 16.

Further evidence that supports the argument that the relationship between security and privacy (or other liberties) is complex can be found in US legislation: the Implementing Recommendations of the 9/11 Commission Act of 2007, which established a reconstituted Privacy and Civil Liberties Oversight Board (PCLOB) as an independent body in the Executive Branch.[30] On the one hand, Title VIII of the Act remained within a 'balancing' framework, charging the PCLOB to: 'analyze and review actions the executive branch takes to protect the Nation from terrorism, ensuring that the need for such actions is balanced with the need to protect privacy and civil liberties'.[31] On the other hand, it preceded this with a quotation from the National Commission on Terrorist Attacks Upon the United States' *9/11 Report* which, it said, had:

> correctly concluded that 'The choice between security and liberty is a false choice, as nothing is more likely to endanger America's liberties than the success of a terrorist attack at home. Our history has shown us that insecurity threatens liberty. Yet, if our liberties are curtailed, we lose the values that we are struggling to defend'.[32]

The RUSI report's construction of the relationship between privacy and the values of democracy resembled this in spirit, and was markedly different from what the ISC (or former Foreign Secretary Hammond) presumed. Recognising the trans-individual importance of privacy to the nation's political and governmental practice, as well as to freedom of the press, it said:

> Privacy is an essential prerequisite to the exercise of individual freedom, and its erosion weakens the constitutional foundations on which democracy and good governance have traditionally been based in this country. [...] Privacy is also a pre-requisite for democracy. It gives people the freedom that is needed to be personally autonomous, to seek out alternative sources of information and to question the status quo. [...]

---

30 US Congress, *Public Law 110–53, 110th Congress—Aug. 3, 2007: Implementing Recommendations of the 9/11 Commission Act of 2007* (Congress.gov, 2007), https://www.congress.gov/bill/110th-congress/house-bill/1; For further discussion and background, see Garrett Hatch, 'Report for Congress Privacy and Civil Liberties Oversight Board: New Independent Agency Status' (Washington DC, 2012).

31 *Public Law 110–53*, p. 121 Stat. 352.

32 *Ibid.*; The quotation is from National Commission on Terrorist Attacks, *The 9/11 Commission Report: Final Report of the National Commission on Terrorist Attacks Upon the United States (Authorized Edition)* (New York: W. W. Norton & Company, 2011), p. 395.

Those who challenge the state — through journalism or legal advocacy, for example — need to be confident they are not spied upon, otherwise they cannot do their jobs effectively, and such jobs are an acknowledged part of a functioning democracy.[33]

This report did use the term 'balance' in referring to various rights, but it immediately veered away from this trope; its understanding of rights was carefully phrased to reflect a sense of their deeper and more intricate mutual dependence:

The concepts of liberty, security and privacy are central to a number of universal rights outlined by important pieces of twentieth-century treaties and legislation [...] These rights are not seen as absolute or unconditional, but rather as qualified rights. This qualification — that these rights are in turn subject to other rights — is important if these rights are to be consistent, balanced and mutually reinforcing. Each right must be protected and respected, to the greatest extent possible, but it cannot exist in isolation. There is no privacy without respect for security; there is no liberty without respect for privacy; security requires both certain liberties and privacy. It is therefore unfruitful (indeed misleading) to cast debates about privacy, liberty and security as a matter of choice or 'balancing' between these rights, still less to think of trade-offs between these rights.[34]

Furthermore, RUSI said:

The relationship between privacy on the one hand, and liberty and security on the other, is complex. Discussions of privacy and security are often described as a matter of finding or striking a 'balance'; this traditional metaphor can be misleading. There is no metric for 'weighing' different rights, or even for comparing the 'weight' of different rights in particular cases. But it is feasible to set out robust standards that must be met in adjusting rights to one another and to devise and establish structures to do so.[35]

Anderson devoted a chapter to exploring the meaning and functions of 'privacy', showing an understanding of the literature as well as the case law that underscored the multifaceted and contextual nature of the concept, its values to the individual and society, its relation to other

---

33 Royal United Services Institute for Defence and Security Studies (2015), pp. ix, 2.10.
34 *Ibid.*, p. 2.3.
35 *Ibid.*, p. 2.6; see also the author's evidence to the ISC inquiry: Independent Reviewer of Terrorism Legislation (2015).

rights and freedoms, and its practical manifestations. For example, the report cited case law in highlighting the importance of privacy:

> A good start is provided by the recent judicial description of privacy protection as 'a prerequisite to individual security, self-fulfilment and autonomy as well as to the maintenance of a thriving democratic society'. As that statement implies, the privacy ecosystem has individual, social and political aspects.[36]

The Anderson report clearly grasped the subtlety of privacy's importance beyond the individual. Although it did use the terms 'balance' and 'balancing' in a more or less conventional way, this was done frequently in a legal framework to show the relevance of the test of *proportionality* that is applied in judicial decision-making and is urged as a principle for political and organisational decision contexts as well. Thus proportionality under Article 8(2) of the European Convention on Human Rights (ECHR) — the 'right to privacy' — 'is determined via a balancing exercise, which may for example require *"the interest of the [...] state in protecting its national security"* to be balanced against *"the seriousness of the interference with the applicant's right to respect for his private life"'*.[37]

This construction invites a more nuanced resolution of the reconciliation — or, indeed, the 'balancing' — of the two values or rights in circumstances where national security is implicated. It shares something of the spirit of the US's Review Group Report, which, like Anderson, discussed the matter within a framework of principles, here putting it in terms of risk, and extending the list of consequences

---

36 Anderson cites the Canadian Supreme Court case of *R v. Spencer*, 2014 SCC 43, involving privacy and anonymity on the Internet and the 'reasonable expectation of privacy'; *A Question of Trust*, p. 27. See Barry Sookman, 'Internet Users' Privacy and Anonymity Protected by Supreme Court: *R v. Spencer*', 13 June 2014, http://www.barrysookman.com/2014/06/13/internet-users-privacy-and-anonymity-protected-by-supreme-court-r-v-spencer/ Anderson cited the Court's differentiation of several types of privacy interest and meaning. Nevertheless, the public's feeling of safety and security may justify the necessary and proportionate overriding of privacy in justifiable circumstances: see *A Question of Trust*, p. 40.

37 Anderson quotes the case of *Leander v. Sweden*, para. 59; emphasis in original: *ibid.*, p. 76. See also *ibid.*, p. 252: 'Central to most of these rights are the concepts of necessity and proportionality. Because those concepts as developed by the courts are adaptable, nuanced and context-specific, they are well adapted to balancing the competing imperatives of privacy and security'. The ISC Report also emphasised the importance of the test of proportionality.

beyond the risk to national security to embrace privacy, civil liberties, international relations, and international commerce.[38]

Policy, oversight and technology

In the US, there has been a long saga regarding the establishment of ancillary machinery for security and intelligence policy and practice.[39] The PCLOB was eventually constituted in 2012 as an independent agency in the Executive Branch, but the independence of such a body had been a matter of contention over the previous eight years. So too have been PLCOB's remit, powers and composition; such arguments continue, with the Review Group Report's recommendation that this body should be supplanted by a Civil Liberties and Privacy Protection (CLPP) Board that would have foreign intelligence within its scope of oversight, and not only anti-terrorism.[40]

As for establishing in the UK something akin to the US's PCLOB, the Government declared an intention to legislate for a Privacy and Civil Liberties Board (PCLB), eschewing the word 'oversight' in its title. Many, including Anderson, looked askance at a PCLB; Anderson's role as IPR, the Independent Reviewer of Terrorism Legislation, it was envisaged, would be replaced by this new body, or at least to be assisted by such a body whose remit and purpose were not clear and appeared unnecessary. In the event, a PCLB was passed into law as the general and opaque Section 46 of the Counter-Terrorism and Security Act 2015, but requiring secondary legislation for its implementation and with no certainty that this would ever be implemented. Its very name — suggesting a privacy-and-civil-liberties function and remit — seems belied by the bare outline of these as given in the Act.[41]

It is a well-grounded observation that technological change outpaces the capacity of law (and lawmakers, judges and overseers)

---

38 The President's Review Group on Intelligence and Communications Technologies (2014), p. 15.
39 For historical details, see Hatch.
40 The President's Review Group on Intelligence and Communications Technologies (2014), pp. 195–99.
41 For critical comment on this, see Cols. 307–18 of the House of Lords, *Lords Hansard Text for 28 Jan 2015 (Pt 0003)* (London: HMSO, 2015), http://www.publications.parliament.uk/pa/ld201415/ldhansrd/text/150128-0003.htm

to catch up for the purpose of regulation in the interest of human rights — including privacy — and other values. This observation is no less relevant to intelligence oversight, in which the practices that are overseen rely heavily on technologically very complex and often arcane means of information gathering and analysis. It is therefore appropriate to mention the way in which recent reports have touched on the question of how technological knowledge can be brought to bear effectively in oversight arrangements. The Review Group Report considered the creation of an Office of Technology Assessment (OTA) within the CLPP Board to be useful 'to assess Intelligence Community technology initiatives and support privacy-enhancing technologies'.[42] As the Report states, '[a]n improved technology assessment function is essential to informing policymakers about the range of options, both for collection and use of personal information, and also about the cost and effectiveness of privacy-enhancing technologies'.[43]

Circumstances within the UK prevent any simple borrowing from the example of other countries' institutions, and technology assessment in the Federal Government has its own institutional and political backstory that shapes present recommendations. But the Review Group Report's suggestion of an OTA may have some greater traction in the UK, owing to an internationally shared need to keep abreast of the information and communication technology (ICT) instruments that are increasingly used in terrorism and crime. In the UK, the ability of overseers, let alone Government, Parliament, and the panoply of Commissioners operating in the security and intelligence field, to keep abreast of information and communication technology (ICT) developments and the worlds of the internet and 'data' remains a problem for the effectiveness of legislation and oversight, as was remarked upon in the three UK reports considered in this chapter.[44] Anderson referred to the views he received

---

42   Privacy impact assessment (PIA) has become a widespread technique for information systems and technologies, see David Wright and Paul De Hert, *Privacy Impact Assessment* (Dordrecht: Springer Netherlands, 2012); among the organisations that conduct PIA is the US's Department of Homeland Security, see Department of Homeland Security, *Privacy Impact Assessments* (24 August 2015), https://www.dhs.gov/privacy-impact-assessments

43   The President's Review Group on Intelligence and Communications Technologies (2014), p. 198.

44   E.g. *A Question of Trust*, Chapter 4; Royal United Services Institute for Defence and Security Studies (2015), Chapter 1.

that emphasised the importance of involving technical specialists in the oversight process, whether as part of the oversight machinery or playing supporting roles.[45] In proposing the creation of an Independent Surveillance and Intelligence Commission (ISIC), he thought ISIC 'should be willing to draw on expertise from the worlds of intelligence, computer science, technology, academia, law and the NGO sector'.[46]

The RUSI report recommended the creation of an Advisory Council for Digital Technology and Engineering as a statutory non-departmental public body. It would:

> keep under review the domestic and international situation with respect to the evolution of the Internet, digital technology and infrastructure, as well as:
> • Provide advice to relevant ministers, departments and agencies on technical measures.
> • Promote co-operation between the public and private sectors.
> • Manage complaints from CSPs [communications service providers] on notices and measures they consider unreasonable.
> • Advance public education.
> • Support research on technology and engineering.[47]

Moreover, this Advisory Council would be a resource for the ISC and for the new proposed National Intelligence and Surveillance Office that is recommended to replace the present array of three Commissioners in this field.[48] Whether any of these alternatives will gain support cannot be foretold. However, as with the recommendation of an OTA in the US, they speak to a glaring need in the operations of security and intelligence oversight and democratic control. Whatever the status of the agencies' own knowledge of new and emerging technologies, overseers need sufficient knowledge to understand the technological side of the work of those they oversee, and to bring to bear upon it their independent critical intelligence and their sense of the rights and values at stake. Such knowledge may help them to shape the questions they ask of agencies — and to interrogate the answers — whose vested interests may not always align with the interests, rights or needs of those whom they

---

45   *Ibid.*, p. 236.
46   *Ibid.*, p. 305.
47   Royal United Services Institute for Defence and Security Studies (2015), pp. 107–08.
48   *Ibid.*, p. 108.

are tasked to protect. This problem is acknowledged universally, but there is no easy, and no prominent, agenda for a solution in the rapidly changing circumstances of threats and of the technological means both to carry them out and to frustrate prevention, detection and apprehension.

Conclusion

This chapter has dealt briefly with some conceptual and practical issues in the oversight of security and intelligence services, and in the wider field of human rights or civil liberties that are affected by these services and by their oversight as well. It has sought to highlight difficulties and ambiguities that stalk the attempt to improve the way a democratic society and political system attempts to 'civilise security', to borrow a term from the academic literature.[49] It is appropriate to end with a question that puts the point clearly:

> What kind of institutional matrix is likely to permit [the state] to be able to exercise sufficient vertical oversight and control over the plurality of agents and agencies who today promise to deliver security, whilst at the same time ensuring that the state anchor remains, in both its delivering and regulatory dimensions, subject to adequate democratic contestation and public and legal scrutiny?[50]

The areas touched on in this chapter resonate with two of the elements of an 'institutional matrix' — rights and resources — proposed by Loader and Walker,[51] but much further analysis is needed to explore how better thinking about privacy, security, independent oversight and its machinery, and technological understanding, might take their place in a matrix, without welding them into a rigid pattern that cannot be altered as new circumstances arise.

---

49   Loader and Walker (2007).
50   *Ibid.,* p. 215.
51   *Ibid.,* Chapter 8.

References

Anderson, David, *A Question of Trust: Report of the Investigatory Powers Review* (London: HMSO, 2015), https://www.gov.uk/government/uploads/system/uploads/attachment_data/file/434399/IPR-Report-Web-Accessible1.pdf

Bellaby, Ross, 'What's the Harm? The Ethics of Intelligence Collection', *Intelligence and National Security*, 27 (2012), 93–117, http://dx.doi.org/10.1080/02684527.2012.621600

Bennett, Colin and Raab, Charles, *The Governance of Privacy: Policy Instruments in Global Perspective* (Cambridge, MA: MIT Press, 2006).

Chandler, Jennifer, 'Privacy Versus National Security: Clarifying the Trade-Off', in *Lessons from the Identity Trail: Anonymity, Privacy and Identity in a Networked Society*, ed. by I. R. Kerr, V. M. Steeves and C. Lucock (Oxford: Oxford University Press, 2009), pp. 121–38.

Cohen, Julie E., *Configuring the Networked Self: Law, Code, and the Play of Everyday Practice* (Yale: Yale University Press, 2012).

Defty, Andrew, 'Educating Parliamentarians About Intelligence: The Role of the British Intelligence and Security Committee', *Parliamentary Affairs*, 61 (2008), 621–41, http://dx.doi.org/10.1093/pa/gsn024

Department of Homeland Security, 'Privacy Impact Assessments' (24 August 2015), https://www.dhs.gov/privacy-impact-assessments

Etzioni, Amitai, *Security First: For a Muscular, Moral Foreign Policy* (Yale: Yale University Press, 2008).

Finn, Rachel L., Wright, David, and Friedewald, Michael, 'Seven Types of Privacy', in *European Data Protection: Coming of Age*, ed. by Serge Gutwirth, Ronald Leenes, Paul de Hert and Yves Poullet (Dordrecht: Springer Netherlands, 2013), pp. 3–32.

Foreign and Commonwealth Office and the Rt Hon Philip Hammond, 'Foreign Secretary Intelligence and Security Speech', Gov.uk, 15 March 2015, https://www.gov.uk/government/speeches/foreign-secretary-intelligence-and-security-speech

Fredman, S., 'The Positive Right to Security', in *Security and Human Rights*, ed. by B. J. Goold and Liora Lazarus (Oxford: Hart, 2007), pp. 307–24.

Gill, Peter, 'Evaluating Intelligence Oversight Committees: The UK Intelligence and Security Committee and the "War on Terror"', *Intelligence and National Security*, 22 (2007), 14–37, http://dx.doi.org/10.1080/02684520701200756

—, 'The Intelligence and Security Committee and the Challenge of Security Networks', *Review of International Studies*, 35 (2009), 929–41, http://dx.doi.org/10.1017/S0260210509990362

—, 'Intelligence, Threat, Risk and the Challenge of Oversight', *Intelligence and National Security*, 27 (2012), 206–22, http://dx.doi.org/10.1080/02684527.2012 .661643

Goold, Benjamin J., 'Surveillance and the Political Value of Privacy', *Amsterdam Law Forum*, 1 (2008), 3–6, http://heinonline.org/HOL/Page?handle=hein. journals/amslawf1&g_sent=1&collection=journals&id=389

Halchin, L. E. and Kaiser, F., *Congressional Oversight of Intelligence: Current Structure and Alternatives* (Washington, DC: Congressional Research Service, 2012).

Hatch, Garrett, *Report for Congress Privacy and Civil Liberties Oversight Board: New Independent Agency Status* (Washington DC, 2012).

House of Lords, *Lords Hansard Text for 28 Jan 2015 (Pt 0003)* (London: HMSO, 2015), http://www.publications.parliament.uk/pa/ld201415/ldhansrd/text/ 150128-0003.htm

House of Lords Select Committee on the Constitution, *Surveillance: Citizens and the State, 2nd Report of Session 2008–09, Hl Paper 18-I* (London: HMSO, 2009), http://www.publications.parliament.uk/pa/ld200809/ldselect/ldconst/18/ 1802.htm

Ilves, Toomas Hendrik, '"Rebooting Trust? Freedom *vs* Security in Cyberspace" Opening Address at Munich Security Conference Cyber', Office of the President, Republic of Estonia (Munich, 31 January 2014), https://vp2006-2016.president.ee/en/official-duties/speeches/9796-qrebooting-trust-freedom-vs-security-in-cyberspaceq

Independent Reviewer of Terrorism Legislation, *Investigatory Powers Review Written Submissions (H-V)* (London: Independent Reviewer of Terrorism Legislation, 2015), https://terrorismlegislationreviewer.independent.gov. uk/wp-content/uploads/2015/06/Submissions-H-Z.pdf

Intelligence and Security Committee of Parliament, 'Privacy and Security Inquiry — Call for Evidence', 11 December 2013, https://b1cba9b3-a-5e6631fd-s-sites.googlegroups.com/a/independent.gov.uk/isc/files/20131211_ISC_ Call_for_papers-Privacy.pdf

—, *Privacy and Security: A Modern and Transparent Legal Framework* (London: HMSO, 2015), https://b1cba9b3-a-5e6631fd-s-sites.googlegroups.com/a/ independent.gov.uk/isc/files/20150312_ISC_P%2BS%2BRpt(web).pdf

Lazarus, L., 'Mapping the Right to Security', in *Security and Human Rights*, ed. by B. J. Goold and Liora Lazarus (Oxford: Hart, 2007), pp. 325–46.

Leigh, Ian, 'Rebalancing Rights and National Security: Reforming UK Intelligence Oversight a Decade after 9/11', *Intelligence and National Security*, 27 (2012), 722–38, http://dx.doi.org/10.1080/02684527.2012.708525

Lever, Annabelle, *Democracy, Privacy and Security* (Rochester: Social Science Research Network, 2015).

Loader, Ian and Walker, Neil, *Civilizing Security* (Cambridge: Cambridge University Press, 2007).

Lukes, Steven, *Power: A Radical View* (Basingstoke and New York: Palgrave Macmillan, 2004).

National Commission on Terrorist Attacks, *The 9/11 Commission Report: Final Report of the National Commission on Terrorist Attacks Upon the United States* (Authorized Edition) (New York: W. W. Norton & Company, 2011).

Nissenbaum, Helen, *Privacy in Context: Technology, Policy, and the Integrity of Social Life* (Stanford: Stanford University Press, 2009).

Phythian, Mark, 'Still a Matter of Trust: Post-9/11 British Intelligence and Political Culture', *International Journal of Intelligence and Counter Intelligence*, 18 (2005), 653–81, http://dx.doi.org/10.1080/08850600500177127

—, 'The British Experience with Intelligence Accountability', *Intelligence and National Security*, 22 (2007), 75–99, http://dx.doi.org/10.1080/026845 20701200822

Raab, Charles, 'From Balancing to Steering: New Directions for Data Protection', in *Visions of Privacy: Policy Choices for the Digital Age*, ed. by C. Bennett and R. Grant (Toronto: University of Toronto Press, 1999), pp. 68–93.

—, 'The Meaning of "Accountability" in the Information Privacy Context', in *Managing Privacy through Accountability*, ed. by D. Guagnin, L. Hempel, C. Ilten, I. Kroener, D. Neyland and H. Postigo (London: Palgrave Macmillan, 2012), pp. 15–32.

—, 'Privacy, Social Values and the Public Interest', in *Politik Und Die Regulierung Von Information*, ed. by A. Busch and J. Hofmann (Baden-Baden: Nomos, 2012), pp. 129–51.

—, 'Privacy as a Security Value', in *Jon Bing: En Hyllest/A Tribute*, ed. by D. W. Schartum, L. Bygrave and A. G. B. Bekken (Oslo: Gyldendal, 2014), pp. 39–58.

Rascoff, Samuel J., 'Presidential Intelligence', *Harvard Law Review*, 129 (2016), 633–717, https://ssrn.com/abstract=2714769

Regan, Priscilla M., *Legislating Privacy: Technology, Social Values, and Public Policy* (Chapel Hill: University of North Carolina Press, 1995).

Royal United Services Institute for Defence and Security Studies, *A Democratic Licence to Operate: Report of the Independent Surveillance Review* (London: Royal United Services Institute for Defence and Security Studies, 2015).

Schattschneider, Elmer E., *The Semisovereign People: A Realist's View of Democracy in America* (New York: Holt, Rinehart and Winston, 1960).

Schoeman, Ferdinand David, ed., *Philosophical Dimensions of Privacy: An Anthology* (Cambridge University Press, 1984).

—, *Privacy and Social Freedom* (Cambridge: Cambridge University Press, 1992).

—, and Solove, Daniel J., *Understanding Privacy* (Cambridge, MA: Harvard University Press, 2008).

Sookman, Barry, 'Internet Users' Privacy and Anonymity Protected by Supreme Court: *R v. Spencer*', 13 June 2014, http://www.barrysookman. com/2014/06/13/internet-users-privacy-and-anonymity-protected-by-supreme-court-r-v-spencer/

Steeves, V., 'Reclaiming the Social Value of Privacy', in *Lessons from the Identity Trail: Anonymity, Privacy and Identity in a Networked Society*, ed. by I. R. Kerr, V. M. Steeves and C. Lucock (New York: Oxford University Press, 2009).

The President's Review Group on Intelligence and Communications Technologies, *The NSA Report: Liberty and Security in a Changing World* (Princeton and Oxford: Princeton University Press, 2014).

US Congress, *Public Law 110–53, 110th Congress — Aug. 3, 2007: Implementing Recommendations of the 9/11 Commission Act of 2007* (Congress.gov, 2007), https://www.congress.gov/bill/110th-congress/house-bill/1

Waldron, Jeremy, 'Security and Liberty: The Image of Balance', *Journal of Political Philosophy*, 11 (2003), 191–210, http://dx.doi.org/10.1111/1467-9760.00174

Wright, David and De Hert, Paul, eds., *Privacy Impact Assessment* (Dordrecht: Springer Netherlands, 2012).

Wright, David and Raab, Charles, 'Privacy Principles, Risks and Harms', *International Review of Law, Computers & Technology*, 28 (2014), 277–98, http://dx.doi.org/10.1080/13600869.2014.913874

Zedner, Lucia, 'The Concept of Security: An Agenda for Comparative Analysis', *Legal Studies*, 23 (2003), 153–75, http://dx.doi.org/10.1111/j.1748-121X.2003. tb00209.x

—, 'Seeking Security by Eroding Human Rights: The Side-Stepping of Due Process', in *Security and Human Rights*, ed. by Benjamin J. Goold and Liora Lazarus (Oxford: Hart, 2007), pp. 257–77.

—, *Security: Key Ideas in Criminology Series* (London and New York: Routledge 2009).

4. Parliamentary Oversight of Intelligence Agencies: Lessons from Westminster

Hugh Bochel and Andrew Defty

While oversight of intelligence agencies can take a number of forms, legislative oversight is often seen as particularly important as it can help ensure agencies' independence from the executive, maintain public confidence and provide legitimacy for the agencies and their actions. This chapter draws on research on oversight of the intelligence and security agencies by the United Kingdom Parliament to consider possible lessons for legislative oversight in emerging states, and in particular, a potentially independent Scotland. It suggests that the challenges associated with such a development have been largely overlooked, and that careful consideration would need to be given to a number of issues, including the capacity and expertise required for intelligence oversight, in addition to the powers of any oversight body and indeed of Parliament as a whole.

https://doi.org/10.11647/OBP.0078.04

As noted elsewhere in this volume (Chapters 5, 6 and 7 in particular), while the Scottish independence referendum of 2014 provided an opportunity for discussion of the role and scrutiny of intelligence agencies in a post-inreferencesdependence Scotland, plans in this area were relatively undeveloped. Moreover, while there was at least some debate about the development of an independent Scottish security and intelligence agency, plans for oversight of the new agency were minimal. The UK Government's analysis, which emphasised the challenges involved in establishing a new intelligence agency, assumed that when it came to oversight, Scotland would simply seek to replicate the mechanisms currently in place in the rest of the UK.[1] Similarly, the Scottish Government's White Paper on independence, which did include consideration of the role of a new Scottish security and intelligence agency, said little about intelligence oversight. It noted that early legislation would set out the 'purpose, duties and powers' and 'the controls that will exist on the use of those powers'. However, aside from asserting that the new agency would be accountable to Scottish ministers and to the Scottish Parliament, there was no discussion as to what form that accountability would take, or, for example, how it might follow or differ from the system currently in operation at Westminster.[2]

This chapter seeks to offer some perspective on the potential approaches and pitfalls in establishing intelligence oversight by drawing on research on the current arrangements for the oversight of the intelligence and security agencies by the United Kingdom Parliament.[3] It provides a brief introduction to the nature of legislative oversight of intelligence, and draws out some of the key findings of the research with regard to the various mechanisms through which parliamentarians have sought to scrutinise the UK intelligence and security agencies. It concludes by considering the implications and possible lessons for oversight, including for emerging states, such as a potentially independent Scotland.

1   HM Government, *Scotland Analysis: Cm. 8741: Security* (London: HMSO, 2013), https://www.gov.uk/government/uploads/system/uploads/attachment_data/file/253500/Scotland_analysis_security.pdf
2   Scottish Government, *Scotland's Future: Your Guide to an Independent Scotland* (Edinburgh: Scottish Government, 2013), http://www.gov.scot/resource/0043/00439021.pdf, p. 266.
3   H. Bochel, A. Defty, and J. Kirkpatrick, *Watching the Watchers: Parliament and the Intelligence Services* (Basingstoke: Palgrave Macmillan, 2014).

Legislative oversight of intelligence agencies

Intelligence oversight can be seen as having a number of functions: ensuring that intelligence agencies do not break the law or abuse the rights of individuals at home or abroad; ensuring that agencies are managed effectively, and that money is spent appropriately and efficiently; and helping to provide legitimacy for the work of the agencies and the use of intelligence gathered by them. Oversight methods vary considerably across states, and may be influenced by history, constitutional and legal systems, and political culture. Born and Leigh have argued that oversight can typically be seen as taking place at several different levels:

> The executive controls the services by giving direction to them, including tasking, prioritising and making resources available. Additionally, the parliament focuses on oversight, which is limited to more general issues and authorisation of the budget. The parliament is more reactive when setting up committees of inquiry to investigate scandals. The judiciary is tasked with monitoring the use of special powers (next to adjudicating wrong-doings). Civil society, think tanks and citizens may restrain the functioning of the services by giving an alternative view (think-tanks), disclosing scandals and crises (media), or by raising complaints concerning wrong-doing (citizens).[4]

It is therefore possible to identify a range of institutions and actors with a role in the oversight of intelligence and the different levels at which oversight can take place. Building on such ideas, Caparini developed a framework for the accountability of intelligence and security agencies based upon three different types of accountability:

- horizontal — the restraint of state institutions by other state institutions, which might therefore include executive, legislative and judicial oversight of agencies;

- vertical — reflecting hierarchical relationships and levels of access and control, and including non-state actors and the public. This enables differentiation between, for example, executive and legislative oversight.

---

4   H. Born and I. Leigh, *Making Intelligence Accountable: Legal Standards and Best Practice for Oversight of Intelligence Agencies* (Oslo: Parliament of Norway, 2005), p. 15, http://www.dcaf.ch/content/download/35100/525417/file/making-intelligence.pdf

- the 'third dimension' — the role of international actors, such as foreign governments and intergovernmental and nongovernmental organisations.[5]

Scrutiny by the legislature, the focus of this chapter, is only one of a number of possible mechanisms for oversight of intelligence agencies. Nevertheless, it is generally viewed as central, since it provides democratic legitimacy and accountability, and some form of legislative oversight has become the norm in most democratic states.[6] It typically ensures that, at a minimum, legislation concerning the agencies and their activities has been subject to parliamentary debate, that they are placed within an existing constitutional framework, and that the agencies are subject to the law. It can also provide for ongoing scrutiny, as with other areas of public policy. While it might be claimed that executive oversight also provides scrutiny by democratically elected politicians, legislative oversight generally involves individuals who are not involved in the process of tasking the intelligence agencies, and who are not the immediate consumers of their work. It should therefore help ensure the independence of the agencies from political pressure. Legislative oversight is also important in maintaining public confidence in the agencies, including by demonstrating more open and accessible oversight than through internal or executive mechanisms, and reassuring the public that the agencies or the government are not abusing their powers.

However, legislative oversight of intelligence does pose a number of distinctive challenges. Gaining the trust of intelligence agencies can be a significant task for legislative oversight bodies. There are risks that parliamentarians might seek to manipulate the oversight process for political advantage, or that they might leak information, accidentally or intentionally. There are also challenges for those involved in the process, which, while not necessarily unique to intelligence issues, are perhaps made greater by the nature of the subject matter. These include: the lack of experience or expertise in intelligence among most parliamentarians; the risk of being misled or diverted from asking difficult questions; and

---

5   M. Caparini, 'Controlling and Overseeing Intelligence Services in Democratic States', in *Democratic Control of Intelligence Services: Containing Rogue Elephants*, ed. by H. Born and M. Caparini (Aldershot: Ashgate, 2007), pp. 3–24.
6   Born and Leigh (2005).

the dangers of becoming seduced by privileged access and 'captured' by the interests that they are supposed to be scrutinising.

Moreover, the degrees of separation between the various levels of oversight may not be as clear as is often implied. In parliamentary systems, where the executive is drawn from the legislature, there is considerable potential for the same individuals to be involved in oversight at different levels, even simultaneously. In some states the membership of legislative intelligence oversight committees may include government ministers. Although this has not been the case in the UK, the membership of the Intelligence and Security Committee has been dominated by parliamentarians who have previously served as ministers with briefs which included the intelligence and security agencies. There has also been considerable movement of personnel between the various institutions involved in oversight, with the House of Lords, in particular, having a number of appointees who have been involved in other forms of oversight as government ministers, judicial commissioners, or former senior members of the intelligence community. While the overlap between different levels of intelligence oversight may be a natural consequence of parliamentary systems which do not entrench a separation of powers, it may also be a result of the relatively small number of individuals with expertise in this area. This may be more acute in small or emerging states in which the pool of individuals with experience or expertise in field of intelligence and national security may be very small.

Parliamentary oversight of intelligence in the UK

Parliamentary oversight of the intelligence and security agencies in the UK is a relatively recent phenomenon. For most of the agencies' one-hundred-year history, oversight was overwhelmingly undertaken by the executive. Legislation during the 1980s and 1990s placed the agencies on a statutory footing, and also established a number of oversight mechanisms, including judicial commissioners to oversee the issue of warrants to intercept communications, and a committee of parliamentarians, the Intelligence and Security Committee (ISC), to oversee the agencies.

The ISC is a statutory committee of parliamentarians established by the Intelligence Services Act 1994. The creation of the ISC represented a significant step forward in the oversight of the UK intelligence and security agencies. The Committee has a membership of nine, drawn primarily from the House of Commons, initially with one member, increased to two from 2010, from the House of Lords. The Committee sets its own agenda, but has on occasion been asked by the government to carry out investigations. Although the ISC's remit was, until recently, confined to the administration, policy and expenditure of the three intelligence and security agencies, it is widely seen as having expanded its mandate, both functionally, to encompass operational matters, and organisationally, to scrutinise other parts of the intelligence community including defence intelligence and the Joint Intelligence Committee.[7] The Committee works almost entirely in secret, but is required by law to publish an annual report on its work. It has also published a number of additional reports covering its inquiries into a wide range of subjects, including intelligence on Iraqi weapons of mass destruction, the handling of detainees by UK intelligence personnel, the murder of Fusilier Lee Rigby, and the role of women in the intelligence community.

In addition to the publication of reports, since 1998 there has been an annual House of Commons debate on the Committee's work. This presented a new and potentially significant opportunity for Parliament to debate intelligence and to scrutinise the Committee. However, the debates have often been squeezed out of the parliamentary timetable, and have typically had fairly low levels of participation, with normally between fifteen and twenty-six speakers, and an average of nineteen, in each debate; perhaps unsurprisingly, current and former ISC members have tended to constitute a significant proportion of those taking part. Moreover, on many occasions debates have been dominated by discussion of the status of the ISC and the relative merits of replacing it with a select committee. While this perhaps reflected the parliamentary appetite for reform of the ISC, it has also displaced time for debate on the content of its reports and more substantive discussion of the work of the agencies. There have also been frequent delays between the publication of ISC reports and the timetabling of debates, and, perhaps more worryingly, the annual debates appear to have fallen into abeyance

---

7   P. Gill and M. Phythian, *Intelligence in an Insecure World* (Cambridge: Polity, 2006); Mark Phythian, 'The British Experience with Intelligence Accountability', *Intelligence and National Security*, 22 (2007), 75–99, http://dx.doi.org/10.1080/02684520701200822

in recent years. The last substantive House of Commons debate on the work of the ISC took place in 2011, and while House of Lords debates on the Committee's work were introduced in 2009, there have, at the time of writing, only been two debates in the Upper House.

The apparent lack of parliamentary interest in the work of the ISC perhaps reflects the Committee's struggle to establish credibility. There have been a number of significant criticisms of the ISC from Parliament and beyond. The ISC's anomalous status as a statutory committee of parliamentarians appointed by and reporting to the Prime Minister, and staffed and funded by the Cabinet Office, led to the criticism that it is too close to those it is responsible for scrutinising.[8] These concerns have perhaps been exacerbated by disquiet about the kind of parliamentarians selected to serve on the Committee. There has been a tendency towards seniority in appointments to the ISC, with more than two thirds of members having previously held Ministerial office, primarily in the fields of security, defence, and foreign affairs, while all but one of the chairs of the Committee have been former cabinet ministers. This has led to an unfortunate perception that membership of the Committee is a compensation for the loss of high office, and that members are less likely to ask difficult questions of the agencies or the Government.[9] These have been reinforced by evidence that the agencies have not always been entirely open with the ISC in relation to the provision of documents, for example on Iraqi weapons of mass destruction and also the 7/7 London bombing.[10]

In recent years a number of reforms have served to increase the powers of the ISC and also sought to enhance its credibility. The reforms reflected an acceptance on the part of successive governments, and some members of the ISC, that the Committee has not always enjoyed the confidence of Parliament. The Justice and Security Act 2013 reconstituted

---

8   Peter Gill, 'Evaluating Intelligence Oversight Committees: The UK Intelligence and Security Committee and the "War on Terror"', *Intelligence and National Security*, 22 (2007), 14–37, http://dx.doi.org/10.1080/02684520701200756; J. Wadham, 'The Intelligence Services Act 1994', *Modern Law Review*, 57, 6 (1994), 916–27.

9   Bochel, Defty, and Kirkpatrick (2014).

10 Intelligence and Security Committee, *Annual Report 2003–2004* (London: HMSO, 2004), https://b1cba9b3-a-5e6631fd-s-sites.googlegroups.com/a/independent.gov. uk/isc/files/2003-2004_ISC_AR.pdf; Intelligence and Security Committee, *Could 7/7 Have Been Prevented: Review of the Intelligence on the London Terrorist Attacks on 7 July 2005* (London: HMSO, 2009), https://fas.org/irp/world/uk/july7review.pdf

the ISC as a committee of Parliament, provided it with greater powers, and expanded its remit to include oversight of operational activity and the wider intelligence community. As a committee of Parliament, members of the ISC are now appointed by Parliament, albeit following nomination by the Prime Minister, in consultation with opposition leaders. The Committee also now reports to Parliament, although it retains the capacity to report directly to the Prime Minister on matters of particular sensitivity. A number of other changes not included in the legislation have also altered the way the ISC operates. The Committee enjoyed a significant increase in resources from 2013, with a doubling of the budget and the number of staff available to it. The Committee also sought to make itself more transparent, including through holding public evidence sessions. Although this has the potential to enhance the profile of the ISC in Parliament and beyond, the unchallenging nature of the Committee's first public cross-examination of intelligence agency heads in November 2013 provided little reassurance that it was capable of rigorous scrutiny.[11]

Most research on legislative oversight in the UK has understandably focused on the ISC,[12] nevertheless, there is evidence of a growth in parliamentary interest in intelligence issues beyond the ISC. This has been prompted in part by the Labour government's use of intelligence to make the case for war in Iraq, the responses of successive governments to the terrorist threat within the UK, and more recently the introduction of legislation designed to enhance the interception powers of the UK intelligence agencies. It is also apparent that wider parliamentary

11 Intelligence and Security Committee of Parliament, 'Uncorrected Transcript of Evidence Given by Sir Iain Lobban, Director, Government Communication Headquarters; Mr Andrew Parker, Director General, Security Service; Sir John Sawers, Chief, Secret Intelligence Service' (London, 7 November 2013), http://isc.independent.gov.uk/public-evidence/7november2013; Andrew Defty, 'Having Security Chiefs Give Evidence to Parliament Is Progress, but Future Sessions Must Dig Deeper' (Democratic Audit UK, 15 November 2013), http://www.democraticaudit.com/2013/11/15/having-security-chiefs-give-evidence-to-parliament-is-progress-but-future-sessions-must-dig-deeper/

12 A. Glees, P. H. J. Davies, and J. N. L. Morrison, *The Open Side of Secrecy* (London: Social Affairs Unit, 2006); Gill (2007); I. Leigh, 'The UK's Intelligence and Security Committee', in Born and Caparini (2007), pp. 177–94; M. Phythian, '"A Very British Institution": The Intelligence and Security Committee and Intelligence Accountability in the United Kingdom', in *The Oxford Handbook of National Security Intelligence*, ed. by L. Johnson (Oxford: Oxford University Press, 2010), pp. 699–718; Leigh (2012).

interest is partly the result of long-term dissatisfaction with the work of the ISC, which has prompted the development of a range of alternative mechanisms to scrutinise the intelligence agencies and the Government's use of intelligence, including through parliamentary questions and debates, the work of all-party parliamentary groups, and most notably, the work of parliamentary select committees.

A number of select committees, particularly the Home and Foreign Affairs committees and the Joint Committee on Human Rights, have sought access to intelligence material and called for greater parliamentary scrutiny of the intelligence and security agencies. The interest of some select committees in intelligence issues pre-dates the creation of the ISC in 1994. For example, in 1985 the Foreign Affairs Committee was granted access to intelligence material in relation to its investigation into the sinking of the Argentine battleship, *General Belgrano*, during the Falklands conflict. Under the 'crown jewels' procedure the Committee was shown intelligence material under supervision in the Foreign Office, with the proviso that they could not take notes.[13] The Home Affairs Committee was at the forefront of calls for greater parliamentary oversight of the intelligence agencies. In 1989 it persuaded the Director General of the Security Service, Stella Rimington, to meet it,[14] and in 1992 recommended that it would be appropriate for the departmental select committees to oversee the work of the agencies, as well as the departments responsible for them.[15]

However, the existence of the ISC has to some extent complicated the work of select committees on intelligence issues and their relationships with the agencies.[16] Requests from several select committees for access to intelligence agency staff and documents have been denied on the grounds that the ISC is the only body responsible and qualified to be allowed access to intelligence material. For example, when the Foreign Affairs Committee invoked the 'crown jewels' procedure in seeking

---

13 Liaison Committee, *First Report — The Work of Select Committees HC323-I* (London: HMSO, 1997), appendix 6, paras 35–38.

14 S. Rimington, *Open Secret: The Autobiography of the Former Director-General of MI5* (London: Hutchinson, 2001), pp. 158–59.

15 Home Affairs Committee, *Accountability of the Security Service, First Report of Session 1992–93, HC 265* (London: HMSO, 1992).

16 See H. Bochel, A. Defty, and J. Kirkpatrick, '"New Mechanisms of Independent Accountability": Select Committees and Parliamentary Scrutiny of the Intelligence Services', *Parliamentary Affairs*, 68 (2015), 314–31.

access to intelligence on the decision to go to war in Iraq, their requests
were declined on the grounds that this was now the responsibility of the
ISC.[17] Similar requests have been denied to the Northern Ireland Affairs
Committee in relation to intelligence on the Omagh bombing, and the
Joint Committee on Human Rights in relation to the interrogation of
terrorist suspects.[18] The withdrawal of access to intelligence material
from select committees, coupled with the anomalous status of the ISC,
prompted a number of select committees to question the role of the ISC
and call for it to be reconstituted as a parliamentary select committee.[19]

Interestingly, while successive governments and the ISC have
resisted closer cooperation with the select committees, there is evidence
of developing engagement between some select committees and the
agencies themselves. The Foreign Affairs Committee and the Home
Affairs Committee have received briefings from MI6 and MI5, although
these are informal and are not recorded as evidence in committee
reports.[20] While this may suggest an appreciation that the ISC does not
have a monopoly over access to the agencies, these briefings are offered
by the agencies and can be withdrawn by them. Moreover, while some
committees have been willing to accept off-the-record briefings, others
have not. The Joint Committee on Human Rights has declined such
offers from the Security Service, arguing that democratic accountability
and public confidence 'cannot be achieved by off the record, secret

17   Foreign Affairs Committee, *The Decision to Go to War in Iraq, Ninth Report of Session
     2002–03, HC 813-I* (London: HMSO, 2003), https://www.gov.uk/government/
     uploads/system/uploads/attachment_data/file/272087/6062.pdf
18   Joint Committee on Human Rights, *Counter-Terrorism Policy and Human Rights
     (Seventeenth Report): Bringing Human Rights Back in, Sixteenth Report of Session 2009–
     10, Hl Paper 86, HC 111* (London: HMSO, 2010), http://www.publications.parliament.
     uk/pa/jt200910/jtselect/jtrights/86/86.pdf; Joint Committee on Human Rights,
     *Counter-Terrorism Policy and Human Rights: Prosecution and Pre-Charge Detention,
     Twenty-Fourth Report of Session 2005–06* (London: HMSO, 2006), https://www.gov.
     uk/government/uploads/system/uploads/attachment_data/file/272344/6920.pdf;
     Northern Ireland Affairs Committee, *The Omagh Bombing: Access to Intelligence*
     (London: HMSO, 2009), http://www.publications.parliament.uk/pa/cm200809/
     cmselect/cmniaf/873/87303.htm
19   For example, Home Affairs Committee, *Accountability of the Security Service, Third
     Report of Session 1998–99, HC 291* (London: HMSO, 1999); Foreign Affairs Committee,
     *Implications for the Work of the House and Its Committees of the Government's Lack of
     Co-Operation with the Foreign Affairs Committee's Inquiry into the Decision to Go to
     War in Iraq* (London: HMSO, 2004), https://www.publications.parliament.uk/pa/
     cm200304/cmselect/cmfaff/440/440.pdf
20   Bochel, Defty, and Kirkpatrick (2015).

briefings'.[21] While the reconstitution of the ISC as a parliamentary committee, although not a select committee, may serve to ameliorate select committee demands, unless the ISC is also prepared to work with the select committees this seems unlikely to address their concerns in full.

There are, then, a range of mechanisms through which the Westminster Parliament and its members have sought to scrutinise the UK intelligence and security agencies. While the ISC is the most important of these, it is not without its flaws and its critics. Partly as a result of this a number of other parliamentary bodies, as well as several enterprising individual parliamentarians, have sought to exert pressure for greater openness and reform in relation both to the work of the agencies, and the operation of the formal oversight mechanisms. After a prolonged period of opposition to further scrutiny, in recent years the UK government has accepted some measure of reform of the oversight mechanisms and the ISC in particular. While the impact of these reforms is not yet clear, the notion that Parliament has a legitimate interest in scrutinising the work of the intelligence agencies and the Government's use of intelligence is now firmly entrenched.

Establishing legislative oversight of intelligence: lessons from the UK Parliament

Clearly, in the event of independence, or even some sharing of responsibility for oversight of the UK intelligence agencies, Scotland would have to consider what form of legislative oversight would be appropriate. The UK's oversight mechanisms, as outlined above, provide one possible model. The establishment of the Intelligence and Security Committee represented a significant step forward in intelligence agency accountability in the UK. It has allowed a small number of parliamentarians wide-ranging access to the intelligence and security agencies, their documents and staff. Moreover, it has expanded its mandate both organisationally and functionally, and recent reforms have considerably enhanced the powers and resources of the Committee. However, the Westminster experience also highlights some of the

---

21   Joint Committee on Human Rights (2010).

challenges involved in establishing intelligence agency accountability, most notably in relation to whether Parliament has sufficient powers and capacity to conduct effective scrutiny in this area.

As a reserved power, the Scottish Parliament has no experience of scrutiny of issues of intelligence and national security. In developing legislative oversight of intelligence it would, therefore, be starting from a very low base. There have been a small number of intelligence-related questions and motions in the Scottish Parliament, primarily in relation to the interception of MSPs' communications, the opening of an MI5 office in Scotland, and the use of Scottish airports in rendition flights (although the latter related mainly to the CIA). However, intelligence-related questions and motions have originated from a relatively small number of members, six MSPs, of whom four came from the SNP and one each from the Scottish Green Party and the Scottish Liberal Democrats. Moreover, the Scottish Government's response to such questions has been to emphasise that as national security is a reserved power it would not be appropriate to comment. The current absence of powers, coupled with the lack of opportunities to ask questions in this area, means there may be very little interest in intelligence issues in the Scottish Parliament, and almost certainly very little expertise.

The Scottish Parliament's involvement in scrutiny in this area is not, however, very different from that of the Westminster Parliament prior to the establishment of the ISC in 1994. When the ISC was established in 1994, the UK intelligence and security agencies had operated for over eighty years with very little external scrutiny, either from Parliament or even the executive. Not only was there no formal mechanism for legislative oversight, for much of their history successive governments refused to avow the existence of the intelligence and security agencies and MPs were prevented from asking questions about them.[22] Indeed, in one important respect a new Scottish oversight body could find itself in a stronger position than the embryonic ISC. Intelligence and security agencies are now an avowed and accepted part of the machinery of state, and legislative oversight bodies to hold them to account exist in most democratic states. As a result, intelligence oversight bodies in newly independent states may need to spend less time seeking to

---

22   Bochel, Defty, and Kirkpatrick (2014).

establish their legitimacy or building a relationship with intelligence agencies. While ISC members claim that the early committees spent a considerable amount of time seeking to gain the trust of the UK intelligence and security agencies, in a newly independent Scotland it is likely that legislative oversight would be established alongside the creation of intelligence and security agencies. While there would still be a need to build trust between the agencies and their overseers, oversight bodies would perhaps be less likely to be viewed as a new and potentially threatening development.

The need to build trust, particularly in states where intelligence agencies are already well established, has also meant that legislative intelligence oversight committees have often started with relatively modest powers, designed to reassure intelligence agencies that parliamentary bodies can be trusted in such a role, and have evolved over time, acquiring extra powers and new roles. As noted above, the ISC, for example, was created with a mandate limited to scrutiny of the administration, expenditure and policy of the three intelligence agencies, and has only recently expanded this to include operational matters and the wider intelligence community. One obvious solution to this is to provide oversight bodies with a more powerful mandate from the outset. A committee modelled on the current ISC would, for example, be considerably more powerful than one which mirrored the powers exercised by the ISC when it was first established. This also emphasises the need to allow for evolution in intelligence oversight mechanisms. Although this has happened in the UK, the pace of intelligence oversight reform has been slow. Indeed there may be real benefits in establishing oversight mechanisms at the same time as intelligence agencies, in that the two processes could inform each other. In this way, executive and legislative oversight bodies, and indeed also civil society, could play a role in ensuring that effective internal procedures are put in place regarding what is and what is not acceptable for intelligence agencies to do, and what powers should be wielded by the different oversight bodies.

Even if a relatively powerful legislative intelligence oversight committee were established, the lack of experience in this area would perhaps still be the most significant challenge involved in establishing legislative oversight of intelligence in a newly independent Scotland. Our research on parliamentary oversight at Westminster found that in addition to the form and powers of legislative intelligence oversight bodies, another crucial factor in their effectiveness is the level of expertise of those involved in oversight. In its first report, published in 1995, the ISC stressed that the Committee was taking a considerable time to 'learn' about its subject, observing that 'the intelligence and security field is a specialist and complex one, about which relatively little is reliably known from the outside'.[23] One possible, although far from ideal, response to this challenge, which has been adopted at Westminster, has been the tendency to appoint ISC members, and particularly committee chairs, with previous ministerial experience in departments involved in the work of the intelligence agencies. Such an approach has its drawbacks. Although this has allowed the ISC to establish a reputation as a well-informed and senior committee, as noted above, it has also led to accusations that ISC members have been too reluctant to criticise the agencies.

Not only is the Scottish Parliament much smaller than the Westminster Parliament, providing a much reduced pool of potential expertise on which to draw, but as national security is at present a reserved power, the number of former ministers with experience in this area is likely to be extremely limited or possibly even non-existent. The possible solution of allowing serving ministers to sit on an intelligence oversight committee, something which is forbidden at Westminster but does take place in other systems, would undermine the independence and credibility of any oversight committee and would be best avoided. While there are likely to be few MSPs with any experience of the UK intelligence agencies, one potentially significant development in this respect was the appointment of an SNP MP, Angus Robertson, to the ISC following the 2015 General Election. Research indicates that ISC members have played an advisory role within their parties by providing informal briefings on intelligence issues for party leaders and frontbench spokespeople.[24] The emergence of a body of MSPs with experience of intelligence oversight at Westminster might therefore be an alternative means of building capacity in the Scottish Parliament.

---

23 Intelligence and Security Committee, *Interim Report of the Intelligence and Security Committee*, Cm. 2873 (London: HMSO, 1995).
24 Defty (2008).

Another means of building capacity in intelligence matters at Westminster, both within the ISC and in Parliament as a whole, has been to use the House of Lords as a reservoir of expertise. As a joint committee, the ISC membership has included a number of members of the House of Lords with experience of working with the intelligence community, including former Ministers, senior civil servants, and a former member of the Secret Intelligence Service, Baroness Ramsay of Cartvale. A high proportion of former members of the ISC have also remained in Parliament through appointment to the House of Lords, while in recent years a number of retired senior members of the intelligence community have been appointed as crossbench peers, including former Directors-General of the Security Service. While this has provided a significant body of experience on intelligence issues in the Upper House, it can also lead to questions about the level of independence of parliamentary scrutiny in this area. Moreover, as a unicameral and entirely elected system these options are not available to the Scottish Parliament, and consideration would therefore have be given to alternative means of building capacity in intelligence expertise within the chamber. This could include, for example: allowing all MSPs greater access to intelligence and security agencies, such as through regular intelligence agency briefings for other parliamentary committees with an interest in this area, like those now provided for select committees at Westminster; public evidence sessions; and opportunities for parliamentarians to visit the agencies.

Opportunities for wider parliamentary debate on intelligence issues, or at least on the work of an oversight committee, are also important both in terms of providing democratic accountability and in building capacity. As noted above, there has been a tendency on the part of British governments to view intelligence as the sole preserve of the ISC, and to use the Committee's existence to prevent wider parliamentary scrutiny of intelligence. However, the experience at Westminster indicates that the existence of a dedicated intelligence oversight committee is unlikely to discourage other parliamentary committees or individual parliamentarians from taking an interest in this area. It is important that legislative intelligence oversight committees are seen as part of Parliament and not as a proxy for wider parliamentary scrutiny. In recent years, the UK government has recognised an overlapping agenda between the ISC and a number of other parliamentary committees, while the appointment of former ISC members to other select committees has facilitated greater cooperation between the ISC and the rest of Parliament. The introduction of annual debates on the work of the ISC is another potentially important development. Although these have been poorly attended at Westminster, and indeed have fallen into abeyance in recent years, they could be a useful means of enhancing the credibility of a committee which operates largely behind closed doors.

Another significant factor in building capacity, particularly in relation to the work of a legislative oversight committee, is the resources available. Unlike other parliamentary committees, the ISC is funded by central government rather than Parliament. Although this naturally raises questions about the Committee's independence, it has also meant that it has been a well-resourced committee, particularly when compared to other parliamentary committees. Given the nature of the subject matter, and the relative lack of expertise of Committee members on appointment, the Committee has relied considerably on building up an independent investigative capacity with staff who are able to go into the agencies and ask questions on the Committee's behalf. In contrast, the Scottish Parliament has been criticised for not having a sufficiently large and well-trained staff, and Scottish parliamentary committees in particular for being under-resourced.[25] The creation of new committees within the Scottish Parliament to cover additional responsibilities would be likely to place extra strain on resources, while finding committee staff with the necessary expertise in this area is also likely to prove challenging.

As noted above, issues of funding and expertise have led to questions about the independence of the ISC. There is clearly a careful balance to be maintained between the desire to provide a well-supported and experienced committee and the need to ensure sufficient distance between it and those it is responsible for overseeing, including the Government. This may be particularly acute in the field of intelligence,

---

25 P. Cairney, 'How Can the Scottish Parliament Be Improved as a Legislature?', *Scottish Parliamentary Review*, 1, 1 (2013), http://www.scottishparliamentaryreview. org/; P. Cairney, 'The Analysis of Scottish Parliament Committees: Beyond Capacity and Structure in Comparing West European Legislatures', *European Journal of Political Research*, 45, 2 (2006), 181–208.

where the monopoly on expertise lies largely with the executive. However, it is crucial that legislative oversight bodies have credibility. It is not sufficient simply to claim to exercise considerable power, particularly if most oversight activities take place behind closed doors. In 2010, the incoming Chair of the ISC, Sir Malcolm Rifkind, observed that the Committee must 'not just be entirely independent in law and in the eyes of its own members. That independence must in practice, be fully respected by all government departments and the ISC perceived to be fully independent, both by Parliament and by the public'.[26] As Rifkind acknowledged, for much of its existence the ISC struggled to establish its credibility. This is, in part, because the Committee itself has paid little attention to its wider public and parliamentary profile and has been somewhat dismissive of attempts at scrutiny by other actors. In a newly emergent state, particularly where one party might be dominant, it would be important, both within Parliament and for the wider public, to ensure that an oversight committee were clearly independent of the executive and the agencies.

Finally, some consideration may need to be given to the question of what protections might be extended to parliamentarians to shield them from scrutiny by the intelligence agencies. Since 1964, UK intelligence agencies have been prevented from intercepting the communications of parliamentarians at Westminster under a convention known as the Wilson doctrine.[27] While there are some limitations to this convention, and it has come under pressure in recent years, it is clearly something that parliamentarians value, and under the Investigatory Powers Act 2016 it will be enshrined in legislation. That legislation will also see the principle extended to members of the devolved assemblies and to UK members of the European Parliament. While this would clearly not protect members of an independent Scottish Parliament from the attentions of UK intelligence agencies, retaining the principle in relation to any new Scottish agency might be important in helping establish trust

---

26 M. Rifkind, 'Intelligence Oversight in the UK: The Intelligence and Security Committee', London: speech delivered at the Royal United Services Institute, 16 November 2010.

27 A. Defty, H. Bochel, and J. Kirkpatrick, 'Tapping the Telephones of Members of Parliament: The 'Wilson Doctrine' and Parliamentary Privilege', *Intelligence and National Security*, 29 (2014), 675–97.

between Parliament and the intelligence agencies in an independent Scotland.

There would, then, be significant challenges involved in establishing legislative oversight of intelligence in an independent Scotland. Some of these challenges are presaged by the experiences at Westminster, but others are likely to be new, or at least more acute, in a newly independent state seeking to establish intelligence agencies and legislative oversight from scratch. Moreover, it is important to note that while the tendency may be to mirror the oversight mechanisms at Westminster, this is not the only possible template for legislative oversight in Scotland. Other states provide a number of alternative models on which to draw, and civil society organisations have also established some notions of best practice in this area.[28] The Parliamentary Intelligence and Security Committee has evolved over time and has recently acquired new powers, but it has not been the most powerful or effective of oversight bodies, and Scotland may want to look to examples from other states, including the Nordic countries or the Netherlands.[29] However, it is also important to note that powerful oversight structures do not always make for more detailed or effective scrutiny. The US has some of the most powerful legislative intelligence oversight committees, but much of the current debate about intelligence agency powers in the US has revolved around whether members of Congressional oversight committees have been willing to wield that power. In establishing legislative oversight of intelligence in a newly-independent Scotland, as much attention should be paid to the composition and capacity of an intelligence oversight body as to its form and powers.

---

28 Born and Leigh (2005).
29 L. Mevik and H. Huus-Hansen, 'Parliamentary Oversight of the Norwegian Secret and Intelligence Services', in Born and Caparini (2007), pp. 143–62; C. Hijzen, 'More Than a Ritual Dance: The Dutch Practice of Parliamentary Oversight and Control of the Intelligence Community', *Security and Human Rights*, 24, 3–4 (2014), 227–38.

References

Bochel, H., Defty, A., and Kirkpatrick, J., *Watching the Watchers: Parliament and the Intelligence Services* (Basingstoke: Palgrave Macmillan, 2014).

—, '"New Mechanisms of Independent Accountability": Select Committees and Parliamentary Scrutiny of the Intelligence Services', *Parliamentary Affairs*, 68 (2015), 314–31, http://dx.doi.org/10.1093/pa/gst032

Born, H. and Leigh, I., *Making Intelligence Accountable: Legal Standards and Best Practice for Oversight of Intelligence Agencies* (Oslo: Parliament of Norway, 2005), http://www.dcaf.ch/content/download/35100/525417/file/making-intelligence.pdf

Cairney, P., 'The Analysis of Scottish Parliament Committees: Beyond Capacity and Structure in Comparing West European Legislatures', *European Journal of Political Research*, 45 (2006), 181–208, http://dx.doi.org/10.1111/j.1475-6765.2006.00295.x

—, 'How Can the Scottish Parliament Be Improved as a Legislature?', *Scottish Parliamentary Review*, 1 (2013), http://www.scottishparliamentaryreview.org

Caparini, M., 'Controlling and Overseeing Intelligence Services in Democratic States', in *Democratic Control of Intelligence Services: Containing Rogue Elephants*, ed. by H. Born and M. Caparini (Aldershot: Ashgate, 2007), pp. 3–24.

Defty, A., 'Educating Parliamentarians About Intelligence: The Role of the British Intelligence and Security Committee', *Parliamentary Affairs*, 61 (2008), pp. 621–41, http://dx.doi.org/10.1093/pa/gsn024

—, 'Having Security Chiefs Give Evidence to Parliament Is Progress, but Future Sessions Must Dig Deeper', Democratic Audit UK, 15 November 2013, http://www.democraticaudit.com/2013/11/15/having-security-chiefs-give-evidence-to-parliament-is-progress-but-future-sessions-must-dig-deeper/

Defty, A., Bochel, H., and Kirkpatrick, J., 'Tapping the Telephones of Members of Parliament: The "Wilson Doctrine" and Parliamentary Privilege', *Intelligence and National Security*, 29 (2014), 675–97, http://dx.doi.org/10.1080/02684527.2013.777606

Foreign Affairs Committee, *The Decision to Go to War in Iraq, Ninth Report of Session 2002–03, HC 813-I* (London: HMSO, 2003), https://www.gov.uk/government/uploads/system/uploads/attachment_data/file/272087/6062.pdf

—, *Implications for the Work of the House and Its Committees of the Government's Lack of Co-Operation with the Foreign Affairs Committee's Inquiry into the Decision to Go to War in Iraq* (London: HMSO, 2004), https://www.publications.parliament.uk/pa/cm200304/cmselect/cmfaff/440/440.pdf

Gill, P. and Phythian, M., *Intelligence in an Insecure World* (Cambridge: Polity, 2006).

—, 'Evaluating Intelligence Oversight Committees: The UK Intelligence and Security Committee and the "War on Terror"', *Intelligence and National Security*, 22 (2007), 14–37, http://dx.doi.org/10.1080/02684520701200756

Glees, A., Davies, P. H. J., and Morrison, J. N. L., *The Open Side of Secrecy* (London: Social Affairs Unit, 2006).

Hijzen, C., 'More Than a Ritual Dance: The Dutch Practice of Parliamentary Oversight and Control of the Intelligence Community', *Security and Human Rights*, 24 (2014), 227–38, http://dx.doi.org/10.1163/18750230-02404002

HM Government, *Scotland Analysis: Cm. 8741: Security* (London: HMSO, 2013), https://www.gov.uk/government/uploads/system/uploads/attachment_data/file/253500/Scotland_analysis_security.pdf

Home Affairs Committee, *Accountability of the Security Service, First Report of Session 1992–93, HC 265* (London: HMSO, 1992).

—, *Accountability of the Security Service, Third Report of Session 1998–99, HC 291* (London: HMSO, 1999).

Intelligence and Security Committee, *Interim Report of the Intelligence and Security Committee, Cm. 2873* (London: HMSO, 1995).

—, *Annual Report 2003–2004* (London: HMSO, 2004), https://b1cba9b3-a-5e6631fd-s-sites.googlegroups.com/a/independent.gov.uk/isc/files/2003-2004_ISC_AR.pdf

—, *Could 7/7 Have Been Prevented: Review of the Intelligence on the London Terrorist Attacks on 7 July 2005* (London: HMSO, 2009), https://fas.org/irp/world/uk/july7review.pdf

Intelligence and Security Committee of Parliament, 'Uncorrected Transcript of Evidence Given by Sir Iain Lobban, Director, Government Communication Headquarters; Mr Andrew Parker, Director General, Security Service; Sir John Sawers, Chief, Secret Intelligence Service', London, 7 November 2013, http://isc.independent.gov.uk/public-evidence/7november2013

Joint Committee on Human Rights, *Counter-Terrorism Policy and Human Rights: Prosecution and Pre-Charge Detention, Twenty-Fourth Report of Session 2005–06* (London: HMSO, 2006), https://www.gov.uk/government/uploads/system/uploads/attachment_data/file/272344/6920.pdf

—, *Counter-Terrorism Policy and Human Rights (Seventeenth Report): Bringing Human Rights Back in, Sixteenth Report of Session 2009–10, Hl Paper 86, HC 111* (London: HMSO, 2010), http://www.publications.parliament.uk/pa/jt200910/jtselect/jtrights/86/86.pdf

Leigh, I., 'The UK's Intelligence and Security Committee', in *Democratic Control of Intelligence Services*, ed. by H. Born and M. Caparini (Aldershot: Ashgate, 2007), pp. 177–94.

—, 'Rebalancing Rights and National Security: Reforming UK Intelligence Oversight a Decade after 9/11', *Intelligence and National Security*, 27 (2012), 722–38, http://dx.doi.org/10.1080/02684527.2012.708525

Liason Committee, *The Work of Select Committees, HC 323-I* (London: HMSO, 1996–1997).

Mevik, L. and Huus-Hansen, H., 'Parliamentary Oversight of the Norwegian Secret and Intelligence Services', in *Democratic Control of Intelligence Services: Containing Rogue Elephants*, ed. by H. Born and M. Caparini (Aldershot: Ashgate, 2007), pp. 143–62.

Northern Ireland Affairs Committee, *The Omagh Bombing: Access to Intelligence* (London: HMSO, 2009), http://www.publications.parliament.uk/pa/cm2008 09/cmselect/cmniaf/873/87303.htm

Phythian, M., 'The British Experience with Intelligence Accountability', *Intelligence and National Security*, 22 (2007), 75–99, http://dx.doi.org/10.1080/0268 4520701200822

—, '"A Very British Institution": The Intelligence and Security Committee and Intelligence Accountability in the United Kingdom', in *The Oxford Handbook of National Security Intelligence*, ed. by L. Johnson (Oxford: Oxford University Press, 2010), pp. 699–718.

Rifkind, M., 'Intelligence Oversight in the UK: The Intelligence and Security Committee' (London: speech delivered at the Royal United Services Institute, 16 November 2010).

Rimington, S., *Open Secret: The Autobiography of the Former Director-General of MI5* (London: Hutchinson, 2001).

Scottish Government, *Scotland's Future: Your Guide to an Independent Scotland* (Edinburgh: Scottish Government, 2013), http://www.gov.scot/resource/0043/00439021.pdf

Wadham, J., 'The Intelligence Services Act 1994', *Modern Law Review*, 57 (1994), 916–27, http://dx.doi.org/10.1111/j.1468-2230.1994.tb01983.x

5. Scotland and the Politics of Intelligence Accountability

Colin Atkinson, Nick Brooke and Brian Harris

This chapter explores the politics of intelligence accountability in the context of the 2014 referendum on Scottish independence and the 2015 General Election in the UK. Drawing upon Peter Gill's model for assessing the effectiveness of security intelligence accountability, it argues that the Scottish Government's proposals for intelligence accountability in an independent Scotland indicated a vague and conservative intention to maintain similar mechanisms to the existing UK political settlement. By exploring the accountability mechanisms for security intelligence in other jurisdictions, this chapter suggests that shortcomings in the Scottish Government's proposals could have been addressed by learning lessons and adopting practices and processes from beyond the UK. The aftermath of the referendum — particularly the landslide victory in Scotland for the pro-independence SNP in the 2015 UK General Election — may herald consequences for both intelligence accountability in the UK and any future plan for accountability mechanisms in an independent Scotland. The previously unconsidered prospect of direct SNP representation on the UK Intelligence and Security Committee (ISC) — now a reality in the UK — raises the scenario that pro-independence politicians will develop the expertise, capital, and political legitimacy necessary for effective intelligence accountability that were lacking in the pre-referendum political landscape.

In a democratic society, accountability is the requirement for those in positions of power to provide answers to those whom they serve. Accountability depends, therefore, upon either the presence of an informed, inquisitive, and engaged public or an array of elected representatives with similar qualities who act on the public's behalf. Although seemingly straightforward, accountability is not a simple administrative task; it poses a series of profound and fundamentally political challenges concerning the shape, composition, scope, power and limitations of any such regime. These challenges are compounded when one seeks to ensure accountability for the actions of intelligence and security agencies, organisations which, by their very nature, operate in conditions of secrecy. It has been argued that the problem here can be easily stated: 'how to provide for democratic control of a governmental function and institutions which are essential to the survival and flourishing of the state but which must operate to a certain extent in justifiable secrecy'.[1] Ensuring the democratic accountability of intelligence services has been a persistent problem for western democracies, a challenge compounded by renewed concerns in the post-9/11 era that will undoubtedly persist in the years to come.[2]

In the UK there are various levels of intelligence accountability; however, the parliamentary Intelligence and Security Committee (ISC) is the principal mechanism that exists to provide for the accountability of the nation's intelligence agencies.[3] Peter Gill has commented upon how the history of the oversight of security intelligence agencies in the UK is short, and how, with one or two exceptions, 'it simply did not exist before the 1970s, though its spread since then has been rapid'.[4] The ISC was first established by the Intelligence Services Act 1994 to examine

---

1   I. Leigh, 'The Accountability of Security and Intelligence Agencies', in *Handbook of Intelligence Studies*, ed. by L. K. Johnson (Abingdon and New York: Routledge, 2007), pp. 67–81 (p. 67).

2   Hans Born and Ian Leigh, 'Democratic Accountability of Intelligence Services', in *Armaments, Disarmament and International Security*, ed. by Institute Stockholm International Peace Research (Oxford: Oxford University Press, 2007), pp. 193–214.

3   Mark Phythian, 'The British Experience with Intelligence Accountability', Intelligence and National Security, 22, 1 (2007), pp. 75–99; H. Bochel, A. Defty, and J. Kirkpatrick, *Watching the Watchers: Parliament and the Intelligence Services* (Basingstoke: Palgrave Macmillan, 2014).

4   Peter Gill, 'Evaluating Intelligence Oversight Committees: The UK Intelligence and Security Committee and the "War on Terror"', *Intelligence and National Security*, 22, 1 (2007), pp. 14–37 (p. 14).

the policy, administration and expenditure of the Security Service, Secret Intelligence Service (SIS), and the Government Communications Headquarters (GCHQ). The Justice and Security Act 2013 reformed the ISC: making it a Committee of Parliament; providing greater powers; and increasing its remit to include oversight of operational activity and the wider intelligence and security activities of Government. Other than the three main intelligence and security agencies, the ISC examines the intelligence-related work of the Cabinet Office including: the Joint Intelligence Committee (JIC); the Assessments Staff; and the National Security Secretariat. The ISC also provides oversight of Defence Intelligence in the Ministry of Defence and the Office for Security and Counter-Terrorism (OSCT) in the Home Office. Members of the ISC are appointed by Parliament and the Committee reports directly to Parliament. The ISC may also make reports to the Prime Minister on matters which are sensitive in relation to national security.[5]

Intelligence oversight in the UK emerged and developed in the late twentieth and early twenty-first centuries; however, the effectiveness of the UK's accountability mechanisms have come increasingly into question. The responses to terrorist attacks on 9/11, the events that led to the Iraq War and the more recent series of disclosures from both Wikileaks and Edward Snowden revealed a range of controversial programs and activities undertaken by the intelligence agencies that were previously unknown to the public, media, and many politicians. It was against this backdrop — and in advance of the 2014 referendum on Scottish independence — that the Scottish Government decided upon the measures it would propose to ensure the accountability of a prospective security and intelligence agency for an independent Scotland. These measures were subsequently published in the White Paper on Scottish independence titled *Scotland's Future: Your Guide to an Independent Scotland*.[6] This chapter evaluates the Scottish Government's proposal for intelligence accountability, locating it in comparative context by understanding the mechanisms that are in place in other

---

5   The Intelligence and Security Committee of Parliament, 'About the Committee' (2016), http://isc.independent.gov.uk/

6   Scottish Government, *Scotland's Future: Your Guide to an Independent Scotland* (Edinburgh: Scottish Government, 2013), http://www.gov.scot/resource/0043/0043 9021.pdf.

similar jurisdictions. It argues that, despite the claim that a range of international comparators were studied,[7] the Scottish Government's plans sought to replicate the existing UK model, without an appreciation of the challenges of such an approach. It concludes by exploring the political aftermath of the both the 2014 Scottish referendum and the 2015 UK General Election, with a particular focus upon the consequences of this new political landscape for intelligence accountability in the UK and in the context of any future referendum on Scottish independence.

Examining the proposed measures for intelligence accountability in an independent Scotland

In evaluating the performance of the ISC, Peter Gill proposed six variables that are important in determining the effectiveness of any committee that oversees security intelligence: its *form, mandate, membership, resources, access to information,* and *reporting*.[8] In Gill's model the *form* of an intelligence oversight committee depends upon the situation and status of the parent assembly. For example Gill makes the distinction between the committee traditions found in the US Congress and those in parliamentary systems, wherein the former offers the potential for independent action in terms of budgets, appointments and investigations, whilst in the latter, parliamentary committees are more likely to be the 'creatures of the executive'.[9] Gill continues that the *mandate* — or terms of reference — for such a committee is likely to be a result of its form. Here Gill discusses the distinction between the relative freedom and independence of the US congressional model and the strictures of the UK statutory model. Considering a UK-style model he concludes that, to the extent that the executive is the dominant force in writing statutes, a committee's powers will reflect government preferences rather than those of an independent legislator.[10] The selection of *membership* for any intelligence accountability committee is critical to its effectiveness and legitimacy. Gill considers that members' independence of the executive will be clearest if the members are chosen

---

7   *Ibid.*, p. 261.
8   Gill (2007).
9   *Ibid.*, p. 16.
10   *Ibid.*

by the assembly itself, as in Argentina and Germany, rather than by the government, as was previously the case in the UK.[11] Both informal, political selection processes and more formal eligibility, selection and vetting procedures will undoubtedly have an impact on the membership composition of an intelligence oversight committee. The inter-related issues of the extent of knowledge and depth of experience of members are also vital in assessing the measures for intelligence accountability. If accountability can be understood as the requirement for those in positions of power to provide answers to those whom they serve, then it is imperative that there is the requisite ability in an oversight committee to ask appropriate questions. Beyond an appropriately skilled and experienced membership, the issue of *resources* is also critical to the effectiveness of an intelligence oversight committee. Whilst Gill remarks upon the plethora of resources available to members in the US system, he also astutely recognises that 'generous resources do not guarantee effectiveness' if there is neither the will nor the skill to use them in the course of business.[12] He continues that intelligence practitioners are highly skilled and can easily subvert the uninitiated outsider, and further contends that 'the first task for any committee is to discover what the right questions are. This, in turn, depends on the expertise, experience and energy of members and staff, if any, and the will to use them'.[13] This leads to the fifth factor that Gill outlines in his model: *access to information*. Gill describes this as 'tokenistic' because, even where legislation formally enables unrestricted access, committees still need to use skill in negotiating with informal gatekeepers in the agencies under scrutiny.[14] The final factor considered by Gill is *reporting*, particularly in the context of the tension between the secrecy of the data to which committee members will have access and the requirement to provide meaningful information on the activities of intelligence agencies to the parent assembly and the public. This leaves parliamentarians or committee members in the 'unenviable but inevitable position of being unable to tell their voters all that they know'.[15]

---

11   *Ibid.*
12   *Ibid.*, p. 17.
13   *Ibid.*
14   *Ibid.*
15   *Ibid.*, p. 18.

Gill's sexpartite model — encompassing form, mandate, membership, resources, access to information, and reporting — offers a useful model to evaluate the effectiveness and performance of an intelligence accountability regime. In his own evaluative study Gill concluded that whilst the ISC had made some appropriate criticisms of the UK intelligence agencies the Committee can be faulted for the essentially managerialist nature of its reports and its failure to provide adequate attention to issues of public education and human rights. Gill's model for evaluation also provides a useful template to assess the measures proposed by the Scottish Government to provide intelligence accountability in the conditions of Scottish independence. The politics of intelligence in Scotland's independence referendum debate were 'hidden' in the sense that both public interest and political debate on this subject were quite limited in scope and intensity.[16] The White Paper on independence outlined the Scottish Government's vision of threats to security in an independent Scotland and how this newly-independent country would respond to such threats. It claimed that upon independence a single security and intelligence agency would be established with a requirement to work with partners to ensure Scotland's national security. The Scottish Government indicated that independence offered an opportunity to build a 'new model' for such work, which was fit for the twenty-first century and which provided a proportionate means of ensuring Scotland's national security.[17] The establishment of a new security and intelligence agency would allow Scotland to 'do things differently, unconstrained by historical structures and precedent'.[18] Crucially in this context the White Paper on independence also indicated the proposed measures for intelligence accountability in an independent Scotland, through the role of legislation, governance and oversight of this new Scottish security and intelligence agency. Considering such matters the White Paper stated that:

---

16   Colin Atkinson, '"The Scottish MI5 Station Will Change to MI6. And You Know What MI6 Does!" Understanding the Hidden Politics of Intelligence in Scotland's Independence Referendum Debate', *Scottish Journal of Criminal Justice Studies*, 21 (2015), 5–24.
17   Scottish Government (2013), p. 261.
18   *Ibid.*

The controls put in place will be wide-ranging and comprehensive. The planned legislation will bring democratic control of our national security to Scotland for the first time. Scottish Ministers will be accountable to the Scottish Parliament for what a Scottish security and intelligence agency does in their name. The Scottish Parliament and the Scottish equivalent of the relevant Commissioners will scrutinise and challenge the work of the agency, including its covert work. They will be given clear legislative powers to support their work, including the power to require documents to be provided and to require the senior management of the agency to give evidence. There will also be detailed budget scrutiny from the Auditor General for Scotland, and the top-level budget will be scrutinised by the Scottish Parliament as part of the Budget Bill. This scrutiny will ensure that the agency is acting properly, legally, efficiently and effectively, in line with international principles for intelligence service oversight. These processes must take transparency as their starting point. But in so doing, they will appropriately and rigorously protect aspects of the agency's work that cannot be made public, and will respect the control principle at all times.[19]

Given that there was no further discussion of intelligence accountability in the White Paper, this represents a useful point at which to apply Gill's six variables in order to determine the effectiveness of any proposed accountability structures and processes for a new Scottish security and intelligence service in an independent Scotland.

The *form* and *mandate* of the prospective regime for intelligence accountability in an independent Scotland was broadly sketched within the constraints of the White Paper, which outlined that 'Scottish Ministers will be accountable to the Scottish Parliament for what a Scottish security and intelligence agency does in their name'. This would include the introduction of 'early legislation', written constitutional rights for Scottish citizens and clear arrangements for investigatory powers that build upon — and update where necessary — the existing UK legislation

---

19   *Ibid.*, p. 266. The control principle, or rule, means that intelligence supplied by one party to another cannot be shared with an additional third-party without the originator's consent. See Stéphane Lefebvre, 'The Difficulties and Dilemmas of International Intelligence Cooperation', *International Journal of Intelligence and Counter Intelligence*, 16, 4 (2003), 527–42 (p. 532). Discussing the difficulties of this principle Robert David Steele reduced the rationale to a clear and parsimonious statement: the default condition of the secret intelligence world is 'do not share'. See R. D. Steele, 'Open Source Intelligence ', in *Strategic Intelligence: Understanding the Hidden Side of Government*, ed. by L. K. Johnson (Westport, CT and London: Praeger Security International, 2007), 95–122 (p. 113).

governing such matters.[20] Moreover, the White Paper detailed that the work of the Scottish security agency would be scrutinised and challenged by both the Scottish Parliament and 'the Scottish equivalent of the relevant Commissioners' — meaning the Intelligence Services Commissioner, the Interception of Communications Commissioner, and the Office of the Surveillance Commissioners under the pre-existing UK arrangement — using 'clear legislative powers'.[21] Beyond the bold claims of the White Paper there clearly remain significant unanswered questions in relation to the form, and subsequently the membership and resources, of such a regime for intelligence accountability. The ISC, for example, is a parliamentary committee comprised of nine members, drawn from both the House of Commons and the House of Lords, with none permitted to be a Minister of the Crown. These members, who are normally seasoned parliamentarians with relevant experience, are nominated by the Prime Minister but their appointment must be approved by parliament. The ISC Chair is selected by its members. It is possible to infer that an ISC equivalent for Scotland was not explicitly mentioned due to the controversial reputation of the ISC in relation to its provision of effective oversight,[22] but there nevertheless remain unanswered questions relating to exactly who, in a prospective Scottish Parliament for an independent Scotland, would be responsible for the scrutiny and oversight of a Scottish security agency, and how they would be selected. Compounding these uncertainties, the issue of specific resources for intelligence accountability were not given any consideration in the White Paper. Resources were only discussed in the context of establishing the new security and intelligence agency itself, and not the accountability mechanisms for this service. In relation to an intelligence agency itself the Scottish Government proposed to maintain a 'comparable level of spending under independence' in relation to Scotland's pre-independence contribution,[23] but this did not take into account any costs that would be associated with establishing the necessary resources to maintain effective oversight and accountability of this new security and intelligence agency. The most recent update

---

20   Scottish Government (2013), p. 266.
21   *Ibid.*
22   See Bochel, Defty, and Kirkpatrick (2014).
23   Scottish Government (2013), p. 266.

from the ISC, following reforms made under the Justice and Security Act 2013, reported that it was supported by ten staff and an investigator, with a total budget of around £1.3 million per annum.[24] There was no indication of the resources available to fund a Scottish mechanism for intelligence accountability.

Access to information and the ability to report such information effectively are vital components of any effective regime for intelligence accountability. The Scottish Government's White Paper was clear that both the Scottish Parliament and relevant commissioners would be given clear legislative powers to support their work, including the powers to require the provision of documents from a Scottish security agency and to require the agency's senior management to give evidence.[25] There was no real clarity in *Scotland's Future* on the ways in which such information would be reported, beyond taking transparency as 'a starting-point' whilst respecting both the need to protect the agency's work where necessary and the control principle. In broadly resonating with the UK legislation and arrangements — and particularly the Justice and Security Act 2013, which reformed and emboldened the ISC — these commitments ultimately appear as a case of *plus ça change, plus c'est la même chose*, a feature that inhabits (or inhibits) much of the thinking on issues of intelligence and security in the Scottish Government's White Paper. The political strategy of such an approach is expedient and understandable: gain public confidence through political reassurance. It is worth recalling here, however, that Gill warned against the 'tokenism' of legislation, highlighting the requirement for the use of skill in negotiating with informal gatekeepers in the agencies under scrutiny.[26] In this context the immaturity of Scotland's political structures in dealing with matters of national security must be considered.

Scotland's Future was explicit in stating that the planned legislation would bring democratic control of national security to Scotland for the first time. A case can certainly be constructed that the existing cadre of 129 elected members in the Scottish Parliament broadly lacks the

---

24   Intelligence and Security Committee of Parliament, *Intelligence and Security Committee of Parliament Annual Report 2015–2016* (London: HMSO, 2016), https://b1cba9 b3-a-5e6631fd-s-sites.googlegroups.com/a/independent.gov.uk/isc/files/2015-2016_ISC_AR.pdf

25   Intelligence and Security Committee of Parliament (2016).

26   Gill (2007), p. 17.

capacity and capability to effectively scrutinise an emerging intelligence and security agency with the same rigour as that of its Westminster counterpart. It is true to say that an intelligence oversight committee in Scotland would have less ground to cover, at least in the longer-term, and would thus require fewer political representatives to function effectively. However, it is unclear as to whether, based on the existing arrangements, there would actually be enough MSPs with the skills, knowledge and experience to provide the necessary level of scrutiny, particularly given the expanded remit of a newly independent Scottish Parliament to provide governance of, and accountability for, whole new swathes of political activity. The provision of additional civil service support would also be necessary, but at least here a case can be made, cost permitting, for the 'poaching' of expertise from the existing UK structures. In considering the Scottish Government's proposal for intelligence accountability a key question thus emerges: would an independent Scotland have the right people asking the right questions, as well as the necessary resources, to hold a developing intelligence and security agency to account effectively? The answer to this question may be informed by a considered analysis of the successes and failures of intelligence oversight and accountability in other European nations that are comparatively similar to Scotland.

Comparison with accountability mechanisms in other jurisdictions

The French security expert Philippe Hayez recently remarked that intelligence and security services have moved from serving princes to serving citizens.[27] Not only do contemporary democratic societies now require their intelligence agencies to be accountable, but the bodies responsible for this task are often overseeing secretive agencies that have been established for a considerable period of time. The White Paper, *Scotland's Future*, argues that this is to Scotland's benefit, allowing Scotland to proceed unburdened by the past; however, as previously argued in this chapter, there are real challenges with regards

---

27 P. Hayez, 'National Oversight of International Intelligence Cooperation', in *International Intelligence Cooperation and Accountability*, ed. by H. Born, I. Leigh, and A. Wills (Abingdon and New York: Taylor & Francis, 2011), pp. 151–69 (p. 151).

to the extent to which the Scottish Parliament would have the capacity and capability to carry out this task. Nevertheless, in comparing an independent Scotland to other similar nations it is clear that Scotland is in a unique position to establish, at the same time, both a new security agency and mechanisms for the oversight of such an agency.

The unique position of Scotland in relation to the simultaneous design and implementation of both an intelligence service and an accountability mechanism is further compounded when one considers the post-'shock' modification of intelligence oversight. Writing on intelligence oversight in the US in the *Handbook of Intelligence Studies*, Loch K. Johnson noted,

> An analysis of intelligence accountability indicates a pattern in recent decades: a major intelligence scandal or failure — a shock — converts perfunctory patrolling into a burst of intense firefighting, which is the followed by a period of dedicated patrolling that yields remedial legislation or other reforms designed to curb inappropriate activities in the future. [...] Once the firestorm has subsided and reforms are in place, however, lawmakers return to a state of relative inattention to intelligence issues.[28]

Johnson's argument, one that has played out frequently in the post-9/11 security landscape, is that the greatest impetus for the progress of oversight is an intelligence failure or scandal that leads to public demand for change. Terrorist attacks by groups linked to Al Qaeda in Madrid and London, the massacre committed by Anders Behring Breivik in Norway, and the killing of Theo van Gogh in the Netherlands all prompted inquiries about intelligence failures. Such inquiries, which fall under the purview of security oversight, were carried out by existing or specially-convened bodies, and from which changes were assumed to follow. Similarly, the intelligence scandals surrounding the recourse to the 2003 Iraq War, the treatment of prisoners in Abu Ghraib, and the revelations from whistle blowers such as Wikileaks and Edward Snowden, have all had a similar impact: leading to inquiries that can be considered within the remit of oversight and intelligence accountability. It is from the shock of intelligence failures and scandals that progress on intelligence

---

28   L. K. Johnson, 'A Shock Theory of Congressional Accountability for Intelligence', in *Handbook of Intelligence Studies*, ed. by L. K. Johnson (Abingdon and New York: Taylor & Francis, 2007), pp. 343–60 (p. 344).

and security oversight is frequently made, thus raising the possibility that the measures for intelligence accountability in Scotland may not be fully effective until a similar shock is experienced. Nevertheless, the effectiveness of intelligence oversight and accountability mechanisms can be evaluated and further developed by considering the process in similar nations.

As highlighted earlier in this chapter, *Scotland's Future* indicated that an independent Scotland would draw from the UK model of security intelligence oversight, with little indication that any such model would be tailored to fit the challenges of the Scottish context. An independent Scotland would have a more limited global reach, presence, and footprint than that of the UK, with the possible implication that Scotland would face a decreased threat from international terrorism, as well as other security risks. This could be termed the 'small nation security dividend'. This section will consider approaches to intelligence oversight and accountability in two states closer in size and global presence to Scotland: Norway and Belgium.[29] The appropriate mechanisms in these two nations will be examined to identify the viability of alternative approaches beyond the replication of the UK model in the context of an independent Scotland.

Norway

Writing about intelligence oversight in Norway before the attacks committed by Anders Behring Breivik, Fredrik Sejersted argued, 'the preconditions for making intelligence accountable are among the most favourable in the world. If democratic oversight is not possible [in Norway], it is not possible anywhere'.[30] The Norwegian model focuses on legislative oversight, with accountability directly falling to the Parliamentary Oversight Committee on Intelligence and the Security Services (known as the EOS Committee). The EOS Committee was

---

29   Ireland, a country with historical, cultural and societal similarities to Scotland, was also considered for comparison, but the absence of a dedicated security agency raises several challenges in relation to a comparative study of intelligence oversight regimes.

30   F. Sejersted, 'Intelligence and Accountability in a State without Enemies: The Case of Norway', in *Who's Watching the Spies?: Establishing Intelligence Service Accountability*, ed. by H. Born, L. K. Johnson, and I. Leigh (Washington DC: Potomac Books, 2005), pp. 119–41 (p. 120).

established in the 1990s based on the recommendations of the Lund Commission, established to consider accusations of illegal surveillance by the security services. This Committee is appointed by and reports directly to Parliament, containing seven non-parliamentary members: an aspect that differs from oversight models in other Western states that draw their personnel from parliamentarians. The Committee operates with a high level of independence from political interference, and conducts oversight in two ways: 'through inspections of the agencies, and by dealing with complaints and inquiries'.[31] Returning to the six key variables outlined by Gill, Norway's accountability mechanisms meet these criteria fully with regards to membership, form and mandate. In addition to the work of the committee, the executive retains control over traditional elements of the oversight infrastructure through traditional governmental administrative structures. The main purpose of the Committee's work is safeguarding individuals against abuses committed by the security agencies (focusing on the protection of civil liberties and restricting intrusive surveillance methods), but it largely refrains from evaluating and analysing the efforts of the security agencies, with this task falling to the executive branch.

In the wake of the terrorist attacks committed by Anders Behring Breivik in July 2011, a ten-person special commission headed by Alexandra Bech Gjørv was established to ascertain the facts behind the attacks and make recommendations to help prevent similar attacks in the future. Their report, delivered in August 2012, indicated that the police could have done more to prevent the bombings and criticised the response to reports of shootings on Utøya, especially the time it took to reach the island itself.[32] The Gjørv report could be considered an extraordinary act of security oversight, coming in the wake of a shock. Norway, so often portrayed by many as a nation from which Scotland would do well to learn lessons, introduced oversight measures in the direct wake of an intelligence scandal in the mid-1990s, and the Breivik attacks on 2011. In line with the social democratic values often associated with Scandinavian states, Norway has chosen to isolate its oversight infrastructure from direct political control by granting the principal

---

31 Sejersted (2005), p. 128.
32 [N.a.], 'Norway Police "Could Have Stopped Breivik Sooner"', *BBC News*, 13 August 2012, http://www.bbc.co.uk/news/world-europe-19241327

committee substantial independence, whilst retaining executive control of the security services. Moreover, the committee's focus on preventing abuses of Norwegian citizens by the security agencies is logical considering the reduced threat of international terrorism faced by Norway.

Belgium

Belgium, is a smaller country geographically than Scotland but twice as populous, with nearly eleven million citizens. Like Scotland, it borders a much larger country that has been directly attacked by actors linked to international terrorist groups in the last decade. Similar to Norway, the Belgian intelligence and security oversight body (the Standing Intelligence Agencies Review Committee, or Committee I) was set up in the 1990s and maintains a public presence. The Committee consists of three individuals, one of whom acts as chairman, a position that must be held by a magistrate.[33] The Belgium Senate appoints these individuals, as well as two substitute members on a six-year term. The principal role of the Committee is described as 'reviewing the activities and functioning of State Security and the General Intelligence and Security Service [...] [and] the functioning of the Coordination Unit for Threat Assessment and the various services that support this coordination unit', focusing on the 'legitimacy (review of observance of the applicable laws and regulations), effectiveness (supervision of the efficiency of the intelligence services), and coordination (the mutual harmonization of the work of the services concerned)' of these bodies.[34]

Broadly similar to Norway and Scotland in international profile, Belgium demonstrates the limits of reliance on the 'small nation security dividend', as the events of 22 March 2016 demonstrated, when thirty-two people were killed by three bombings in the capital, Brussels: the first two at the city's airport, the latter on the Metro. This attack came only months after the November 2015 Paris attack, carried out by a Belgian-based group of Islamic State supporters, of whom some were

---

33   [N.a.], 'A Review Committee Acting as an Jurisdictional Body. The New Role of the Belgian Committee within the Framework of Reviewing Special Intelligence Methods', in Workshop on Best Practices for Intelligence and Intelligence Oversight, Montreux, 1–2 March 2010.
34   *Ibid.*

Belgian-born.[35] Previous to this, Belgium has witnessed the threat from its own citizens returning from the conflicts in Syria and Iraq in a deadly attack on a Jewish Museum in Brussels in June 2014 and the killing of two 'suspected jihadists' who had been suspected by police of an imminent attack in January 2015.[36] This rapid series of events has led to suggestions that Belgian intelligence is 'regarded as weak [...] more divided than most and more beset with scandals and charges of inefficiency'.[37] In response to these attacks, and to questions about the ability of the Belgian intelligence services, the president of Committee I, Guy Rapaille, pushed back, stating, 'these attacks show that more coordination with the United States is clearly desirable [...] but you have to remember that big powers guard their intelligence very closely'.[38] Furthermore, another member of the oversight committee publicly suggested, 'we are paying for our *naïveté* [...] it's not a weakness in intelligence. It's a weakness in society'.[39] Thus, in a short space of time Belgium has gained experience in the necessity of responding to the threat of international terrorism and it seems likely that Committee I will have a substantial role to play in investigating the extent to which the intelligence agencies failed, and how these inadequacies can be addressed.

The most visible component of Committee I is its Investigation Service, which can carry out investigations based on 'its own initiative, on the request of the Senate, the Chamber of Representatives or the competent minister or authority,[40] or on the request of a citizen or a

---

35   [N.a.], 'Paris and Brussels Bombers' Links Uncovered', *BBC News*, 9 April 2016, http://www.bbc.co.uk/news/world-europe-35879401

36   [N.a.], 'Belgian Anti-Terror Raid in Verviers Leaves Two Dead', *BBC News*, 16 January 2015, http://www.bbc.co.uk/news/world-europe-30840160

37   John Lloyd, 'The World's Spies Agree Belgian Intelligence Is Broken', *Reuters*, 24 March 2016, http://blogs.reuters.com/great-debate/2016/03/24/how-the-worlds-intelligence-services-rate-each-other/

38   Mark Hosenball, 'U.S. Frustration Simmers over Belgium's Struggle with Militant Threat', *Reuters*, 24 March 2016, http://www.reuters.com/article/us-belgium-blast-usa-intelligence-idUSKCN0WQ0BU

39   Adam Nossiter, 'Brussels Attacks Underscore Vulnerability of an Open European Society', *The New York Times*, 25 March 2016, http://www.nytimes.com/2016/03/23/world/europe/belgium-security.html

40   When asked to carry out an investigation by Parliament or by Ministers of Justice, Defence or the Interior, Committee I is required to carry out the investigation. Standing Intelligence Agencies Review Committee, 'Home' (2016), http://www.comiteri.be/index.php/en/. See Peter De Smet, 'Excerpt of the Speech Held at the 6th International Intelligence Review Agencies Conference ('Does Setting Priorities Mean "to Lose"?')', in *6th International Intelligence Review Agencies Conference* (New Zealand, 2008).

civil servant who lodges a complaint or files a denunciation' or 'in the framework of a parliamentary enquiry'.[41] The Committee is a powerful body: it can compel the security services to provide all documents relating to an investigation that it chooses to undertake, and because all members and employees of the committee hold security clearance, they can request classified material. Furthermore, the Committee has the power to 'advise' the Belgian courts on the legality of 'special and exceptional methods' and 'forbid the further use of the method in question' if deemed illegal.[42] Additionally, the Committee can summon anyone to undertake an interview and may require the individual to testify under oath, as well as having strong reporting capacities. Committee I is extraordinarily powerful when it comes to requesting information and testimony. Thus, there are many similarities between these two cases: operating independently from parliament with strong investigative powers.

Reflections on the Scottish case

Scotland has, in different ways, much in common with the two countries considered here. Whilst it is tempting to rely on the small-nation dividend when considering the security implications for an independent Scotland the series of terrorist attacks conducted, or planned, in Belgium between 2014 and 2016, and the attacks of Anders Breivik in Norway, caution against complacency, particularly if an independent Scotland sought to remain a close ally of both the UK and the US. With particular regards to intelligence accountability, Scotland could benefit from considering the examples of Norway and Belgium in the appointment of non-parliamentary experts to the oversight committees. This would alleviate the problem that results from the lack of experience, expertise and skill in overseeing the functions of the intelligence security services among the vast majority of the existing cadre of Scottish parliamentarians. Furthermore, these cases demonstrate some of the advantages of legislative independence of the primary security and intelligence oversight bodies, and Scotland would be well served if a similar model were adopted. Yet when it comes to

---

41   *Ibid.*
42   *Ibid.*

security oversight there is no model that Scotland should adopt in its entirety, and the requirement would remain to structure a security and intelligence service and accountability mechanisms to meet the challenges faced by an independent Scotland.

Post-referendum politics and intelligence accountability

The 2014 Scottish referendum on independence and the 2015 UK General Election remain fresh in the collective political consciousness, not least given the decision of the UK electorate in June 2016 to leave the European Union. Considered and dispassionate analysis of post-referenda politics has therefore been limited in volume, breadth and rigour. It is clear that, whilst Scotland voted to remain part of the UK, the electoral landscape of both Scottish and UK politics was transformed by the landslide victory for the pro-independence SNP in the 2015 UK General Election, which returned 56 Scottish representatives to Westminster from a possible total of 59. Whilst there is some scholarship and commentary on the most prominent issues affecting this post-referendum political landscape — from tax powers[43] to Trident[44] — the impact of the Scottish referendum White Paper, debate, result and subsequent electoral outcomes on the accountability of the intelligence agencies in the UK has attracted little to no attention. The nature of this now transformed post-referendum politics, however, may possibly herald some important consequences for both intelligence accountability in the UK and any future plan for accountability mechanisms in an independent Scotland.

The most immediate outcome for intelligence accountability in post-referendum politics in the UK was apparent in the third variable in Gill's sexpartite model: the change in membership of the Intelligence and Security Committee. The dissolution of parliament in advance of the 2015 General Election necessitated the parallel dissolution of the ISC. Previous ISC members ceased to be so. Similarly, the election of a new government required that a new ISC membership be established.

---

43   J. Aitken, 'The Continuing Battle for Scottish Tax Powers', in *After Independence: The State of the Scottish Nation Debate*, ed. by G. Hassan and J. Mitchell (Edinburgh: Luath Press Ltd, 2013).

44   W. Walker, 'Trident's Insecure Anchorage', in Hassan and Mitchell (2013).

Following the electoral success of the SNP there emerged some support for the inclusion of an SNP member on this new ISC, with initial reports suggesting that Scotland's former First Minister, Alex Salmond, would be the front-runner for such a post.[45] The inclusion of SNP representation on the ISC, whoever the member would be, received a mixed response from some quarters. For example, a small number of Unionist MPs voiced concern over the SNP stance on key issues of defence and security, whilst others accepted the requirement for SNP representation on the ISC as part of the democratic process.[46] Following the 2015 General Election the SNP was given representation on the ISC: on 9 September 2015 the Rt Hon Angus Robertson MP was nominated to this committee and subsequently appointed by the Prime Minister. The appointment of Robertson, the parliamentary group leader of the SNP at Westminster, is notable not only for his support for independence and his opposition to the UK nuclear deterrent capability, but also for his views on the role and remit of the ISC. Robertson has been, for example, critical of the UK Government in relation to parliamentary oversight of UK drone strikes in Syria.[47] The impact of the change in ISC membership may, however, extend beyond a shift in the nature of intelligence accountability in the UK context; the inclusion of SNP representation on the ISC may also provide valuable experience, capital, and political legitimacy that could deepen and enhance any future plans for intelligence accountability in an independent Scotland.

The 2014 referendum on Scottish independence was undertaken on the shared proviso that it would be a 'once in a generation' event;[48]

---

45   See 'Salmond Lined up for Role as Top Spy Chief', *Sunday Post*, 10 May 2015, https://www.sundaypost.com/news/scottish-news/salmond-lined-up-for-role-as-top-spy-chief/ This speculation was seemingly predicated on two factors. Firstly, that ISC members are by convention also Privy Councillors, and Alex Salmond was then the only Privy Councillor in the SNP's ranks. Secondly, that Salmond had ruled himself out of other important roles at Westminster.

46   Michael Settle, 'Tory Fears over Allowing SNP Role in UK Security', *Herald*, 22 May 2015, http://www.heraldscotland.com/news/13214836.Tory_fears_over_allowing_SNP_role_in_UK_security/

47   House of Commons, *House of Commons Hansard Debates for 09 Sep 2015 (Pt 0001)* (London: HMSO, 2015), http://www.publications.parliament.uk/pa/cm201516/cmhansrd/cm150909/debtext/150909-0001.htm#15090926000005

48   Karen McVeigh, 'Scottish Referendum: Yes and No Agree It's a Once-in-a-Lifetime Vote', *Guardian*, 17 September 2014, https://www.theguardian.com/politics/2014/

however, the issue of a second referendum has remained very much in the political spotlight.[49] As previously argued in this chapter, the mechanism for intelligence accountability sketched in *Scotland's Future* offered little deviation from the existing UK model. In the context of a future referendum on Scottish independence, however, one of the most significant political consequences of the revised membership of the ISC may be the experience and, more importantly, political legitimacy, gained through SNP representation on the ISC, and the associated capital and credibility that would be accrued as a result. As Bochel, Defty, and Kirkpatrick noted in *Watching the Watchers*,

> Like the departmental select committees, the ISC has allowed a small number of parliamentarians to acquire specialist knowledge in a particular policy area, and moreover one in which few parliamentarians have had any prior experience.[50]

Nevertheless, there will remain challenges for a prospective intelligence accountability mechanism in Scotland, particularly given that the ISC has, to a great extent, relied upon the experience of its members from both chambers of the UK parliament.[51] The nature of the now transformed post-referenda political landscape in the UK — where Nationalist representation at Westminster is stronger than ever before and the prospect of a second referendum on Scottish independence remains a clear possibility — may result in some significant changes in the practices of intelligence accountability in the UK and the rigour of any proposed mechanisms for intelligence accountability in an independent Scotland.

---

sep/17/scottish-independence-referendum-yes-no-agree-once-in-lifetime-vote; Keely Lockhart, 'Alex Salmond: "This Is a Once in a Generation Opportunity for Scotland"', *Telegraph*, 14 September 2014, http://www.telegraph.co.uk/news/uknews/scottish-independence/11095210/Alex-Salmond-This-is-a-once-in-a-generation-opportunity-for-Scotland.html

49 [N.a.], 'Nicola Sturgeon Asks Opponents to Back Second Independence Referendum', *BBC News*, 24 September 2015, http://www.bbc.co.uk/news/uk-scotland-scotland-politics-34333394; Jon Stone, 'Second Scottish Independence Referendum Is Inevitable, Says Nicola Sturgeon', *Independent*, 12 October 2015, http://www.independent.co.uk/news/uk/politics/another-scottish-independence-referendum-is-inevitable-says-nicola-sturgeon-a6690586.html

50 Bochel, Defty, and Kirkpatrick (2014), p. 77.

51 *Ibid.*, p. 79.

Conclusion

This chapter has explored the politics of intelligence accountability in the context of the 2014 referendum on Scottish independence and the 2015 General Election. It examined and evaluated the Scottish Government's vision for the accountability of a proposed new security and intelligence service in Scotland, exploring the consequences of the decision to remain in the UK and the 2015 electoral outcome on both intelligence accountability mechanisms in the UK and for a future independent Scotland. Drawing upon Gill's model for assessing the effectiveness of security intelligence accountability, the chapter argued that the Scottish Government's proposals for accountability mechanisms were vague, but inherently conservative, indicating a continuation of similar mechanisms used in the existing UK political settlement. This issue was brought into particular focus by exploring the accountability mechanisms for security intelligence in other jurisdictions, a process that highlights how shortcomings in the Scottish Government's proposals could have been addressed by learning lessons and adopting practices and processes from beyond the UK. Despite Scotland's decision to remain part of the UK, the aftermath of the referendum, particularly the landslide victory in Scotland for the pro-independence SNP in the 2015 UK General Election, may herald some important consequences for both intelligence accountability in the UK and any future plan for accountability mechanisms in an independent Scotland. The previously unconsidered prospect of direct SNP representation on the ISC — now a reality in the UK — raises the issue that pro-independence politicians will develop the expertise, capital, and political legitimacy necessary for effective intelligence accountability that were lacking in the pre-referendum political landscape.

References

[N.a.], 'A Review Committee Acting as an Jurisdictional Body. The New Role of the Belgian Committee within the Framework of Reviewing Special Intelligence Methods', paper presented at 'Workshop on Best Practices for Intelligence and Intelligence Oversight', Montreux, 1–2 March 2010.

—, 'Norway Police "Could Have Stopped Breivik Sooner"', *BBC News*, 13 August 2012, http://www.bbc.co.uk/news/world-europe-19241327

—, 'Belgian Anti-Terror Raid in Verviers Leaves Two Dead', *BBC News*, 16 January 2015, http://www.bbc.co.uk/news/world-europe-30840160

—, 'Nicola Sturgeon Asks Opponents to Back Second Independence Referendum', *BBC News*, 24 September 2015, http://www.bbc.co.uk/news/uk-scotland-scotland-politics-34333394

—, 'Paris and Brussels Bombers' Links Uncovered', *BBC News*, 9 April 2016, http://www.bbc.co.uk/news/world-europe-35879401

Aitken, J., 'The Continuing Battle for Scottish Tax Powers', in *After Independence: The State of the Scottish Nation Debate*, ed. by G. Hassan and J. Mitchell (Edinburgh: Luath Press Ltd, 2013).

Atkinson, Colin, '"The Scottish MI5 Station Will Change to MI6. And You Know What MI6 Does!" Understanding the Hidden Politics of Intelligence in Scotland's Independence Referendum Debate', *Scottish Journal of Criminal Justice Studies*, 21 (2015), 5–24.

Bochel, H., Defty, A., and Kirkpatrick, J., *Watching the Watchers: Parliament and the Intelligence Services* (Basingstoke: Palgrave Macmillan, 2014).

—, '"New Mechanisms of Independent Accountability": Select Committees and Parliamentary Scrutiny of the Intelligence Services', *Parliamentary Affairs*, 68 (2015), 314–31, http://dx.doi.org/10.1093/pa/gst032

Born, Hans and Leigh, Ian, 'Democratic Accountability of Intelligence Services', in *Armaments, Disarmament and International Security*, ed. by Stockholm International Peace Research Institute (Oxford: Oxford University Press, 2007), pp. 193–214.

De Smet, Peter, 'Excerpt of the Speech Held at the 6th International Intelligence Review Agencies Conference ('Does Setting Priorities Mean "to Lose"?')', in *6th International Intelligence Review Agencies Conference* (New Zealand, 2008).

Gill, Peter, 'Evaluating Intelligence Oversight Committees: The UK Intelligence and Security Committee and the "War on Terror"', *Intelligence and National Security*, 22 (2007), 14–37, http://dx.doi.org/10.1080/02684520701200756

Hayez, P., 'National Oversight of International Intelligence Cooperation', in *International Intelligence Cooperation and Accountability*, ed. by H. Born, I. Leigh, and A. Wills (Abingdon and New York: Taylor & Francis, 2011), pp. 151–69.

Hosenball, Mark, 'U.S. Frustration Simmers over Belgium's Struggle with Militant Threat', *Reuters*, 24 March 2016, http://www.reuters.com/article/us-belgium-blast-usa-intelligence-idUSKCN0WQ0BU

House of Commons, *House of Commons Hansard Debates for 09 Sep 2015 (Pt 0001)* (London: HMSO, 2015), http://www.publications.parliament.uk/pa/cm201516/cmhansrd/cm150909/debtext/150909-0001.htm#15090926000005

Intelligence and Security Committee of Parliament, *Intelligence and Security Committee of Parliament Annual Report 2015–2016* (London: HMSO, 2016), https://b1cba9b3-a-5e6631fd-s-sites.googlegroups.com/a/independent.gov.uk/isc/files/2015-2016_ISC_AR.pdf

——, 'About the Committee' (2016), http://isc.independent.gov.uk/

Johnson, L. K., 'A Shock Theory of Congressional Accountability for Intelligence', in *Handbook of Intelligence Studies*, ed. by L. K. Johnson (Abingdon and New York: Taylor & Francis, 2007), pp. 343–60.

Lefebvre, Stéphane, 'The Difficulties and Dilemmas of International Intelligence Cooperation', *International Journal of Intelligence and CounterIntelligence*, 16 (2003), 527–42, http://dx.doi.org/10.1080/716100467

Leigh, I., 'The Accountability of Security and Intelligence Agencies', in *Handbook of Intelligence Studies*, ed. by L. K. Johnson (Abingdon and New York: Routledge, 2007), pp. 67–81.

Lloyd, John, 'The World's Spies Agree Belgian Intelligence Is Broken', *Reuters*, 24 March 2016, http://blogs.reuters.com/great-debate/2016/03/24/how-the-worlds-intelligence-services-rate-each-other/

Lockhart, Keely, 'Alex Salmond: "This Is a Once in a Generation Opportunity for Scotland"', *Telegraph*, 14 September 2014, http://www.telegraph.co.uk/news/uknews/scottish-independence/11095210/Alex-Salmond-This-is-a-once-in-a-generation-opportunity-for-Scotland.html

McVeigh, Karen, 'Scottish Referendum: Yes and No Agree It's a Once-in-a-Lifetime Vote', *Guardian*, 17 September 2014, https://www.theguardian.com/politics/2014/sep/17/scottish-independence-referendum-yes-no-agree-once-in-lifetime-vote

Nossiter, Adam, 'Brussels Attacks Underscore Vulnerability of an Open European Society', *The New York Times*, 25 March 2016, http://www.nytimes.com/2016/03/23/world/europe/belgium-security.html

Phythian, Mark, 'The British Experience with Intelligence Accountability', *Intelligence and National Security*, 22 (2007), 75–99, http://dx.doi.org/10.10 80/02684520701200822

Picken, A., 'Salmond Lined up for Role as Top Spy Chief', *Sunday Post*, 10 May 2015, https://www.sundaypost.com/news/scottish-news/salmond-lined-up-for-role-as-top-spy-chief/

Scottish Government, *Scotland's Future: Your Guide to an Independent Scotland* (Edinburgh: Scottish Government, 2013), http://www.gov.scot/resource/0043/00439021.pdf

Sejersted, F., 'Intelligence and Accountability in a State without Enemies: The Case of Norway', in *Who's Watching the Spies?: Establishing Intelligence Service Accountability*, ed. by H. Born, L. K. Johnson and I. Leigh (Washington DC: Potomac Books, 2005), pp. 119–41.

Settle, Michael, 'Tory Fears over Allowing SNP Role in UK Security', *Herald*, 22 May 2015, http://www.heraldscotland.com/news/13214836.Tory_fears_over_allowing_SNP_role_in_UK_security/

Standing Intelligence Agencies Review Committee, 'Home' (2016), http://www.comiteri.be/index.php/en/

Steele, R. D., 'Open Source Intelligence ', in *Strategic Intelligence: Understanding the Hidden Side of Government*, ed. by L. K. Johnson (Westport, CT and London: Praeger Security International, 2007), pp. 95–122.

Stone, Jon, 'Second Scottish Independence Referendum Is Inevitable, Says Nicola Sturgeon', *Independent*, 12 October 2015, http://www.independent.co.uk/news/uk/politics/another-scottish-independence-referendum-is-inevitable-says-nicola-sturgeon-a6690586.html

Walker, W., 'Trident's Insecure Anchorage', in *After Independence: The State of the Scottish Nation Debate*, ed. by G. Hassan and J. Mitchell (Edinburgh: Luath Press Ltd, 2013).

6. 'Hardly a Moment's Discussion'? Intelligence and the Scottish Referendum[1]

Sandy Hardie

This chapter offers an account of 'intelligence' in the Scottish Referendum, the first occasion on which the subject had featured in a British political contest. It documents and assesses the strategic dimension in UK national security, its visibility to voters, the presentation and impact of arguments for and against separate arrangements, and the professional and political constraints on the Yes and No camps. Press coverage emerges as reasonable and fair if largely reactive, while the broadcasters were distinctly cautious, and overall treatment of the cyber threat to an independent Scotland was inadequate. The chapter concludes with a forward look to the likely profile of intelligence in the event of a second referendum.

---

1   My thanks to the organisers of the CeSeR launch conference 'The Future of Security Research: Multidisciplinary Perspectives' for their kind invitation to speak, and to participants for a stimulating panel discussion. This essay was produced on the basis of the public record, personal recollections, and meetings with a wide range of campaign participants, observers and former national security practitioners, to all of whom I am grateful for sharing knowledge and perspectives.

https://doi.org/10.11647/OBP.0078.06

'In the debate about Scotland's future, there has hardly been a moment's discussion about how best to protect Scotland's security in the event of independence'. Such was Sir Menzies (now Lord) Campbell's conclusion just two weeks before the referendum.[2] Was he right? Two years on, with a possible second referendum a live issue, the profile of 'intelligence' in the campaign calls for review.

This was the first political contest in Britain in which intelligence had featured as an issue. There was no precedent either in time of national crisis or in the post-war process of de-colonisation.[3] At Westminster, following 'avowal' of the agencies in 1994, intelligence had largely been a bipartisan matter.[4] The workings of the intelligence community and its performance in the run-up to the war in Iraq had of course been the subject of unprecedented public scrutiny in the Butler Review of 2004. Yet when questioned by the Foreign Affairs Committee on the intelligence implications of Scottish separation, a Foreign Office minister observed 'it is one of the frustrating things as a minister that you cannot rightly talk about this'.[5] He was voicing a continuing, and generally shared, constraint on open exchange. But given the profound implications of separation for future security on both sides of the border, the intelligence dimension simply had to be acknowledged and addressed.[6] In addition, the prospect of a new security apparatus alongside the recently-centralised Scottish police authority raised major issues around oversight and civil liberties, and these too called for public

---

2   Menzies Campbell, 'Sir Menzies Campbell: We Are Safer Together', Scottish Liberal Democrats, 5 September 2014, http://www.scotlibdems.org.uk/intervention_from_ intelligence_chief_shows_we_are_safer_together

3   For the immediate pre-war period, however, Churchill's 1939 speech in the House of Commons praising SIS as 'the finest service of its kind in the world' and warning Chamberlain and Halifax against ignoring its product, stands out: see Richard Aldrich and Rory Cormac, *The Black Door: Spies, Secret Intelligence and British Prime Ministers* (London: HarperCollins, 2016), pp. 83–84.

4   'Avowal': a standard term for the process of acknowledging the existence of the intelligence agencies, represented by the Intelligence Service Act.

5   Richard Lidington, cited in Foreign Affairs Committee, *Foreign Policy Considerations for the UK and Scotland in the Event of Scotland Becoming an Independent Country, Sixth Report of Session 2012–2013* (London: HMSO, 2013), Ev. 66, Q 341., http://www. publications.parliament.uk/pa/cm201213/cmselect/cmfaff/643/643.pdf

6   Just one commentator challenged this proposition at the time: Alex Massie, 'Theresa May's Grubby Little Warning: An Independent Scotland Will Be out in the Cold', *Spectator*, 29 October 2013, http://blogs.spectator.co.uk/2013/10/theresa-mays-grubby-little-warning-independent-scotland-will-be-left-out-in-the-cold/

scrutiny and submission to the voters. I took part in the No campaign through 2013 and 2014 as a Scot living in Scotland, and as a former foreign service officer. The questions to be addressed in what follows arise from that experience, and its pro-Union perspective. How visible was the strategic intelligence dimension to Scottish voters? How were the issues and arguments presented, and what impact did they have? What constraints were in play? And how well was the public served by media coverage?

At the outset, public interest in intelligence appeared to be low. On the central campaign battleground it was eclipsed by the more visible and emotive matters of the armed forces, Trident, and NATO membership. Campbell himself conceded that there probably weren't many votes in intelligence and security issues. Yet that assumption seems not to have been tested with campaign focus groups. And for what it may be worth, the *Sunday Express* of 7 September 2014 listed 'British Intelligence' seventh out of '25 things we'll miss in independent Scotland'; then again, on 19 September, the *Scottish Daily Mail* put 'intelligence services' sixth in its list of the 'twenty real reasons' No-voters wanted to keep the Union 'but are too polite to admit'.[7] Whether 'quiet No-voters' had a larger appetite for the subject than campaign managers were prepared to admit is now beyond verification, but by 18 September there was at least some sense that security and intelligence had edged out of the shadows and into the light.

The first effort to get to grips with the subject came from Westminster. The Foreign Affairs Committee (FAC) opened their hearings in late 2012;[8] their report, published on 1 May 2013, offered what is still the most thoughtful exploration of the wider-world dimension to Scottish separation; the likely threat environment; the correlation of external intelligence work and domestic security; the infrastructure requirements of an independent Scotland; and the question of assistance from the rUK. Expert witnesses argued that a Scottish administration would need a new, independent intelligence and security infrastructure, and would

7 Borland, Ben, '25 Things We'll Miss Independent Scotland' [*sic*], *Scottish Express*, 7 September 2014, pp. 38–39; Jonathan Brocklebank, 'Fear and Laughing in the Ad Campaigns as We Reveal What Really Drove Better Together', *Scottish Daily Mail*, 19 September 2014, pp. 14–15.
8 Foreign Affairs Committee (2013).

face substantial set-up costs and formidable technical challenges over an extended timeframe. They foregrounded cyber security (the threats of cyber espionage, fraud, and potential sabotage), but they suggested that, within the field of cryptography, there was no certainty that even a small-scale ('mini-GCHQ') project would be feasible.[9] Nobody denied Scottish capacity to put some sort of infrastructure in place, given time, resources, effective direction and the good will of partners, but new structures could not replicate the levels of protection afforded by MI5, MI6 and GCHQ, and the ability of a Scottish government to protect its citizens at home and abroad would likely be diminished.

Oral and written evidence stressed the objective rUK interest in helping develop Scottish capabilities, and one submission argued that close institutional cooperation between the rUK and Scotland would be needed if the present UK National Security Strategy itself was to be implemented effectively.[10] But witnesses also stressed that bilateral assistance would be contingent on the conditions and mood of separation, including the defence and external approach of an independent administration.[11] Policy on Trident, and its impact on the NATO alliance (US perceptions in particular), would bear upon rUK attitudes and interests. For its part, the FAC acknowledged that the rUK could well have an interest in advising and assisting an embryonic Scottish intelligence community, not least given the risk that under-investment could result in perceptions of Scotland as a 'weak link' in counter-terrorism and cyber defences and as the easy way to attack the rUK, with loss of security on both sides of the border.[12] But it concluded that 'it remains unclear how much support the rUK might be willing *or indeed able* to give and what impact this might have on its other foreign policy priorities, budgets and resources'.[13] Here was a warning that the rUK's perception of its own interests would be conditioned by existing alliances as well as by reformulated requirements in relation to the British land mass, and that the quality of start-up assistance to Scottish agencies would be determined in the light of the strategic situation in its entirety and not by Scottish considerations, however immediate,

---

9   *Ibid.*
10   *Ibid.*, Ev 86 (Dr Malcolm Chalmers), Ev 92 (Dr Daniel Kenealy).
11   *Ibid.*, Ev 25–31.
12   *Ibid.*, Ev 31, Para 125, citing Sir David Omand (Q154).
13   *Ibid.*, p. 54 (my emphasis).

alone. In adding 'or indeed able', the FAC hinted at constraints on rUK freedom of action. The point was made more explicitly by the former Director of GCHQ, Sir David Omand, commenting on GCHQ's 'deep technical assessment':[14]

> Whether an independent Scotland would benefit from that, and from the American underpinning of it is a bigger question about the relationship in the whole intelligence sphere between an independent Scotland and the rest of the United Kingdom and, indeed, the United States.

In other words, the rUK would be unable, on its own authority, simply to pass on the technical or intelligence products of its strategic alliance with the US. A good deal of later discussion, it might be added, focussed on whether Scotland might join the Five Eyes intelligence alliance (Australia, Canada, New Zealand, UK and US).[15] However, early Scottish accession to this group, and its security protocols, was never a realistic prospect and arguably served as a distraction from more immediate issues, including cooperation with the principal European agencies (the latter, for their part, seem to have shown scant awareness of what was afoot in Scotland until well into 2014).

On what the Chair rightly described as 'a very important occasion', the FAC took evidence from Nicola Sturgeon, the then Deputy First Minister (DFM), in Edinburgh on 28 January 2013. The SNP had resolved in October 2012 that 'a cyber security and intelligence infrastructure to deal with new threats and protect key national economic and social infrastructure' should be maintained, and now, the FAC was seeking a closer view of Scottish Government (SG) proposals.[16] Sturgeon envisaged a Scottish threat environment broadly familiar from the UK's current National Security Strategy (NSS): 'cyber threat, international terrorism [...] global instability and failed states, serious international organised crime'.[17] She did not suggest, as others were, that a distinctive

---

14   *Ibid.*, Ev 25.
15   See for example Rob Dover, 'Cutting the Ties That Bind? Intelligence in an Independent Scotland', *PSA Political Insight*, 4 November 2013, https://www.psa.ac.uk/insight-plus/blog/cutting-ties-bind-intelligence-independent-scotland
16   [N.a.], 'In Full: SNP Resolution on Nato', 16 July 2012, http://www.scotsman.com/news/politics/in-full-snp-resolution-on-nato-1-2414919
17   Foreign Affairs Committee (2013), Q309. Cf. HM Government, *A Strong Britain in an Age of Uncertainty: The National Security Strategy* (2010), http://webarchive.nationalarchives.gov.uk/20121015000000/http://www.direct.gov.uk/prod_consum_dg/groups/dg_digitalassets/@dg/@en/documents/digitalasset/dg_191639.pdf

external posture would lead to reduced levels of threat. She spoke of 'independent domestic intelligence machinery […] sitting alongside our police service', but questions as to an external intelligence capability were parried by reference to a 'substantial piece of work' then under way.[18] SG understanding of how Scottish intelligence-gathering might relate to the acknowledged international dimensions of the threat environment was not further probed. Rather, the DFM referred to future 'shared arrangements' with the rUK: but what she (or those who compiled her brief), understood by this was quite uncertain.[19] It was thus left unclear whether the SG actually envisaged shared responsibility for the security of Scotland in the period following 24 March 2016. Her performance drew sharply critical comment from Baroness Ramsay, a former senior officer of MI6.[20]

To her credit, Sturgeon had offered to come back to the FAC for detailed discussion of the SG's preparatory work, which would be published 'in the lead-up to and in the White Paper'.[21] In the event, no separate publication took place. In response to a Freedom of Information (FOI) request, I was informed that 'a public statement, paper or event on Defence and Security (and external affairs in general) was initially scheduled for April 2013, then rescheduled to follow Mr Brown's [Keith Brown, MSP, the then SG Secretary for Transport and Veterans Affairs] House of Commons defence committee appearance on 2 July.[22] Official records do not discuss why the paper was not published'. The successive postponements disclosed in this response suggest emerging SG/SNP awareness of a major weakness in the area of national security and they point to a political decision taken around mid-2013 to bury Defence and Security proposals within the White Paper, thereby

---

18   Foreign Affairs Committee (2013), Ev 62.
19   *Ibid.*
20   Meta Ramsay, 'Security Service Can Take Nothing for Granted', *Scotsman*, 17 February 2013, http://www.scotsman.com/news/opinion/meta-ramsay-security-service-can-take-nothing-for-granted-1-2795918
21   Foreign Affairs Committee (2013), Ev 62.
22   In response to a request for a meeting with Scottish Government officials, I was told by telephone on 7 October 2015 that SG ministers' positions on security and intelligence remained unchanged from those set out in Chapter 7 of the White Paper of November 2013 (cited below, n. 29). I regret that this opportunity for a closer, more developed, approach to SG thinking was passed up. The SG's response to an FOI request on issues arising from Nicola Sturgeon's evidence to the Foreign Affairs Committee in January 2013, communicated in a letter dated 23 December from the SG Safer Communities Directorate, is reproduced in the main text.

limiting exposure. At all events, the failure to publish in advance of the White Paper, together with the FAC's own failure to follow up the DFM's offer of further discussions on intelligence and security matters, meant that no Scottish leader was again to face purposeful questioning on SG proposals or on the 'substantial piece of work' to which Sturgeon referred. Indeed the exchange with the FAC marked the closure of the SG's active engagement in public discussion of the subject. And in that respect certainly, Campbell was right.

A sceptical FAC drew its own conclusions. Here is what it said:

> By the Scottish Government's own assessment, in the event of independence Scotland would need both internal and external security and intelligence capabilities to deal with the many diverse potential threats it believes it could face. Yet Scotland has no external intelligence structure to build upon. With just a year to go before the referendum takes place [in fact, over fifteen months], it is not at all clear that the Scottish Government has a costed and coherent vision of the security and intelligence infrastructure it needs to put in place to protect Scottish citizens, business and economic interests.[23]

A further conclusion foreshadowed what was to become fertile ground for pro-Independence counterclaims that the UK Government was bluffing on the key issue of future set-up support and intelligence-sharing:

> [...] there appears to be a working presumption on the part of the Scottish Government that the rUK would fill the intelligence shortfall that would emerge in the short term, but possibly over a longer time frame too. The basis for this position is not at all clear. Scotland would undoubtedly remain of strategic interest to the rUK and in the vast majority of cases it is likely that it would be in the rUK's interests to assist Scotland.

The FAC report received fair exposure in pro-Union parts of the Scottish press. Sturgeon called it 'partisan', with 'rare examples of even-handedness', and claimed that the FAC's aim was 'to undermine the case for independence'.[24] By contrast, the Foreign Secretary

---

23   Foreign Affairs Committee (2013), Para 137.
24   Severin Carrell, 'Scottish Independence Quest Hampered by Policy Gaps, MPs Say', *Guardian*, 19 July 2013, https://www.theguardian.com/politics/2013/may/01/scottish-independence-hampered-policy-gaps; Matt Chorley and Alan Roden, 'Voters Need Facts About Scottish Independence, Hague Says as MPs Warn Rest of the UK's Global Reputation Is at Stake', *Daily Mail*, 1 May 2013, http://www.dailymail.co.uk/news/article-2317689/Voters-need-facts-Scottish-independence-Hague-says-MPs-warn-rest-UKs-global-reputation-stake.html

William Hague noted, not without humour, 'the dependence that an independent Scotland would still have on rUK'.[25] Intelligence and security, in other words, both exemplified a fundamental ambiguity in the SNP's conception of 'independence' later noted by (Yes-voting) Iain Macwhirter and (No-voting) Alex Massie:[26] its attempt to square sovereignty with a network of continuing dependencies on its large neighbour.

The FAC added this observation on voter-awareness: 'it is crucial that the Scots are aware that the rUK's intelligence and security help would be discretionary, based on self-interest and could not be taken for granted'. Unsurprisingly, there were large gaps in Scottish public awareness of intelligence matters, and it was the UK Government's responsibility to put the facts before the voters. Whitehall had the benefit of a body of research into communicating strategic issues around national security to the public.[27] Of course, 'communications' in a divisive campaign was a quite different proposition from building public trust in a national security strategy. Yet Whitehall's experience of what might be said about security and resilience, in what level of detail, by whom and to which constituencies was certainly relevant to the referendum campaign.

A major cross-Whitehall effort, co-ordinated by the Cabinet Office, went into a briefing package published in October 2013.[28] This was the product of extended drafting and a sharply defined internal debate that prompted the intervention of Danny Alexander, now in command of the tactical interface between coalition and campaign. From the London

---

25   HM Government, *Sixth Report from the Foreign Affairs Committee of Session 2012–13: Foreign Policy Considerations for the UK and Scotland in the Event of Scotland Becoming an Independent Country. Response from the Secretary of State for Foreign and Commonwealth Affairs. Cm. 8644* (London: HMSO, 2013), https://www.gov.uk/government/uploads/ system/uploads/attachment_data/file/210012/30944_Cm_8644_Web_Accessible. pdf, para 20.

26   Cf. Iain Macwhirter, *Disunited Kingdom: How Westminster Won a Referendum but Lost Scotland* (Glasgow: Cargo Publishing, 2014); Alex Massie, 'Why I Am Voting No', *Spectator*, 9 September 2014, http://blogs.spectator.co.uk/2014/09/ why-i-am-voting-no/

27   R. Mottram, 'Protecting the Citizen in the Twenty-First Century: Issues and Challenges', in *The New Protective State: Government, Intelligence and Terrorism*, ed. by Peter Hennessy (London and New York: A&C Black, 2008), pp. 42–65 (pp. 61–63).

28   HM Government (2013). The account that follows is based on private information from various sources.

perspective, the published document represented a preference for factual presentation over sharper, more confrontational, lines of approach. *Scotland Analysis: Security* laid out the machinery and its underlying principles in fine detail, largely eschewing hype.[29] One of a series of thirteen papers rolled out as sceptical commentary on separation, and as a resource to inform discussion, it made no pretension to direct voter-appeal. However, its core message was an unambiguous constitutional reality: as a separate state, Scotland would have sovereign responsibility for its own security.

This meant that Scotland would necessarily cease to participate in the near-seamless arrangements that join MI5 and the National Crime Agency to the external operational work of MI6 and GCHQ. It could not expect others to be proactive on its behalf. rUK and Scotland would no doubt work together, to mutual self-interest: but no external liaison, however close, could replicate the intimacy and immediacy of integration within the United Kingdom. In short, if the Scots were to choose separation, they could not still 'share' as though separation had not happened: 'two countries, one system', to reverse Deng's characterisation of the Hong Kong settlement, was not a constitutional option for the security of a dis-integrated country.[30] Such was the united view of the coalition government, though individual emphases varied from time to time. The Foreign Secretary put it thus:[31] 'Although it is likely that Scottish and rUK interests would largely coincide in this area [...] Scotland would lose access to the many benefits that it currently derives from being part of the UK'. Implicitly responding to criticism of Better Together negativity, the Prime Minister was to go further in May 2014, conceding that an independent Scotland would 'of course' have a share of defence and security resources.[32] But that is to run ahead of the story.

William Hague had taken the wider-world arguments for the Union to Edinburgh in June 2013 and had touched on the intelligence services

---

29   HM Government (2013).
30   Deng Xiaoping, 'One Country, Two Systems' (22 June 1984), http://en.people.cn/dengxp/vol3/text/c1210.html
31   HM Government (2013), Para 20.
32   [N.a.], 'The Pros and the Cons of Negativity', *Herald*, 16 May 2014, http://www.heraldscotland.com/opinion/13160648.The_pros_and_the_cons_of_negativity/

as 'some of the most capable and professional [...] in the world'.[33] But the task of presenting *Scotland Analysis: Security* in Edinburgh fell to the then Home Secretary, Theresa May. Given her lead on Counter-Terrorism, and the paper's emphasis on the protection of people, property and prosperity, this made sense; despite divided ministerial responsibilities for the agencies, it served to underline the strategic integration of external and domestic capabilities with policing across the UK. Arguably, too, it made political sense to detach what was said about the external agencies from considerations of Britain's place in the world, an arena where Nationalist accusations of post-imperial hubris carried undeniable appeal in the long, fractious aftermath of the Iraq war.[34]

Yet Theresa May could have been forgiven for apprehension as she travelled north on 29 October. What Alex Salmond had called the 'phoney war' was at an end, and with the advent of Autumn the big beasts were locking horns.[35] Visiting Conservative ministers were already fair game for SNP accusations of 'lecturing the Scots' (primed by the new Secretary of State for Scotland Alistair Carmichael's not very private admonitions to his coalition colleagues).[36] A recent addition to the politics of security was the disclosure of UK/US intercept capabilities by the rogue National Security Agency contractor, Edward Snowden, later to be elected Rector of Glasgow University (*in absentia*). Moreover, as the Foreign Secretary had found in June, dotty allegations of MI5 pro-Union 'dirty tricks' could still command headlines, a minor symptom not just of fringe paranoia but of popular distrust of Westminster and all

33 William Hague, 'Foreign Secretary's Speech: The United Kingdom: Stronger Together', Foreign and Commonwealth Office, Gov.uk, 20 June 2013, https://www.gov.uk/government/speeches/foreign-secretarys-speech-the-united-kingdom-stronger-together

34 Cf. Harry Reid, 'Decent Case for a Scots Foreign Policy', *Herald*, 2 October 2012, http://www.heraldscotland.com/opinion/13075312.Decent_case_for_a_Scots_foreign_policy; Harry Reid, 'Case for Knowing Our Place in the World', *Herald*, 26 August 2014, http://www.heraldscotland.com/opinion/13176691.Case_for_knowing_our_place_in_the_world/

35 Jason Cowley, 'Alex Salmond: "This Is the Phoney War. This Is Not the Campaign"', *New Statesman*, 25 June 2013, http://www.newstatesman.com/2013/06/phoney-war-not-campaign

36 Magnus Gardham, 'Carmichael Tells Cabinet Not to Give Lectures on Independence', *Herald*, 11 October 2013, http://www.heraldscotland.com/news/13126815.Carmichael_tells_Cabinet_not_to_give_lectures_on_independence/

its works.[37] In a further illustration of the febrile atmosphere, the then Chief Constable of Police Scotland Sir Stephen House declined to meet the Home Secretary in the course of her visit.[38]

Here, at all events, was the set-piece Edinburgh presentation of national security issues as seen from London. Print and broadcast coverage was extensive and largely factual, though it added a harder, 'Scotland to be frozen out', edge to what was actually said. Headlines focused on counter-terrorism and narcotics, with cyber security some way back. Given Scottish sensitivities, however, there was always a risk that the effort to inform would be spun as London didacticism, that questions addressed to the SG would be heard as threats, even that acknowledgement of likely co-operation might be dismissed as condescension. The challenge of bringing this occasion off was underlined in the acerbic comments of the Scotland editor of *The Spectator*. Intelligence, Alex Massie claimed, was a 'bother-with-it-later' item to be addressed as and when independence materialised.[39] Was Theresa May, he asked, trying to persuade '[t]he poor sap who might vote Yes but can be security-theatred into voting No?' More predictable was the SNP response, voiced by Christine Grahame: 'This is Project Fear at its worst — trying to politicise issues of security and anti-terrorism in this way is the height of irresponsibility'.[40]

Were the Archangel Gabriel to have materialised in Surgeon's Hall that day, one suspects he'd have been charged with scurrilous scaremongering and talking down Scotland. Even so, it's worth pausing to ask how a presentational remix might have fared.[41] Suppose, for the sake of

---

37   [N.a.], 'UK spies "not trailing SNP"; Hague dismisses "Scots paranoia"', *Daily Star*, 21 June 2013; Paula Murray, 'MSP Margo Convinced MI5 Spying in Nat Camp', *Scottish Sunday Express*, 23 June 2013; cf. Jonathan Brown, 'SNP Veteran Blames MI5 for Trolling over Independence', *Independent*, 14 June 2014; Tom McTague, 'One in Four Scots Believe UK Spies Are Working against Independence', *Daily Mail*, 8 September 2014, http://www.dailymail.co.uk/news/article-2747809/One-four-Scots-believe-British-spies-secretly-working-against-Yes-independence-campaign.html

38   Private information.

39   Alex Massie, *Spectator*, 29 October 2013.

40   Cited from Richard Ford, 'SNP Accuses May of Scaremongering', *The Times*, 30 October 2013.

41   For relevant reflections on George Osborne's presentation of the currency issue, see David Torrance, *100 Days of Hope and Fear: How Scotland's Referendum Was Lost and Won* (Edinburgh: Luath Press Ltd, 2014), p. 113.

argument, that the Home Secretary had foregrounded common security interests, accentuated continuity, conceded the likelihood of purposeful engagement and a measure of technical support, and then registered the constraints on the rUK and the practical challenges that would confront the architects of a new security apparatus. A case could certainly have been made for some such approach. But the political assessment, at least in retrospect, was that the SNP/SG would have pocketed the first half and ignored the qualifications (much as it did with selective quotation from *Scotland Analysis: Security* in the White Paper).[42] Furthermore, from the pro-Union perspective, it would have spun any such soft-sell as evidence that Westminster was bluffing, and bluffing also on the central campaign issues. Be that as it may, claims that the UK Government position was pre-negotiation posturing were in my view wide of the mark.[43] In mid to late 2013, Scottish independence following a Yes vote was a hypothetical situation which UK ministers did not expect to arise. No substantive departmental or agency work was done to anticipate this eventuality. The cabinet ruling (late 2012-early 2013) against contingency planning was observed, though subject to parliamentary criticism (to be repeated during the EU referendum) from Lord Hennessy.[44] Whether the ruling was entirely appropriate within the intelligence and security community, given what would have been at stake, was and is open to question. In any case, it can be assumed that in the run-up to the vote heads of agencies were aware of the issues that would arise, and of immediate actions that would need to be taken, had London's anticipation of a No vote been proven misguided. But it would be wrong to suppose that contingency thinking informed the Home Secretary's presentation on 29 October. This was no pre-negotiation posture, because no requirement for negotiating positions had been anticipated.

Around this time, two Scottish universities made welcome interventions: the Edinburgh Economic and Social Research Council series 'Security in Scotland, with or without Constitutional Change' had

---

42   Scottish Government (2013), pp. 264–65.
43   Cf. Andrew W. Neal, 'Comment: Scotland Wouldn't Be Out of Security Loop', *Scotsman*, 11 November 2013, http://www.scotsman.com/news/opinion/comment-scotland-wouldn-t-be-out-of-security-loop-1-3184490
44   Lord Hennessy of Nympsfield, *Lords Hansard, Col. 1361–1451* (London: HMSO), https://www.publications.parliament.uk/pa/ld201314/ldhansrd/text/140130-0001.htm#14013072000875. Mark Carney revealed in August 2014 that the Bank of England had drawn up contingency plans in the event of a Yes vote.

kicked off at Holyrood on 4 October, and the Glasgow conference 'Global Security, National Defence, and the Future of Scotland', followed on 8–9 November. Each initiative offered a forum for exchange, questioning, and exploration, and each put appreciably more information into the public domain. And yet, discussion overall remained distinctly asymmetrical: publication of the White Paper had been delayed until St Andrew's Day, and SG officials were understandably keeping a low profile.

In compiling the White Paper, the SG was obliged rapidly to develop policies in 'reserved' subject-areas of which it had no experience in government.[45] National security, including intelligence, was one such area. Even allowing for absence of expertise, the route by which the SG arrived at its proposal is oddly opaque. An endnote on methodology refers to 'a range of expert inputs'.[46] Informal feelers had gone out to the intelligence community in London, to former practitioners, and to Euro-structures in Brussels, and one or two unofficial advisory engagements took place in Scotland.[47] There were contacts, too, with academic specialists, and no doubt the websites of European agencies were trawled for data and ideas,[48] but the process as a whole remains to be documented. Chapter 7 advanced a proposal for a 'single security and intelligence agency' that would embrace cyber security as well as counter-terrorism.[49] It was claimed that this arrangement would 'avoid any barriers between different agencies', and it may be that the authors had in mind the scale of overall effort that might be required to protect a population of just five million.[50] But it represented an unusual (perhaps

---

45   Torrance (2014), p. 17.
46   Scottish Government (2013), p. 639.
47   Private information.
48   David Leask, 'Scottish Civil Servants Probe Plans for "Nordic" Intelligence Services after Independence', *Sunday Herald*, 28 July 2013, http://www.heraldscotland.com/news/13115795.Scottish_civil_servants_probe_plans_for__Nordic__intelligence_services_after_independence/; Scottish Government (2013), pp. 639, endnote 284. The White Paper lists, as international comparators 'studied', Belgium, the Czech Republic, Denmark, Finland, Germany, the Netherlands, New Zealand, Norway, Sweden, Switzerland. It is unlikely that SG officials were briefed by any service of the countries listed.
49   Scottish Government (2013), pp. 261–67.
50   Cf. the claim by Allan Burnett that 'UK security is a long way from being perfect. Multiple organisations fight for power and influence and inappropriate UK Government interference is rife'. As evidence for this nonsense, he cited the UK Border Agency (not, of course, a security agency). [N.a.], 'Former Senior Police Officers Clash on Independence Security Report', *STV News*, 26 October 2013, http://stv.tv/news/politics/245660-graeme-pearson-and-allan-burnett-clash-on-independence-security-report/

unique) concentration of functions, professional cultures and personal authority, one that historically had been rejected for the UK agencies.[51]

More conspicuously, Chapter 7 failed to define either a strategic role for the new agency or a Scotland-specific context in which it would exercise its functions. The 'functions' themselves were a list of activities, not a statement of the responsibilities that the agency would exist to discharge. The issue of external intelligence gathering was ducked. As for cyber security, it was stated that 'our strategy will be to protect Scotland from attack': an aspiration, not a strategy. The assumption of 'joint working' with the rUK remained without definition. On the civil liberties front, no case was presented for placing the full panoply of state investigative capabilities under the same political authority as Police Scotland, and the authors attracted further flak with a pictorial mock-up of a future personal data retention system.[52]

This was an unhappy compilation. Mired in detail, it failed to provide a persuasive strategic narrative and it offered instead an easy target for opponents of independence. It all suggested that the SG leadership had learned little from public discussion of Scottish security over the previous twelve months. They had failed to take on board the magnitude, costs, and urgency of the security challenge they had set themselves. Behind closed doors, it must be added, one or two senior figures gave an impression of almost wilful refusal to acknowledge threat realities, not least in the domain of electronic and cyber-attack.[53] The fragility of the entire Chapter 7 edifice was encapsulated in the assertion that a new capability would be up and running by 'day one of independence', 24 March 2016: this was an undertaking which could not have been delivered even had rUK assistance been instantly negotiated and as rapidly deployed.[54]

---

51 See, e.g., Keith Jeffery, *MI6: The History of the Secret Intelligence Service 1909–1949* (London and New York: A&C Black, 2010), pp. 595–616; Aldrich and Cormac (2016), pp. 158–59.
52 Cf. Mark Howarth, 'SNP under Fire over "ID Register" Plans', *Scottish Daily Express*, 24 January 2015; Scottish Government (2013), p. 262.
53 Private information.
54 Scottish Government (2013), p. 262. The phrase first appears in Nicola Sturgeon's evidence to the Foreign Affairs Committee (2013), p. 62.

The sceptical, but largely wait-and-see tone of specialist comment shifted to outright hostility.[55] This surfaced in the House of Lords debate on Scotland on 30 January.[56] Hostile media comment spiked in March 2014 around a major intervention by the Scots-born architect of the UK counter-terrorism strategy, David Omand, who suggested that the White Paper showed a 'basic misunderstanding of intelligence'.[57] Simultaneously, an analysis by the Royal United Services Institute (RUSI) more or less advised the SG to scrap their proposals and start again. Two months later, RUSI's Director General, Professor Michael Clarke, observed that 'an independent Scotland without an effective intelligence agency will be a very attractive niche for terrorists and organised crime'.[58]

---

55 For earlier comment, see Peter Jackson, 'How an Independent Scotland Can Run Its Own Intelligence Service', *Sunday Herald*, 30 June 2013, http://www.pressreader.com/uk/sunday-herald/20130630/281560878374529; John Holmes, 'A Note by the Director "the Future of Scotland: International Implications and Comparisons — the Ditchley Foundation"', Ditchley Foundation, July 2013, http://www.ditchley.co.uk/conferences/past-programme/2010-2019/2013/the-future-of-scotland; Sandy Hardie, 'The SNP Have Set Themselves Major Challenges to Make Scotland Secure', *Herald*, 8 November 2013, http://www.pressreader.com/uk/the-herald/20131108/282243778354838; David Omand, 'Keynote Speech: Thinking Strategically About Security', in *Glasgow Global Security Network International Conference 2013* (Glasgow University, 8 November 2013).

56 See Lord Browne of Ladyton, *Lords Hansard* (London: HMSO, 30 January 2014), http://www.publications.parliament.uk/pa/ld201314/ldhansrd/text/140130-0001.htm; Baroness Neville-Jones, *Lords Hansard* (London: HMSO, 30 January 2014), http://www.publications.parliament.uk/pa/ld201314/ldhansrd/text/140130-0001.htm

57 Ben Riley-Smith, 'Head-to-Head: How the SNP and Sir David Omand Disagree on Intelligence', *Telegraph*, 13 March 2014, http://www.telegraph.co.uk/news/uknews/scottish-independence/10694066/Head-to-head-how-the-SNP-and-Sir-David-Omand-disagree-on-intelligence.html; Ben Riley-Smith, 'Scotland 'More Vulnerable' after Independence under Alex Salmond's Security Plans', *Telegraph*, 13 March 2014, http://www.telegraph.co.uk/news/uknews/scottish-independence/10694022/Scotland-more-vulnerable-after-independence-under-Alex-Salmonds-security-plans.html

58 Charlie Edwards, Clare Ellis, and Calum Jaffray, *Scotland's Blueprint for a Security and Intelligence Agency: An Initial Assessment* (London: RUSI, 2014); Riley-Smith, *Telegraph*, 13 March 2014; Kerry Gill, 'Think-Tank Warns Separate Scotland Could Be "Soft Underbelly" for Anti-UK Terror', *Daily Express*, 15 May 2014, http://www.express.co.uk/news/uk/475986/Think-tank-warns-separate-Scotland-could-be-soft-underbelly-for-anti-UK-terror; A less critical account is offered by the summary of a discussion held on 31 January in the University of Edinburgh: Andrew W. Neal, *The Threat Environment of the UK and Scotland in the Context of the UK National Security Strategy* (Edinburgh: Centre on Constitutional Change, 2014).

The SNP, SG and Yes Scotland proceeded to form a kind of defensive triangle that displayed impressive discipline under sustained assault. Waves of criticism were met by steady return fire along the lines of: 'Scotland will have/could develop first class security arrangements'; 'Scotland will get rid of Trident, will not wage illegal wars, and will therefore face reduced levels of threat'; 'Scotland has the skill base on which to build effective cyber and counter-terrorist defences'; 'Scotland will be welcomed as a trusted intelligence ally'. Mr Allan Burnett, a former Assistant Chief Constable deployed by Yes Scotland as their expert spokesman, had claimed in June 2013 that the UK Government had cut off debate on post-independence intelligence sharing by refusing to discuss the matter.[59] Wisely, the SNP had not pursued this particular line of defence, for by then or soon after, the leadership evidently recognised its vulnerability on intelligence and security and retreated into damage-limitation mode: contain exposure; repeat assurances; play the critic, not the ball. But Burnett's mirror-imaging claim that Westminster had closed down debate had an ironic sequel in a BBC interview with the then Chief Constable which generated the headline 'Police discuss post-Yes intelligence and security sharing'.[60] This was not the only occasion on which a policy-light area was disguised by the suggestion that contingency discussions with London were indeed under way.[61]

The SG could have made a more persuasive presentational case than it did. It might have been better advised to acknowledge the challenges, the likely dependencies and the requirement for a sincere bilateral effort to create a security architecture that would ensure continued mutual protection. It might even then have reached out to Scottish security

---

59 David Leask, 'Former Security Chiefs Clash over How an Independent Scotland Could Protect Itself from Terrorism', *Sunday Herald*, 30 June 2013; For comment on SNP 'closing down discussion on mass collection of data' from the civil liberties perspective, cf. Henry Porter, 'All We Ask Is for Transparency to Inform the Surveillance Debate', *The Observer*, 3 November 2013, https://www.theguardian.com/commentisfree/2013/nov/03/nsa-surveillance-security

60 Reevel Alderson, 'Scottish Independence: Police Discuss Post-Yes Intelligence and Security Sharing', *BBC News*, 20 March 2014, http://www.bbc.co.uk/news/uk-scotland-26651783; cf. also 'Talks Take Place on Shared Intelligence after "Yes" Vote', *The Times (Scotland)*, 21 March 2014.

61 Cf. James Titcomb, 'Bank of England Flatly Denies Scottish Currency Talks', *Telegraph*, 14 August 2014, http://www.telegraph.co.uk/finance/currency/11034881/Bank-of-England-flatly-denies-Scottish-currency-talks.html

practitioners who, irrespective of their views on independence, could have helped sustain public and agency confidence if independence had materialised. As it was, SG messaging was badly flawed both in tone and in substance. Part of the problem was the absence of a senior advisor with genuine, up-to-date experience of strategic intelligence.[62] This was more than a matter of presentation: it placed a question mark over the quality of advice reaching SG/SNP leaders, and their willingness to listen. The *Financial Times* was not alone in concluding that 'the deception in the Nationalist campaign lies in the assertion that everyone else would bend to Edinburgh's will and allow Mr Salmond to dictate his own terms'.[63] The risks were self-evident: lacking a first-hand sense of the threat environment, the SNP might really believe that Scotland could (in the *FT*'s phrase) 'inoculate itself against the harsh realities of the wider world'; and lacking sufficiently robust advice on the practicability of their own intelligence proposals, they might have come to believe that Scottish technical and personnel resources were more sophisticated than is the case, and that for any skill shortfall they could depend on the enthusiastic support of the rUK and other governments.[64] The *FT*'s emphasis on the personality of the then First Minister was telling: herein, it seemed, lay the prospect of miscalculation, or else (what would have amounted to the same thing) of preparedness to take a strategic gamble on public security against the prize of a popular majority on 18 September. As the polls narrowed, the spectre of an extended and messy transition, with diminished security defences on both sides of the border, started to move beyond the realm of the hypothetical.

Yet the UK Government did not press any 'weak link' line of argument.[65] This, it was judged, would have played into the SNP claim that the rUK would have to fall in with 'shared arrangements'. Nor

---

62   Dame Mariot Leslie, a former Director-General Defence and Intelligence at the FCO who declared herself a Yes supporter in early September 2014, confined her public comments to Scotland's prospects for NATO membership: Tom Peterkin, 'Scottish Independence: "Scots Welcome in Nato"', *Scotsman*, 3 September 2014, http://www.scotsman.com/news/politics/scottish-independence-scots-welcome-in-nato-1-3529122

63   Philip Stephens, 'Alex Salmond Brushes Aside the Foreign Policy Facts for Scotland', *Financial Times*, 16 September 2014, https://www.ft.com/content/4460 7564-3d8b-11e4-b782-00144feabdc0

64   *Ibid.*

65   It was however echoed in May 2014 by Professor Michael Clarke, Director-General of RUSI, cited in Gill (2014).

would the agencies have wished to draw further hostile attention to hypothetical vulnerabilities. In the event, the intelligence debate went quiet over the summer of 2014. In the background lay reluctance in London to take this most sensitive subject, alongside confidential capabilities and relationships, into the campaign bear pit (certainly, it would have been out of place in the televised Darling-Salmond debates). Again, there would have been no appetite among Whitehall officials for making life more difficult for SG counterparts, especially at a time when UK inputs into security arrangements for the Commonwealth Games (starting on 23 July), already the subject of intensive discussion, were being implemented. In Glasgow, the Better Together website carried items on national security, but there were gaps in coordination, and neither the political leadership nor campaign staff seemed comfortable with a subject that they felt was better left to 'experts'. Consequently, in Blytheswood Square and the Savoy Centre, it languished until a Better Together sub-group, 'Forces Together', embracing defence, security and intelligence, sought to re-focus interest.

In September, just two weeks before the vote, two interventions summed up the 'intelligence' case for retaining the Union. In the first, Sir David Omand focused on cyber security and added this: 'as a Scot, I want security for Scotland. So were independence to come, it must leave the people on both sides of the border no less secure than today, at no greater cost. The SNP White Paper is fundamentally flawed on how either part of that condition could be achieved'.[66] By way of response, Allan Burnett was quoted as saying 'Sir David is wrong and this is another example of Project Fear at its worst — trying to politicise issues of security and anti-terrorism in this way is the height of irresponsibility'.[67] The second intervention, by Sir John Scarlett, former Chief of MI6, followed the next day, 5 September. He too questioned the White Paper proposals and then reflected on the wider world: 'we live in unstable times. We must follow and understand jihadi extremism and related terrorist threats; deep-rooted regional instability; the policies

---

66 [N.a.], 'Scottish Independence Cyber Plans "Flawed"', *Scotsman*, 4 September 2014, http://www.scotsman.com/news/politics/scottish-independence-cyber-defence-plans-flawed-1-3530887
67 Cited from [n.a.], *Scotsman*, 4 September 2014. Compare Christine Grahame's identical response to Theresa May, in Richard Ford, 'SNP Accuses May of Scaremongering', *The Times*, 30 October 2013.

and ambitions of authoritarian states; the ever-present threat of inter-state conflict, including now on our own continent on the borders of our NATO alliance. And all this against the background of rapid economic, demographic, social and technological change and fundamental shifts in the global balance of power'.[68] The two interventions prompted further statements from Menzies Campbell, Scottish Conservative leader Ruth Davidson, and Shadow Defence Minister, Gemma Doyle.[69] The Prime Minister added a reference to 'some of the best security and intelligence services anywhere in the world' at the end of the NATO conference in Wales.[70] Yet perhaps for reasons to do with the preservation of broadcast 'balance', Omand and Scarlett did not achieve the extended replay by the BBC and STV that might have opened out their arguments to a larger audience.

In undertaking this review, I had the impression that there really had been 'hardly a moment's discussion'. And indeed so far as SNP/ SG engagement was concerned, Menzies Campbell was right. But my title acquired its question mark when a trawl turned up rather more coverage than I had been aware of at the time. The Scottish press has taken a good deal of flak in recent years for declining standards of journalism.[71] It is true that the most significant interventions on the subject of intelligence came through London-based papers and their Scotland correspondents. Much Scotland-based coverage spiked around political and media inputs that originated south of the border. The SG's defensive posture could, and should, have been probed more deeply and directly from Edinburgh and Glasgow. Yet print and online media interest was quite widespread, with informative coverage from unexpected quarters: the Aberdeen *Press and Journal*, for example, and

---

68   John Scarlett, 'A Yes Vote Brings Grave Security Dangers', *The Times*, 5 September 2014, http://www.thetimes.co.uk/tto/opinion/columnists/article4197050.ece

69   Gemma Doyle: quoted in Ben Riley-Smith, 'Scotland Would Be less Protected after Independence under SNP's Intelligence Plans, Former MI6 Head Warns', *Telegraph*, 5 September 2014, http://www.telegraph.co.uk/news/uknews/scottish-independence/11077028/Scotland-would-be-less-protected-after-independence-under-SNPs-intelligence-plans-former-MI6-head-warns.html; 'Davidson Slams SNP Defence Plans', *Evening News*, 4 September 2014, http://www.eveningtimes.co.uk/news/13290481.Davidson_slams_SNP_defence_plans; Campbell (2014).

70   Rob Reid, 'Scotland Will Be Safer in Dangerous World by Remaining with UK Says David Cameron', *Daily Record*, 5 September 2014, http://www.dailyrecord.co.uk/news/politics/scotland-safer-dangerous-world-remaining-4172507

71   See, for example, Macwhirter (2014), pp. 72–95.

the *Sunday Post* in particular.[72] The overall impression is one of fair, if largely reactive, press reportage, but of a subject the broadcast media found almost too hot to handle.[73]

By 18 September, then, there had been rather more public discussion of 'intelligence' than Menzies Campbell allowed. But there is a king-sized qualification on cyber security. On any professional analysis, the most immediate threat confronting an independent Scotland on 24 March 2016 would have come from cyber-attack, and not from terrorism. This threat had been covered in *Scotland Analysis: Security* (though it lost visibility amidst a plethora of detail); it was underlined in Omand's interventions; and an outstanding presentation to the second Edinburgh ESRC seminar in January 2014 was available online in summary form.[74] One mainstream Scottish journalist made the connection between cyber-attack and the 'business voter',[75] and BBC Scotland carried a short piece, pairing Allan Burnett and myself. Astonishingly, however (given the availability of Scottish expertise), no media outlet offered anything like 'the plain man's guide to cyber and the Indy-vote'.

Cyber-spying, along with long-range cyber-crime, is moving with an exponential growth in technical sophistication.[76] The capacity to discover, diagnose and take counter-measures, which underpins an effective cyberspace strategy, requires technological resources of a high order, together with a rapid response capability and robust international collaboration. Within the UK, this capability resides with GCHQ. This is why the UK Government can claim a competitive security edge for the

---

72 To the academic commentaries already listed, add Professor Rhodri Jeffreys-Jones' thoughtful reflections on Scottish expertise in intelligence gathering: Rhodri Jeffreys-Jones, 'Masters of the Spying Game', *Scotsman*, 8 May 2013, http://www.scotsman. com/news/opinion/rhodri-jeffreys-jones-masters-of-spying-game-1-2922226

73 For a survey of press coverage (pro- and anti-independence and neutral), see David Patrick, 'Bought and Sold or Hype in Bold? Newspaper Framing of the Scottish Independence Debate', Scottish constitutional futures forum (15 September 2014), http://www.scottishconstitutionalfutures.org/OpinionandAnalysis/ViewBlogPost/ tabid/1767/articleType/ArticleView/articleId/4255/David-Patrick-Bought-and-Sold-or-Hype-in-Bold-Newspaper-Framing-of-the-Scottish-Independence-Debate.aspx

74 Neal, pp. 8–9.

75 Terry Murden, 'Comment: More Needed to Tackle the Cost of Cybercrime', *Scotsman*, 12 June 2014. Mr. Murden, then Business Editor of *The Scotsman*, was unable to follow this through, for unconnected reasons.

76 On cyber-crime, see Sir David Omand, 'The Dark Net: Policing the Internet's Underworld', *World Policy Journal* (Winter 2015), http://www.worldpolicy.org/ journal/winter2015/dark-net

UK as business location and as a destination for foreign investment. For an independent Scotland, critically dependent as its economy would be upon innovative technology, this was not a luxury. Nor could the loss of GCHQ capability have been made good by commercial products, however persuasive the sales pitch. For families dependent for employment in, for example, pharmaceuticals, offshore hydrocarbon technology, or advanced IT products, the present level of protection of intellectual property within UK cyberspace — though admittedly far from perfect — is of a higher order than anything in Europe, and for that reason it remains a must-have. In its absence, Scottish firms would face a growing incidence of unseen penetration of their systems, to be spotted only when something very like their products appeared on foreign competitors' websites. At that point, Alex Massie's derisive slogan, 'Vote No to remain beneath the GCHQ umbrella', might have seemed not so very far from reality.

That the price of independence would have included at least the partial loss of GCHQ/UK protective support for Scottish jobs and prosperity was not at all clear to voters. We in the No campaign had not succeeded in getting that story across, and in retrospect, the national security debate had not moved beyond the familiar images of terrorist outrage to the more potent, more immediate, yet less visible threat of the cyber-spy. If the cyber debate were to be re-run, with the lessons of some high-profile lapses in corporate security in view, growing public awareness of the costs of cyber-crime, and renewed focus on the threat presented by China and Russia, the level of coverage might be very different.

Yet two years on, with the rise of so-called Islamic State and the spread of domestic radicalisation, the counter-terrorist environment too has changed. The use of Belgium as an operating base by those responsible for the Paris shootings of November 2015 and for the terrorist attacks of March 2016 in Brussels itself have served notice that no country, however remote from the geopolitical epicentre in the Middle East, can assume it will remain immune to the new levels of threat.[77] In a broadcast response that attracted the headline 'Independent Scotland "would have better intelligence services than MI5", says Alex Salmond', the former First Minister predictably sought to play down domestic

---

77 See Chapter 5, pp. 138–40, for a discussion of the Belgian comparison.

implications.[78] Symptomatic of renewed public interest in the politics of security, however, was the prominence of European intelligence cooperation as an issue in the EU referendum of June 2016.[79] In contrast to Scotland in 2014, political figures were prepared to engage (whether or not they knew very much about what they were saying). Meanwhile former heads of agency, in public disagreement as to the likely impact of Brexit, were given air time by the BBC, as was an American perspective from Mike Hayden, former Director of the National Security Agency and of the CIA.

A second independence referendum, should one materialise, would take place in quite different circumstances from the first. With changes in political leadership, the UK's departure from the EU, and a fast-developing threat environment, the tone and content of a renewed intelligence and security debate would likely move on. This would no longer be unknown public-political territory. A wider range of external perspectives might be on view, and might also (with the arrival in Edinburgh of Russia's *Sputnik* 'news' agency) embrace that of Mr Putin.[80] The SNP, through its presence at Westminster and its representation on the Intelligence Services Committee and the FAC, would have the advantage of closer engagement with national security issues (and the SG could quietly jettison Chapter 7). The media, print and broadcast, with the benefit of their 2014 experience, might set about drilling into the issues and questioning the principals with renewed vigour; and in putting out facts and findings, they could help voters take a second, better informed, look at the intelligence dimension of separation.

By way of conclusion, I would recall the odd mixture of business-as-usual and political touchiness surrounding security and Scotland in 2014, sharpened as it was by the Commonwealth Games. UK specialists, drawing on the 2012 Olympics, worked with Scottish authorities through the long lead-up to ensure the all-round security of the event and the

---

78 John Ashmore, 'Independent Scotland "Would Have Better Intelligence Services Than MI5", Says Alex Salmond', *Holyrood*, 24 March 2016, http://www.holyrood.com/articles/news/independent-scotland-would-have-better-intelligence-services-mi5-says-alex-salmond

79 The topic features briefly in Craig Oliver, *Unleashing Demons: The Inside Story of Brexit* (London: Hodder & Stoughton, 2016), p. 220.

80 Kenny Farquharson, 'Putin Is Gatecrashing Scotland's House Party', *The Times*, 12 August 2016, http://www.thetimes.co.uk/article/putin-is-gatecrashing-scotlands-house-party-ml5r9n5p9

safety of the participants. These joint efforts were not acknowledged by the SG, which went to some lengths to minimise public awareness of its reliance on national assets.[81] By late August, it would have been open to the UK Government to celebrate the combined endeavour: a triumph for Glasgow and Scotland, quietly secured. That nothing of the sort was proclaimed is a reflection of the professional reticence of those most closely engaged. But more than that, London's silence was a gesture of respect for Scottish colleagues whose lot it was to work on as public servants, in the eye of the campaign storm.[82]

---

81   Private information.
82   On this general subject, see Matt Foster, 'Civil Service "Should Remain Unified" Says Senior Scottish Government Official', *Holyrood*, 5 October 2015.

References

[N.a.], 'In Full: SNP Resolution on Nato', *Scotsman*, 16 July 2012, http://www.scotsman.com/news/politics/in-full-snp-resolution-on-nato-1-2414919

—, 'UK Spies "Not Trailing SNP"; Hague Dismisses "Scots Paranoia"', *Daily Star*, 21 June 2013

—, 'Former Senior Police Officers Clash on Independence Security Report', *STV News*, 26 October 2013, http://stv.tv/news/politics/245660-graeme-pearson-and-allan-burnett-clash-on-independence-security-report/

—, 'Talks Take Place on Shared Intelligence after "Yes" Vote', *The Times (Scotland)*, 21 March 2014.

—, 'The Pros and the Cons of Negativity', *Herald*, 16 May 2014, http://www.heraldscotland.com/opinion/13160648.The_pros_and_the_cons_of_negativity/

—, 'Scottish Independence Cyber Plans "Flawed"', *Scotsman*, 4 September 2014, http://www.scotsman.com/news/politics/scottish-independence-cyber-defence-plans-flawed-1-3530887

—, 'Davidson Slams SNP Defence Plans', *Evening News*, 4 September 2014, http://www.eveningtimes.co.uk/news/13290481.Davidson_slams_SNP_defence_plans/

Alderson, Reevel, 'Scottish Independence: Police Discuss Post-Yes Intelligence and Security Sharing', *BBC News*, 20 March 2014, http://www.bbc.co.uk/news/uk-scotland-26651783

Aldrich, Richard and Cormac, Rory, *The Black Door: Spies, Secret Intelligence and British Prime Ministers* (London: HarperCollins UK, 2016).

Ashmore, John, 'Independent Scotland "Would Have Better Intelligence Services Than MI5", Says Alex Salmond', *Holyrood*, 24 March 2016, https://www.holyrood.com/articles/news/independent-scotland-would-have-better-intelligence-services-mi5-says-alex-salmond

Borland, Ben, '25 Things We'll Miss Independent Scotland' [*sic*], *Scottish Express*, 7 September 2014, pp. 38–39.

Brocklebank, Jonathan, 'Fear and Laughing in the Ad Campaigns as We Reveal What Really Drove Better Together', *Scottish Daily Mail*, 19 September 2014, pp. 14–15.

Brown, Jonathan, 'SNP Veteran Blames MI5 for Trolling over Independence', *Independent*, 14 June 2014.

Campbell, Menzies, 'Sir Menzies Campbell: We Are Safer Together', Scottish Liberal Democrats, 5 September 2014, http://www.scotlibdems.org.uk/intervention_from_intelligence_chief_shows_we_are_safer_together

Carrell, Severin, 'Scottish Independence Quest Hampered by Policy Gaps, MPs Say', *Guardian*, 19 July 2013, https://www.theguardian.com/politics/2013/may/01/scottish-independence-hampered-policy-gaps

Chorley, Matt and Roden, Alan, 'Voters Need Facts About Scottish Independence, Hague Says as MPs Warn Rest of the UK's Global Reputation Is at Stake', *Daily Mail*, 1 May 2013, http://www.dailymail.co.uk/news/article-2317689/Voters-need-facts-Scottish-independence-Hague-says-MPs-warn-rest-UKs-global-reputation-stake.html

Cowley, Jason, 'Alex Salmond: "This Is the Phoney War. This Is Not the Campaign"', *New Statesman*, 25 June 2013, http://www.newstatesman.com/2013/06/phoney-war-not-campaign

David Leask, 'Former Security Chiefs Clash over How an Independent Scotland Could Protect Itself from Terrorism', *Sunday Herald*, 30 June 2013.

Dover, Rob, 'Cutting the Ties That Bind? Intelligence in an Independent Scotland', *PSA Political Insight*, 4 November 2013, https://www.psa.ac.uk/insight-plus/blog/cutting-ties-bind-intelligence-independent-scotland

Edwards, Charlie, Ellis, Clare, and Jaffray, Calum, *Scotland's Blueprint for a Security and Intelligence Agency: An Initial Assessment* (London: RUSI, 2014).

Farquharson, Kenny, 'Putin Is Gatecrashing Scotland's House Party', *The Times*, 12 August 2016, http://www.thetimes.co.uk/article/putin-is-gatecrashing-scotlands-house-party-ml5r9n5p9

Ford, Richard, 'SNP Accuses May of Scaremongering ', *The Times*, 30 October 2013.

Foreign Affairs Committee, *Foreign Policy Considerations for the UK and Scotland in the Event of Scotland Becoming an Independent Country*, Sixth Report of Session 2012–2013 (London: HMSO, 2013), http://www.publications.parliament.uk/pa/cm201213/cmselect/cmfaff/643/643.pdf

Foster, Matt, 'Civil Service "Should Remain Unified" Says Senior Scottish Government Official', *Holyrood*, 5 October 2015, https://www.holyrood.com/articles/news/civil-service-should-remain-unified-says-senior-scottish-government-official

Gardham, Magnus, 'Carmichael Tells Cabinet Not to Give Lectures on Independence', *Herald*, 11 October 2013, http://www.heraldscotland.com/news/13126815.Carmichael_tells_Cabinet_not_to_give_lectures_on_independence/

Gill, Kerry, 'Think-Tank Warns Separate Scotland Could Be "Soft Underbelly" for Anti-UK Terror', *Daily Express*, 15 May 2014, http://www.express.co.uk/news/uk/475986/Think-tank-warns-separate-Scotland-could-be-soft-underbelly-for-anti-UK-terror

Hague, William, 'Foreign Secretary's Speech: The United Kingdom: Stronger Together', Foreign and Commonwealth Office, Gov.uk, 20 June 2013, https://www.gov.uk/government/speeches/foreign-secretarys-speech-the-united-kingdom-stronger-together

Hardie, Sandy, 'The SNP Have Set Themselves Major Challenges to Make Scotland Secure', *Herald*, 8 November 2013, http://www.pressreader.com/uk/the-herald/20131108/282243778354838

HM Government, 'A Strong Britain in an Age of Uncertainty: The National Security Strategy' (2010), http://webarchive.nationalarchives.gov.uk/20121015000000/http://www.direct.gov.uk/prod_consum_dg/groups/dg_digitalassets/@dg/@en/documents/digitalasset/dg_191639.pdf

—, *Scotland Analysis: Cm. 8741: Security* (London: HMSO, 2013), https://www.gov.uk/government/uploads/system/uploads/attachment_data/file/253500/Scotland_analysis_security.pdf

—, *Sixth Report from the Foreign Affairs Committee of Session 2012–13: Foreign Policy Considerations for the UK and Scotland in the Event of Scotland Becoming an Independent Country. Response from the Secretary of State for Foreign and Commonwealth Affairs. Cm. 8644* (London: HMSO, 2013), https://www.gov.uk/government/uploads/system/uploads/attachment_data/file/210012/30944_Cm_8644_Web_Accessible.pdf

Holmes, John, 'A Note by the Director "the Future of Scotland: International Implications and Comparisons — the Ditchley Foundation"', Ditchley Foundation (July 2013), http://www.ditchley.co.uk/conferences/past-programme/2010-2019/2013/the-future-of-scotland

Howarth, Mark, 'SNP under Fire over "ID Register" Plans', *Scottish Daily Express*, 24 January 2015.

Jackson, Peter, 'How an Independent Scotland Can Run Its Own Intelligence Service', *Sunday Herald*, 30 June 2013, http://www.pressreader.com/uk/sunday-herald/20130630/281560878374529

Jeffery, Keith, *MI6: The History of the Secret Intelligence Service 1909–1949* (London and New York: A&C Black, 2010).

Jeffreys-Jones, Rhodri, 'Masters of the Spying Game', *Scotsman*, 8 May 2013, http://www.scotsman.com/news/opinion/rhodri-jeffreys-jones-masters-of-spying-game-1-2922226

Leask, David, 'Scottish Civil Servants Probe Plans for "Nordic" Intelligence Services after Independence', *Sunday Herald*, 28 July 2013, http://www.heraldscotland.com/news/13115795.Scottish_civil_servants_probe_plans_for__Nordic__intelligence_services_after_independence/

Lord Browne of Ladyton, *Lords Hansard* (London: HMSO, 30 January 2014), http://www.publications.parliament.uk/pa/ld201314/ldhansrd/text/140130-0001.htm

· Lord Hennessy of Nympsfield, *Lords Hansard, Col. 1361–1451* (London: HMSO, 30 January 2014), http://www.publications.parliament.uk/pa/ld201314/ldhansrd/text/140130-0001.htm#14013072000875

Macwhirter, Iain, *Disunited Kingdom: How Westminster Won a Referendum but Lost Scotland* (Glasgow: Cargo publishing, 2014).

Massie, Alex, 'Theresa May's Grubby Little Warning: An Independent Scotland Will Be Out in the Cold', *Spectator*, 29 October 2013, http://blogs.spectator.co.uk/2013/10/theresa-mays-grubby-little-warning-independent-scotland-will-be-left-out-in-the-cold/

—, 'Why I Am Voting No', *Spectator*, 9 September 2014, http://blogs.spectator.co.uk/2014/09/why-i-am-voting-no/

McTague, Tom, 'One in Four Scots Believe UK Spies Are Working against Independence', *Daily Mail*, 8 September 2014, http://www.dailymail.co.uk/news/article-2747809/One-four-Scots-believe-British-spies-secretly-working-against-Yes-independence-campaign.html

Mottram, R., 'Protecting the Citizen in the Twenty-First Century: Issues and Challenges', in *The New Protective State: Government, Intelligence and Terrorism*, ed. by Peter Hennessy (London and New York: A&C Black, 2008), pp. 42–65.

Murden, Terry, 'Comment: More Needed to Tackle the Cost of Cybercrime', *Scotsman*, 12 June 2014.

Murray, Paula, 'MSP Margo Convinced MI5 Spying in Nat Camp', *Scottish Sunday Express*, 23 June 2013.

Neal, Andrew W., 'Comment: Scotland Wouldn't Be Out of Security Loop', *Scotsman*, 11 November 2013, http://www.scotsman.com/news/opinion/comment-scotland-wouldn-t-be-out-of-security-loop-1-3184490

—, *The Threat Environment of the UK and Scotland in the Context of the UK National Security Strategy* (Edinburgh: Centre on Constitutional Change, 2014).

Neville-Jones, Baroness, *Lords Hansard* (London: HMSO, 30 January 2014), http://www.publications.parliament.uk/pa/ld201314/ldhansrd/text/140130-0001.htm

Oliver, Craig, *Unleashing Demons: The Inside Story of Brexit* (London: Hodder & Stoughton, 2016).

Omand, David, 'Keynote Speech: Thinking Strategically About Security', paper presented at Glasgow Global Security Network International Conference 2013, Glasgow University, 8 November 2013.

—, 'The Dark Net: Policing the Internet's Underworld', *World Policy Journal*, Winter (2015), http://dx.doi.org/10.1177/0740277515623750

Patrick, David, 'Bought and Sold or Hype in Bold? Newspaper Framing of the Scottish Independence Debate', Scottish Constitutional Futures Forum (15 September 2014), http://www.scottishconstitutionalfutures.org/Opinion andAnalysis/ViewBlogPost/tabid/1767/articleType/ArticleView/articleId/ 4255/David-Patrick-Bought-and-Sold-or-Hype-in-Bold-Newspaper-Framing-of-the-Scottish-Independence-Debate.aspx

Peterkin, Tom, 'Scottish Independence: "Scots Welcome in Nato"', *Scotsman*, 3 September 2014, http://www.scotsman.com/news/politics/scottish-independence-scots-welcome-in-nato-1-3529122

Porter, Henry, 'All We Ask Is for Transparency to Inform the Surveillance Debate', *The Observer*, 3 November 2013, https://www.theguardian.com/ commentisfree/2013/nov/03/nsa-surveillance-security

Ramsay, Meta, 'Security Service Can Take Nothing for Granted', *Scotsman*, 17 February 2013, http://www.scotsman.com/news/opinion/meta-ramsay-security-service-can-take-nothing-for-granted-1-2795918

Reid, Harry, 'Decent Case for a Scots Foreign Policy', *Herald*, 2 October 2012, http://www.heraldscotland.com/opinion/13075312.Decent_case_for_a_ Scots_foreign_policy

—, 'Case for Knowing Our Place in the World', *Herald*, 26 August 2014, http:// www.heraldscotland.com/opinion/13176691.Case_for_knowing_our_place_ in_the_world

Reid, Rob, 'Scotland Will Be Safer in Dangerous World by Remaining with UK Says David Cameron', *Daily Record*, 5 September 2014, http:// www.dailyrecord.co.uk/news/politics/scotland-safer-dangerous-world-remaining-4172507

Riley-Smith, Ben, 'Head-to-Head: How the SNP and Sir David Omand Disagree on Intelligence', *Telegraph*, 13 March 2014, http://www.telegraph.co.uk/ news/uknews/scottish-independence/10694066/Head-to-head-how-the-SNP-and-Sir-David-Omand-disagree-on-intelligence.html

—, 'Scotland "More Vulnerable" after Independence under Alex Salmond's Security Plans', *Telegraph*, 13 March 2014, http://www.telegraph.co.uk/ news/uknews/scottish-independence/10694022/Scotland-more-vulnerable-after-independence-under-Alex-Salmonds-security-plans.html

—, 'Scotland Would Be less Protected after Independence under SNP's Intelligence Plans, Former MI6 Head Warns', *Telegraph*, 5 September 2014, http://www. telegraph.co.uk/news/uknews/scottish-independence/11077028/Scotland-would-be-less-protected-after-independence-under-SNPs-intelligence-plans-former-MI6-head-warns.html

Scarlett, John, 'A Yes Vote Brings Grave Security Dangers', *The Times*, 5 September 2014, http://www.thetimes.co.uk/tto/opinion/columnists/article 4197050.ece

Scottish Government, *Scotland's Future: Your Guide to an Independent Scotland* (Edinburgh: Scottish Government, 2013), http://www.gov.scot/resource/0043/00439021.pdf

Stephens, Philip, 'Alex Salmond Brushes Aside the Foreign Policy Facts for Scotland', *Financial Times*, 16 September 2014, https://www.ft.com/content/44607564-3d8b-11e4-b782-00144feabdc0

Titcomb, James, 'Bank of England Flatly Denies Scottish Currency Talks', *Telegraph*, 14 August 2014, http://www.telegraph.co.uk/finance/currency/11034881/Bank-of-England-flatly-denies-Scottish-currency-talks.html

Torrance, David, *100 Days of Hope and Fear: How Scotland's Referendum Was Lost and Won* (Edinburgh: Luath Press Ltd, 2014).

Xiaoping, Deng, 'One Country, Two Systems' (22 June 1984), http://en.people.cn/dengxp/vol3/text/c1210.html

7. Press Scrutiny and the Proposals for Security and Intelligence in an Independent Scotland[1]

Eamonn P. O'Neill

This chapter examines the scrutiny by the press in Scotland and the wider UK, before, during and after the publication of issues related to the proposals presented in the Scottish Government's independence White Paper *Scotland's Future* in November 2013. It outlines the various categories of media coverage in common usage and examines a selection of coverage in depth. It argues that, with some exceptions, the coverage was narrow and formulaic. It suggests more investigative projects could have widened and deepened the coverage and led to a more informed debate.

1   I am grateful to Dr Andrew Neal and colleagues who attended the ESRC seminar series at the University of Edinburgh for their work and patience. Also colleagues in the media in Scotland, especially at *BBC Scotland* and *The Herald*, for their input and contributions.

When the Scottish Government's White Paper *Scotland's Future* was published in November 2013, most media attention was focused on its proposals for the economy, social welfare, currency and defence matters. When the latter was mentioned, coverage focused on the issue of Trident and the implications that would have for the economy. Coverage of the SNP's claims regarding a 2002–2012 Defence 'underspend' of £7.4 billion, for example, featured extensively in the media, as was the policy of an independent Scotland having a total of 15,000 regular and 5000 reserve personnel across land, air and maritime forces by 2026. There was also widespread coverage of the SNP's policy of maintaining a £2.5 billion annual military budget in an independent Scotland. Whilst these military plans were covered by the press, it appeared that little or no real attention and scrutiny was paid to the proposals for intelligence and security matters within an independent Scotland.

It might be argued that this was down to the fact that the proposals were mentioned across a mere handful of pages in an otherwise lengthy policy document. The word count for these proposals ran to little more than 1500 words across 6 pages of the 670 page publication. Yet this in itself was surprising given some of the implications the proposed establishment of the new Scottish Security and Intelligence Agency (SSIS) had for both Scotland itself and its relationship with the other countries within existing UK borders.

The short content of the White Paper and its subsections did, within their limitations, present a deceptively wide range of issues which could have acted as starting points for journalists to examine in a variety of ways across all publication platforms. Potential subjects for scrutiny included — but were not limited to — the following five areas. Firstly, the structure and operation of the new SSIS: this included the proposal to create a single domestic intelligence agency rather than two or more that could also focus on foreign intelligence, the ways in which the SSIS would assess and investigate threats and gather and analyse intelligence, and how it would be scrutinised by the Scottish Government. Secondly, the transition to independence: whether a 'seamless'[2] transition in the early period of independence would really be possible to 'ensure

---

2   Scottish Government, *Scotland's Future: Your Guide to an Independent Scotland* (Edinburgh: Scottish Government, 2013), http://www.gov.scot/resource/0043/00439021.pdf, p. 262

the security of both countries [Scotland and rUK]'[3] was continuously maintained, what the legislative timetable for the establishment of the SSIS would be, how the new agency would protect Scotland's critical infrastructure during the transition and after independence, and how it would recruit and train its staff, with or without the assistance of the remaining UK.

The third area includes the challenges that would have been involved in working with partners, both foreign and domestic: how a cooperative relationship with the remaining UK and its agencies would be guaranteed and maintained, what the planned role for Scottish universities and businesses would be and whether there were any early signs of cooperation from these bodies, and what the relationship and oversight arrangements between the new single Police Scotland force and the planned SSIS would be. Fourthly, the adequacy of the estimated £206m budget (calculated from the current Scottish contribution and spending based on population in the UK budget) could have been questioned, as well as whether the expected significant investment in establishing an agency would be factored into an independence settlement agreement from the rest of the UK; and fifthly, the plans and structures that would have been in place for dealing with cyber terrorism could have been explored, including how this would align with Scotland's critical infrastructure protection aims (e.g. protecting oil production facilities and output), and whether the planned return of proportionate funding from the UK's Cyber Security Programme would adequately fund the new Scottish plans.

The Scottish media coverage in the twelve months before the referendum devoted relatively modest resources to the proposals themselves, the issues they might have represented, or indeed the Westminster Government's response to them. The narrow amount of coverage that did appear was varied in quality and content, and came from both Scotland itself and England. The coverage published across all platforms (e.g. digital/print/broadcast) tended to break down into distinct categories: (a) recounting the policy briefly and uncritically in news articles; (b) analysis in news articles or news feature articles; (c) framing the policy announcement in feature articles or comment and

---

3   *Ibid.*, p. 474.

opinion pieces that themselves were sometimes presented in overtly accessible and populist terms (e.g. headlines which mention 'Scottish James Bonds' etc.).[4] Scant attention was given in investigative contexts which might have been reasonably expected to go into considerably more depth about the proposals and their myriad implications.

This chapter asks whether there was sufficient and informed debate in the wider UK press and Scottish media about these issues. It examines output from a selected range of sources that I believe were broadly indicative of the wider underlying trends of coverage. The first section of the chapter identifies the theoretical and practical understandings of each output category. The second section focuses in more depth on the press output on this issue with these definitions and categories in mind. The third section concludes with an analysis of what this output meant and introduces my own experience working on a BBC project discreetly connected to this debate, arguing that investigative journalism could have played a more productive and focused part in this process.

News categories and shifting rules

News articles, by their nature, are meant to be pertinent, factual and balanced. They are designed to cover ongoing events which are of relevance to the public audience. 'News values' are the shifting sands of journalism practice, identifiable as an array of tests by which the professional (and, increasingly, the amateur unpaid blogger too) uses to decide which story, subject, or issue to focus on. This model has been articulated as: 'an attempt to render the daily, instinctive decisions of professionalism journalism tangible'.[5] I can see the wisdom in this interpretation but caveats do apply. Each journalist has their own accumulated professional (and life) experiences which shape their own

---

4   Kevin McKenna, 'Would Independent Scotland Have Its Own Spies?', *Japan Times*, 8 April 2014, http://www.japantimes.co.jp/opinion/2014/04/08/commentary/world-commentary/would-independent-scotland-have-its-own-spies. I use this *Japan Times* version of a deceptively informed article to show the global reach of the author and the subject. The 'Scottish James Bond' theme was a clever way of cloaking a serious topic in an accessible headline and in no way is meant to criticise the professional aims of the author which I recognise were serious and complex.

5   A. Smith and M. Higgins, *The Language of Journalism: A Multi-Genre Perspective* (New York and London: Bloomsbury Publishing, 2013).

professional code in the field and the office. This means any journalistic news values are constantly changed and challenged. Smith and Higgins are correct to use 'attempt' in their analysis since, in most cases, that is all it may be. However, in other cases, where strict editorial pressure is applied throughout the working day and week, journalists will adhere to the model under the threat of losing their jobs if they fail to deliver.

These can include simplistic tests that state 'if it bleeds, it leads!' — meaning that if human life and limb are at stake, then the story might merit attention; 'all news is local' is another dictum, meaning the 'relevance' criterion is mostly geographical and demands local demographic impact as well; 'hold the powerful to account' is another traditional guideline which invokes the role of the press in questioning the so-called 'power elite' whether they be individuals, groups, organisations, or government departments; and the reliable old maxim 'man bites dog' suggests the 'unusual' story is always best to consider when ranking a subject for media attention.[6] Other factors which are in common use to determine the newsworthiness of a story on any given day of the week in newsrooms up and down the UK could include a mix of the following (in no particular order): celebrity (is someone with a news profile in the mix?); shocking and/or 'bad news' issues which might involve human tragedy; 'good' news or 'nice surprises' — reversing the previous category; 'follow-ups' or 'new chapter' stories which return to a previous topic and add a new body of research, slant or interpretation (these sometimes follow the pattern of more serious investigative articles); 'exclusives' which the news organisation has decided merit their own resources, attention and interpretation — these can range from a tabloid 'splashing' on the front page with a tale of celebrity sex, drugs and anything else to hand, or

---

6   I have witnessed this in action during a visit to a Scottish courtroom where a case was being heard involving a suspect accused of a knife crime. This in itself is not an unusual scenario. However, the accused's defence lawyer successfully argued the stabbing victim had launched herself onto the blade which the accused happened to be holding. The jury returned a Not Proven verdict. Press coverage in Scottish courts has declined markedly in recent years. This is primarily due to resourcing by publications and professional companies employing court reporters. This means fewer cases are covered in the press which, in itself, is a challenge to the democratic process to have court process and practice recorded and monitored in an open way. This can affect complex cases which have later resulted in miscarriages of justice.

a broadsheet reporting on its front page and website the results of a several-years' long investigation into phone hacking.[7]

Depending on the news organisation involved, they also frequently have to be constructed according to internal ethical guidelines. Broadcast news organisations, like the BBC for example, adhere to the concept of journalistic 'balance' by timing input from 'sides' of the debate in an effort to present arguments from the main parties within the same amount of air-time.

Feature articles tend to be on the inside pages of publications and are afforded more space for in-depth coverage and analysis. They are sometimes investigative in nature and incorporate more facts, expert opinion, analysis and comment. They are also the place for journalists to express more colour and flair in their writing. News features, as the name implies, are something of a hybrid of news and features. The latter form would have been ideal print territory for news organisations to have carried coverage of an in-depth nature of an independent Scotland's likely security landscape. Randall's ideal that there is no great difference between the standards in either form would have applied here.[8]

Comment or opinion pieces have more room for debate, subjective opinion and polemical approaches. This can lead to articles which vary considerably in terms of content, analysis and factual underpinning. Humour, 'devil's advocacy' and colourful language feature heavily. Personal 'lifestyle' and 'diary' narratives can sometimes dominate this genre. However, as Hobsbawm and Lloyd have argued persuasively, there are columnists from both ends of the print-press spectrum who are fully paid-up members of a 'commentariat [...] taken seriously by most of those who constitute the political class'.[9]

'Investigative' articles form a notoriously difficult journalism category to pin down. As I have demonstrated elsewhere there are many disputes

---

7   [N.a.], 'Phone Hacking | Media', *Guardian* (2016), https://www.theguardian.com/media/phone-hacking
8   D. Randall, *The Universal Journalist*, 4th edn. (London: Pluto Press, 2011).
9   J. Hobsbawm and J. Lloyd, *The Power of the Commentariat: How Much Do Commentators Influence Politics and Public Opinion?: A Report* (Oxford: Editorial Intelligence, 2008).

about the roots of the term, the genre and its practices.[10] In practical terms it endeavours to challenge the perceived ill of 'passivity'.[11]

Its definition is also hotly disputed. The criteria adopted by this author and based on the founding principles of the US's Investigative Reporters and Editors (IRE) group are that: the project must be the result of the author's own work and not simply the result of passive receipt of other's labours; it must be a subject that others wish to conceal from wider public knowledge; it must be relevant and have, where possible, impact and ramifications in the legal and/or legislative and policy realms. This three-point checklist is, by even seasoned journalists' standards, difficult to fulfil regularly. Aiming for at least two out of these three points usually produces hard-hitting journalism with investigative qualities.

The genre of modern investigative reporting is usually regarded as being from the Watergate era onwards — meaning from the mid-1970s. The primacy and impact of this form of journalism has been challenged, however. Both Schudson and Pilger, for example, have questioned its social and industry impact and challenged whether the myth of Watergate has been helpful to delivering agenda-changing stories and questioning the deeper, often hidden political motives which lie behind news headlines.[12] There are many constraints — inside and outside news organisations — on the ability of, and opportunity for, a journalist or group of journalists to engage in investigative journalism. Lack of finance, lack of training and specialisation, restricted access to legal advice, and a dearth of editorial encouragement and ambition in the workplace are just a few constraining factors. Lack of a guaranteed outcome in terms of a headline-grabbing story and follow-on articles (or indeed a cast-iron assurance that the entire project won't become a magnet for expensive litigation) are common reasons, often cited, for not pursuing such projects. Within the last decade, the use of Freedom of Information (FOI) laws; data journalism techniques; cross-border

---

10   E. O'Neill, 'Digging Deeper', in *Investigative Journalism: Dead or Alive?*, ed. by J. Mair and R. L. Keeble (Bury St Edmunds: Arima Publishing, 2011), pp. 291–307.

11   T. Harcup, *Journalism: Principles and Practice* (London, Thousand Oaks, New Delhi and Singapore: SAGE Publications, 2015); O'Neill (2011).

12   J. Pilger, *Tell Me No Lies: Investigative Journalism and Its Triumphs* (London: Vintage, 2005); M. Schudson, *Watergate in American Memory: How We Remember, Forget, and Reconstruct the Past* (New York: Basic Books, 1993).

projects, and other online developments, have ensured something of an evolution and resurgence of the genre. Within the UK, conferences, crowd-funded initiatives, two dedicated university masters' degrees and a plethora of major national and international stories related to the genre have assured its public and industry profile remains high.

In theoretical terms, investigative journalism is regarded highly by many as a 'watchdog' on those in power and a 'voice for the voiceless'. It therefore tends to take on myriad political meanings within that sphere and its attendant discourse. Within the more general realm of accountability post-Watergate it is broadly seen as a contributory factor in the process of ensuring a healthy democracy: '[investigative journalism has a role as] the tribune of the commoner, exerting on his or her behalf, the right to know, to examine and to criticise'.[13] In theory the pursuit of investigative projects is a noble one and its normative role within society as a force for good is a position with which I readily concur. I agree with the argument that investigative journalism involves a 'morally engaged voice' and stakes out this argument within the normative landscape discussed by Ettema and Glasser, marking out its practitioners as 'custodians of conscience'.[14] Yet, equally, I acknowledge the difficulty of the current terrain, especially within a Scottish print press context, where it is extremely difficult to do investigations for the reasons stated earlier. Individual journalists do their utmost and others on certain 'beats' co-opt investigative approaches as the need arises. This results in a patchy picture in terms of output and consistency.

The media and Scottish security pre-referendum

Taking a qualitative, methodologically-narrow approach, looking at monthly output across broadsheet newspapers in the UK, I found a cluster of articles about Scottish security in the run up to the referendum. Initially, the articles featured mainly in publications that have their headquarters in London, and take a critical tone towards the issue.

---

13 H. de Burgh, *Investigative Journalism: Context and Practice* (Abingdon and New York: Routledge, 2000), p. 282.
14 J. S. Ettema and T. L. Glasser, *Custodians of Conscience: Investigative Journalism and Public Virtue* (New York: Columbia University Press, 1998), p. 4.

In January 2013, for example, following oral evidence heard in Edinburgh by the House of Commons Foreign Affairs Committee, censorious headlines were generated in several newspapers by what was perceived as a lacklustre performance by then Deputy First Minister Nicola Sturgeon. In evidence she stated, for example, that £200 million would be budgeted for security and intelligence. This was challenged by Rory Stewart MP, who said that was for running costs only and did not include the billions of pounds required to establish the agencies required to overcome the threats she identified. Despite criticism over the lack of detail forthcoming from the Deputy First Minister, the information contained in these reports about the Scottish Government's plans was not markedly different from that which was eventually published in November of that year. The reporting of this was less widespread in Scotland-based newspapers than one might have anticipated. In-depth coverage came from the London-based papers, in particular *The Guardian*, for example, which had then only one full-time Edinburgh-based correspondent. Its report raised many of the core issues which would come, in my view, to bedevil the SNP Government's plans as the year progressed.[15] The article was in technical terms a news feature which was published in both print and digital editions.

In Scotland and in contrast, the left-leaning tabloid *The Daily Record* ran a news feature article which was largely uncritical of the SNP Government's plans and Sturgeon's evidence about a future Scottish intelligence agency. Its headline and content reported the plans outlined at her appearance but indicated little about the sceptical line of questioning to which she had reportedly been exposed.[16]

Other newspapers in England continued in a similar vein in 2013. Whilst this chapter examines, in the main, the media scrutiny of the intelligence issues contained in the White Paper, many articles surveyed tended to fold the issue in with the general SNP 'defence' plans. Others ignored this and reported the whole issue of defence in negative terms within news articles. The reporting of *The Daily Telegraph* throughout

---

15   Severin Carrell, 'Scotland Facing "Enormous" Costs for Independent Security', *Guardian*, 28 January 2013, https://www.theguardian.com/uk/2013/jan/28/scotland-enormous-costs-independent-security

16   [N.a.], 'Deputy First Minister Says Independent Scotland Will Have Its Own Security Service', *Daily Record*, 28 January 2013, http://www.dailyrecord.co.uk/news/scottish-news/scottish-government-will-set-up-its-own-security-1560814

the summer and early autumn of 2013 was indicative of the general tone and nature of its coverage of the wider defence issue.[17]

The Independent in September 2013 publicised that the Commons Defence Select Committee believed that the £2.5 billion Scottish defence budget was too low in a news feature piece. This was a full two months before *Scotland's Future* was published. *The Daily Telegraph* followed suit in November with almost precisely the same theme in another news article.[18]

Whitehall's response to the possible move to independence came in its paper *Scotland analysis: Security* in November 2013. This was taken at face value by most English newspapers in news articles which covered it and was similar in tone and content to other coverage which was critical of an independent Scotland's future security and intelligence plans. This was a subtle but nevertheless crucial issue inasmuch as little interrogation of this paper's contents were undertaken, despite their significance in relation to the separate SNP Scottish Government plans in its own White Paper.

One of the few exceptions was *The Guardian*, which scrutinised its language, factual accuracy and claims in an in-depth analysis piece by defence specialist Richard Norton-Taylor. The latter included a detailed inference that the remaining UK would not necessarily share its intelligence with an independent Scotland and that the EU and NATO wouldn't necessarily welcome an independent Scotland into the fold of either. It also noted in a somewhat sceptical tone:

> The Home Office paper also includes tendentious arguments suggesting that one of the problems would be the lack of accountability of new Scottish security and intelligence agencies.

---

17   Simon Johnson, 'Philip Hammond Pours Scorn on SNP's "Incoherent" Scottish Defence Plan', *Telegraph*, 14 March 2013, http://www.telegraph.co.uk/news/uknews/scotland/9928041/Philip-Hammond-pours-scorn-on-SNPs-incoherent-Scottish-defence-plan.html; Simon Johnson, 'MPs 'Unconvinced' by SNP Defence Plan for Independent Scotland', *Telegraph*, 27 September 2013, http://www.telegraph.co.uk/news/uknews/scotland/10337718/MPs-unconvinced-by-SNP-defence-plan-for-independent-Scotland.html

18   Nigel Morris, 'Alex Salmond's SNP Plans for Scottish Independence Criticised for Lacking Crucial Detail over Defence Plans', *Independent*, 26 September 2013, http://www.independent.co.uk/news/uk/politics/alex-salmonds-snp-plans-for-scottish-independence-criticised-for-lacking-crucial-detail-over-defence-8842555.html

As a 'separate state', Scotland could not 'share' the UK's security and intelligence agencies 'for reasons of sovereignty and democratic accountability', it says. 'They would instead continue to operate in the national interest of the continuing UK'.[19]

It adds: 'The UK could not share secret intelligence with an independent Scottish state that had been passed to it by another country without the originator's consent'.[20]

The Home Office paper continues: 'It takes time to build this trust and confidence. Other states would only share with an independent Scottish state what it was in their own interests to share'.[21]

The paper went on to explain that automatic access to the Five Eyes group of allies would not be on the cards. The Home Office makes Scotland seem as though it is just coming out of the backwoods of an unknown continent.

The conclusion that might be cautiously drawn from the coverage was that, by and large, the English-based press in news, and news features, was sceptical, critical and sometimes outright hostile to the Scottish Government's plans for security and intelligence. This was the case before and after the publication of the White Paper in November 2013. This could arguably be explained in editorial terms, by the fact that this policy was of key importance to the UK Government since an independent Scotland created, at the very least, a significant alteration to its existing defence profile. It was also an issue which might be regarded as a 'hot button' topic which could resonate with the reading public. More cynically, if editors were minded, it was also easily moulded into a scare story which cast Scotland as the 'soft underbelly' of a disunited Kingdom.

The Scottish press were focused on the myriad other policy issues related to the referendum, but when it did turn its attention — which was not often — to the issues of security and intelligence plans, it registered a less critical tone. This may have been because it was examining issues that were perhaps seen as more relevant to the average reader, or because it was simply not editorially minded to commit resources

---

to reviewing the complex nature of intelligence and security matters, a subject that requires cultivation of sources and journalistic commitment.

Others may arrive at different conclusions, of course. For example, in Chapter 6 of this volume Sandy Hardie argues that a rigorous understanding of the intelligence landscape at UK level, including the complex weave of its partnership with Scotland at multiple levels, was cold-shouldered by the Scottish media as something too hot to handle. He might be correct in some ways. However, as someone with a long professional track record in the investigative field in Scotland and elsewhere, and as someone who engaged in a BBC project directly related to this matter in the same timeframe, I sensed a more *multi-layered* series of challenges within the media when it came to covering security and intelligence issues. These were not easily explained and, even with the benefit of hindsight, remain infuriatingly complex and, at times, contradictory. However there were exceptions and I would argue that some individual case studies might be as helpful as a more sweeping approach, since they reveal how some journalists recognised that very same gap but did — within professional constraints — deliver engaging output nonetheless.

The Herald newspaper was a rare example of a newspaper regularly following this subject and reporting with detail, balance and perspective. In my view it was, with, perhaps, *The Guardian*, the exception that proved the rule. An article on 30 June 2013, for example, rebutted the widespread and more common claims that the SNP intelligence proposals were poorly planned. This piece argued that the plans were feasible and the existing institutional experience within the Scottish police ranks could adapt to the proposed new arrangements. Using their own source, an authority figure with a professional track record in this arena, they laid out an alternative view than that heavily featured in mostly London-based sources in previous articles:[22]

> Allan Burnett insisted security services could be 'readily created' and traditional alliances easily maintained if Scots vote Yes next year.
> His remarks come as figures close to the UK security establishment warn that SNP strategists have 'naïvely' underestimated how much time and money it will take to create a secret police service.

---

22   David Leask, 'Spy Wars', *Herald*, 30 June 2013, http://www.heraldscotland.com/news/13111636.Spy_wars/

Burnett was the old Strathclyde Police's head of intelligence and Scotland's counter-terrorism co-ordinator before retiring in 2010 with the rank of assistant chief constable, and endorsing the SNP.

He believes Scottish policing — with the biggest Special Branch outside London and substantial existing capacity to deal with terrorists and organised crime — already has the basis of a strong MI5-style domestic security service.

He has accused UK authorities of refusing to discuss post-independence intelligence sharing in order 'to cut off debate' on the issue.

Burnett said: 'Their studied intention is to fill the discussion gap they have created with scurrilous scaremongering. "The Americans won't share intelligence with you", "you're leaving yourselves open to terrorist attack". The truth is that an independent Scotland would face less of a threat, intelligence institutions will be readily created, and allies will remain allies'.

The Herald followed this up with another news piece a month later at the end of July 2013, which lent another fresh perspective on the issue. This suggested that Scottish civil servants were exploring Scandinavian intelligence models which might be transplanted into a Scottish context in a future independent Scotland:

Scottish civil servants are investigating how to create Nordic-style intelligence services post-independence.

The Sunday Herald understands government officials have been sounding out international experts on security for more than a year.

Their focus, sources stress, is firmly on developing the kind of counter-espionage and counter-terrorist capacity developed in NATO members Norway and Denmark and neutral Sweden.[23]

The report continued with details of how Scottish academics and members of the Scottish government had met to discuss Nordic models of a post-independence security and intelligence model. Unlike the consistently negative tones woven through earlier articles in London-based newspapers, this article introduced new information (e.g. the Nordic model) into the debate, emphasising their relatively small intelligence operations while pointing out that they were still trusted

---

23   David Leask, 'Scottish Civil Servants Probe Plans for "Nordic" Intelligence Services after Independence', *Herald*, 28 July 2013, http://www.heraldscotland.com/news/13115795.Scottish_civil_servants_probe_plans_for__Nordic__intelligence_services_after_independence/

western partners. The piece still aimed for balance by continuing with comments from sceptical contributors whose backgrounds were mentioned for context:

> Pro-UK politicians have cast doubts on the ability of any Nordic-style Scottish domestic security service to quickly become a trusted ally of MI6 and the CIA.
> Former MI6 officer Meta Ramsay — a Labour peer — has called SNP rhetoric on the issue 'extremely naive'.
> However, Ramsay, who served in Finland and Sweden during the Cold War, is also an admirer of Nordic intelligence services.
> But she also disagrees on how easy it would be to create a Nordic-style domestic security service, perhaps on the basis of existing police special branch capability.
> Other intelligence experts contacted by the Sunday Herald acknowledge Scotland would take time to build up relationships — but stressed the country would have information that it could bargain for access to the intelligence services of western allies.[24]

The article then concluded with 'official' comment from the Scottish Government itself:

> Asked about the civil servants investigation into creating a Nordic-style intelligence service a Scottish Government spokesperson said: 'The Scottish Government is engaging with a wide range of experts and stakeholders in developing its proposals for independence.
> This engagement includes informal discussions as well as consideration of proposals by leading experts in panels such as the Fiscal Commission Working Group, the Welfare Commission, and the Expert Commission on Energy Regulation announced earlier this month.[25]

This article conforms to a 'new chapter' or 'follow-up' news piece. It contains revelations on the basis of original reporting and aims at balance and to provide context throughout. Neither side in the debate is given favourable status. The tone of the piece is one of revelation and veracity. The official source — in this case the UK Government — is quoted only at the end and it is therefore not elevated to a status of higher-truth or authoritative knowledge.

Earlier in July 2014 *The Herald* ran a brief but significant opinion piece regarding the 'pros and cons' of an independent Scotland establishing

---

24   *Ibid.*
25   *Ibid.*

its own cyber-security strategy. This was written by Dr Neil Anderson, Security Director at the FarrPoint consultancy, and conformed to the model of being an 'expert' authored piece, written without any political view or agenda that the host newspaper might retain, aiming for verifiable factual accuracy and a degree of professional balance in his capacity as a consultant. The article introduced the 'both sides' approach, detailing the opportunities and potential pitfalls of an independent Scotland having to organise its own cyber defences. It listed the potential challenges and structural focus the new operation would potentially need to plan for:

> Clearly, the move to an independent government would lead to a change in priorities for the security services, which could include:
> • Moving away from mass surveillance and a dragnet approach to intelligence gathering.
> • Concentrating cyber security defences on critical economic and commercial interests, building on the experience of other European countries such as Estonia. Estonia is considered to be the world leader in national cyber defence after a co-ordinated Russian cyber attack in 2007.
> • Making domestic counter-insurgency and counter-terrorism work, such as that undertaken by GCHQ and MI5, less of a priority.
> • Supervision of the intelligence service becoming open and democratically accountable.[26]

There are significant caveats around a Scottish intelligence agency's room for manoeuvre on some of these points. The physical network layout throughout Scotland and the UK means that very few connections from other countries land in Scotland, with most landing in Cornwall near GCHQ's listening post at Bude. This means that, at least in the medium term, internet and corporate network traffic would be subject to UK Government surveillance, regardless of the wishes of the Scottish Government. It is likely that a condition of support from allied intelligence agencies would be cooperation in sharing signals intelligence with other agencies.[27]

---

26   Neil Anderson, 'Agenda: Pros and Cons of an Independent Scotland's Cyber Security Strategy', *Herald*, 10 July 2014, http://www.heraldscotland.com/opinion/13169217. Agenda__Pros_and_cons_of_an_independent_Scotland_s_cyber_security_strategy/
27   *Ibid.*

The piece continues with an analysis of the situation should independence not be chosen in the referendum, suggesting that there is perhaps something to be said for Scotland having access to the UK's intelligence services and their output, but also reflecting on the implications for Scotland's own cyber-defence's strategic priorities within a system that regards anti-terrorism as its own top priority. It concludes: 'Whichever way the vote goes, it is clear that there are opportunities and risks for Scotland on both sides'.[28]

The article introduced a fresh and important perspective to the debate inasmuch as it moved away from the debate about how 'safe' an independent Scotland would be, towards another perspective which asks what should Scotland be defending which is different from the current UK-wide model? The information and detail published in the article answer that from a detached point of view, laying out facts and views which were not politically partial or partisan in language.

Part of the connective tissue of the independent Scotland and intelligence issue debate was the long-held belief in some quarters that the UK security services had covertly interfered in the political arena in the past, were currently interfering, and would interfere at some unspecified point in the future. As far back as 2007, for example, *Scotland On Sunday* reported that:

> THE SNP was spied on by British secret service agents, previously classified Government files seen by *Scotland on Sunday* have finally proved.
> Claims of surveillance of nationalist politicians by intelligence officers have circulated for years, but the new papers provide the first incontrovertible evidence that the state spied on the SNP in the 1950s.
> Agents from MI5 and Special Branch infiltrated the party as part of a campaign to undermine support for Scottish independence, the papers show.
> The revelations have put First Minister Alex Salmond — who in opposition complained about closed Government files on the SNP — under pressure to close a legal loophole that allows the secret services to intercept the calls of Scottish parliamentarians.

---

28 *Ibid.*; Gerry Braiden, 'Inside Track: MI5 Input in the Independence Debate', *Herald*, 7 July 2014, http://www.heraldscotland.com/opinion/13168760.INSIDE_TRACK__MI5_input_in_the_independence_debate/

The files, which have been opened and placed in the UK National Archives in Kew, show that throughout the 1950s Special Branch officers posed as Nationalist supporters and attended party meetings and rallies.

> The dossiers contain first-hand accounts from numerous unnamed agents of party meetings, and also include names of SNP members and sympathisers. They also provided transcripts of speeches and give particular attention to members they believed were on the more radical and militant wing of the party.[29]

The same theme was updated in early June 2013 when *The Herald* ran an article about a letter sent by a leading high-profile Nationalist (a popular and influential MSP, but not a member of the governing SNP, it should be noted) to the then head of MI5 asking for assurance that the agency was not interfering in the referendum debate and process. The letter acted as the 'peg' for the article, thus allowing the topic to be aired without any hard evidence of the interference being a reality. The MSP, and the article itself, then referred back to the 1970s and the allegations surrounding the UK security services being complicit in undermining the Wilson government. The article aims to balance this approach towards the end when a source with security credentials is asked about the likelihood of MI5 interfering in the referendum process. His answer suggests any involvement would be benign, even helpful:

> Crispin Black, a former intelligence adviser to ex-prime minister Tony Blair and the Joint Intelligence Committee, said he believed MI5 would monitor the independence debate: 'My guess is that MI5 would have the referendum on its radar, primarily to ensure its fairness. There's definitely a national security angle to Scottish independence that the security services would be aware of, but my sense is that they would be stopping dirty tricks, rather than trying to initiate them'.[30]

In July 2014, an opinion column in *The Herald* returned briefly to the same issue, urging readers to take the issue seriously in light of some historical and recent developments in the intelligence world. This was

---

29 [N.a.], 'Files Prove That MI5 Spied on SNP', *Scotsman*, 16 June 2007, http://www.scotsman.com/news/politics/files-prove-that-mi5-spied-on-snp-1-1423283

30 Paul Hutcheon, 'MI5 Spies Told: Stay out of Referendum', *Herald*, 9 June 2013, http://www.heraldscotland.com/news/13108551.MI5_spies_told__stay_out_of_referendum/

a piece that was rightly labelled as 'opinion' since, although timely and thought-provoking, it did not deliver fresh revelations to support its thesis.[31]

The same newspaper ran another piece reporting on another news organisation's opinion poll which stated that 25% of the 1084 individuals polled by YouGov in previous weeks thought that MI5 would try to 'prevent' a Yes vote or 'rig' the outcome.[32] It was a headline that could have gone in several directions, since the statistics suggested an overwhelming majority of people were sceptical of the thesis that MI5 was carrying out 'skullduggery' in the ten days before the referendum vote, and indeed the poll was split when the additional question of UK concealment of oil fields was asked.[33] Read another way, the poll results could have produced very different headlines. Moreover, the response to the proposition, without any special knowledge or insight on either the pollsters' or the participants' parts rendered the results merely indicative of a vague belief without any verifiable information with which to work.[34] This piece, which broadly conforms to the 'news feature' model was constrained by the reporting of a separate news organisation's poll findings, and had no control over the questions asked and played no role in the design of the study. This perhaps accounted for the timing of the article and its inherent limitations of meaning, resonance and depth.

On a freelance basis, during 2014, and against the press background examined in this chapter, I began researching the issues surrounding this debate for a BBC Radio Scotland documentary. Initially this was aimed at being a pre-referendum production but eventually it was strongly suggested that it would work better after the referendum. BBC Scotland at that time, and indeed since, came under criticism for their coverage of the referendum, mostly from pro-independence campaigners. In recent times the BBC's own Audience Council in Scotland also levelled

---

31 Braiden, *Herald*, 7 July 2014.

32 David Leask, 'One-Quarter Fear MI5 Will Try to Prevent Yes Vote', *Herald*, 8 September 2014, http://www.heraldscotland.com/news/13178861.One_quarter_fear_MI5_will_try_to_prevent_Yes_vote/

33 *Ibid.*

34 *Ibid.*

criticism at the broadcaster for being too 'anglicised' in its coverage.[35] In this atmosphere a project looking at 'Spying in the 21st Century' was potentially a difficult one to undertake. The usual worries about producer's guidelines, balance, and impartiality were aired. Little additional investigative work of this type on this topic was undertaken by colleagues. This was probably due to the normal budgetary concerns (i.e. investigative projects are usually more expensive and require specialisation, editorially and sometimes legally) and the news-value judgement that other topics related to, for example, the economy, health, and currency, might be more important to audiences. Due to the fact that some sources I consulted were retired ex-intelligence officers, I also had to consult the BBC's own lawyers in case security was breached during interviews.

One key area, which everyone was sensitive to, was the matter of reviewing the Scottish Government's White Paper in a way which might, as one producer put it, be seen, 'after the fact'. Producers felt it was unfair and potentially damaging to scrutinise the issue a few months after the referendum result — No — had been delivered by the Scottish electorate on 18 September 2014. I therefore had to focus on the history of Scots in the security services; the role of the intelligence community in Scotland; and briefly, the implications for security if Scotland had become — or were to become — an independent nation. Former Special Branch, MI5 and MI6 officers, as well as security experts and academics in security research, were consulted. This was my attempt to bring an investigative slant to the debate, utilise some of the primary and secondary material available as an academic, access the press reporting mentioned throughout this chapter, and deliver a project which might be, at least, thought-provoking around the wider theme. It was never designed to be definitive or the last word on the issue — rather it aimed to be part of the discussion. What was significant, however, was the availability of sources willing to shed light on all aspects of the debate under discussion. This suggests that if other journalists and editors had chosen to look at this issue in a committed and consistent form before

---

35   [N.a.], 'BBC Urged to Review Scottish Coverage in Wake of Independence Row BBC Urged to Review Scottish Coverage in Wake of Independence Row', *Guardian*, 14 July 2015, https://www.theguardian.com/media/2015/jul/14/bbc-scottish-coverage-independence-row-referendum

the independence referendum then it could have been achievable. This assumes both editorial and financial support and, for the journalist, a realistic amount of time to investigate the matter and, where applicable, the resources to scrutinise it in depth across the UK. Specialised security experience and contacts within the sector would have helped focus and refine this undertaking and assisted in the quality of the final report.

Conclusions

The majority of the journalism looking at the issue of the referendum and the implications for Scotland's intelligence capabilities fell into the categories of news, features, opinion and contributing commentary. There was little, if any at all, investigative journalism pre-referendum as commonly defined within the industry or indeed the academy's definitions. Even under the constraints mentioned, this was enormously regrettable, since it would have probably widened, deepened and added illumination to this debate within the public sphere.

London-based publications by and large produced articles which sounded concern and even alarm for the perceived wider negative implications for UK security of the prospect of Scottish independence. Some Scottish publications implicitly followed this line. Most were predicated upon press releases, briefings and interviews from London-based sources, although some did use Scotland-based sources too. The quality of these in terms of balance, research, verifiable fact and impartiality varied. Scotland-based publications' interest in the issue also varied. *The Herald* consistently added new information to the debate, whilst making a genuine attempt to bring fresh voices and wider understanding to the topic. Their output looking at MI5 involvement, and the late poll supporting this notion, was not developed. For the most part, critical voices challenging their 'top line' themes were not avoided and their readers may have benefitted from this work. Amongst all the publishers they were potentially best placed to deliver a significant investigative contribution to the mix had they been so minded.

My own contribution was undertaken against a post-referendum landscape where, arguably, appetite for anything related to the process was diminished. Its contents were refined during the editorial process to reflect a wider historical and cultural context with less emphasis on investigating the contents of the Scottish Government's security and intelligence plans. Instead, the discussion of these issues was explored in the last quarter of the programme. It is for others to judge how successful this was at analysing the contents of the plans laid out for the Scottish people and as an attempt at looking at the matter through the approach of investigative journalism.[36]

---

36   [N.a.], 'Spying in the 21st Century: How Safe Are You?', BBC Radio Scotland, 13 January 2015, http://www.bbc.co.uk/programmes/b04xrv6c

References

[N.a.], 'Files Prove That MI5 Spied on SNP', *Scotsman*, 16 June 2007, http://www.scotsman.com/news/politics/files-prove-that-mi5-spied-on-snp-1-1423283

——, 'Deputy First Minister Says Independent Scotland Will Have Its Own Security Service', *Daily Record*, 28 January 2013, http://www.dailyrecord.co.uk/news/scottish-news/scottish-government-will-set-up-its-own-security-1560814

——, 'Spying in the 21st Century: How Safe Are You?', BBC Radio Scotland, 13 January 2015, http://www.bbc.co.uk/programmes/b04xrv6c

——, 'BBC Urged to Review Scottish Coverage in Wake of Independence Row', *Guardian*, 14 July 2015, https://www.theguardian.com/media/2015/jul/14/bbc-scottish-coverage-independence-row-referendum

——, 'Phone Hacking | Media', *Guardian* (2016), https://www.theguardian.com/media/phone-hacking

Anderson, Neil, 'Agenda: Pros and Cons of an Independent Scotland's Cyber Security Strategy', *Herald*, 10 July 2014, http://www.heraldscotland.com/opinion/13169217.Agenda__Pros_and_cons_of_an_independent_Scotland_s_cyber_security_strategy/

Braiden, Gerry, 'Inside Track: MI5 Input in the Independence Debate', *Herald*, 7 July 2014, http://www.heraldscotland.com/opinion/13168760.INSIDE_TRACK__MI5_input_in_the_independence_debate/

Carrell, Severin, 'Scotland Facing "Enormous" Costs for Independent Security', *Guardian*, 28 January 2013, https://www.theguardian.com/uk/2013/jan/28/scotland-enormous-costs-independent-security

de Burgh, H., *Investigative Journalism: Context and Practice, Investigative Journalism: Context and Practice* (Abingdon and New York: Routledge, 2000).

Ettema, J. S. and Glasser, T. L., *Custodians of Conscience: Investigative Journalism and Public Virtue* (New York: Columbia University Press, 1998).

Harcup, T., *Journalism: Principles and Practice* (London, Thousand Oaks, New Delhi and Singapore: SAGE Publications, 2015).

Hobsbawm, J. and Lloyd, J., *The Power of the Commentariat: How Much Do Commentators Influence Politics and Public Opinion?: A Report* (Oxford: Editorial Intelligence, 2008).

Hutcheon, Paul, 'MI5 Spies Told: Stay Out of Referendum', *Herald*, 9 June 2013, http://www.heraldscotland.com/news/13108551.MI5_spies_told__stay_out_of_referendum/

Johnson, Simon, 'Philip Hammond Pours Scorn on SNP's "Incoherent" Scottish Defence Plan', *Telegraph*, 14 March 2013, http://www.telegraph.co.uk/news/uknews/scotland/9928041/Philip-Hammond-pours-scorn-on-SNPs-incoherent-Scottish-defence-plan.html

—, 'MPs "Unconvinced" by SNP Defence Plan for Independent Scotland', *Telegraph*, 27 September 2013, http://www.telegraph.co.uk/news/uk news/scotland/10337718/MPs-unconvinced-by-SNP-defence-plan-for-independent-Scotland.html

Leask, David, 'Spy Wars', *Herald*, 30 June 2013, http://www.heraldscotland.com/ news/13111636.Spy_wars/

—, 'Scottish Civil Servants Probe Plans for 'Nordic' Intelligence Services after Independence', *Herald*, 28 July 2013, http://www.heraldscotland. com/news/13115795.Scottish_civil_servants_probe_plans_for__Nordic__ intelligence_services_after_independence/

—, 'One-Quarter Fear MI5 Will Try to Prevent Yes Vote', *Herald*, 8 September 2014, http://www.heraldscotland.com/news/13178861.One_quarter_fear_ MI5_will_try_to_prevent_Yes_vote/

McKenna, Kevin, 'Would Independent Scotland Have Its Own Spies?', *The Japan Times*, 8 April 2014, http://www.japantimes.co.jp/opinion/2014/04/08/ commentary/world-commentary/would-independent-scotland-have-its-own-spies/ - .WEFgFqKLSgQ

Morris, Nigel, 'Alex Salmond's SNP Plans for Scottish Independence Criticised for Lacking Crucial Detail over Defence Plans', *Independent*, 26 September 2013, http://www.independent.co.uk/news/uk/politics/alex-salmonds-snp-plans-for-scottish-independence-criticised-for-lacking-crucial-detail-over-defence-8842555.html

Norton-Taylor, Richard, 'Scotland: Playing Games with Britain's Security', *Guardian*, 7 November 2013, https://www.theguardian.com/uk-news/ defence-and-security-blog/2013/nov/07/scotland-security-shipbuilding

O'Neill, E., 'Digging Deeper', in *Investigative Journalism: Dead or Alive?*, ed. by J. Mair and R. L. Keeble (Bury St Edmunds: Arima Publishing, 2011), pp. 291–307.

Pilger, J., *Tell Me No Lies: Investigative Journalism and Its Triumphs* (London: Vintage, 2005).

Randall, D., *The Universal Journalist*, 4th edn. (London: Pluto Press, 2011).

Schudson, M., *Watergate in American Memory: How We Remember, Forget, and Reconstruct the Past* (New York: Basic Books, 1993).

Scottish Government, *Scotland's Future: Your Guide to an Independent Scotland* (Edinburgh: Scottish Government, 2013), http://www.gov.scot/ resource/0043/00439021.pdf

Smith, A. and Higgins, M., *The Language of Journalism: A Multi-Genre Perspective* (New York and London: Bloomsbury Publishing, 2013).

8. To Speak Security or Not to Speak Security? Responsibility and Deference in the Scottish Independence Debate

Andrew W. Neal

This chapter is about how and why security was debated and not debated in the Scottish independence referendum campaigns. It begins with a summary of the security content of the campaigns in the run up to the vote, arguing that 'security' was not entirely absent but not prominent either. The main focus is to discuss the political implications of speaking security, using the lens of securitisation theory. It argues that more security talk is not necessarily a good thing, because it may ramp up fear and mobilise security apparatuses. The chapter then considers the implications of staying silent on security, which are not innocent either. This is because historically, the power and authority of the state to declare and define security threats depended on the silent deference of the wider political class. By demonstration, the chapter compares the quietude of security politics in Scotland with the history and transformation of security politics at Westminster.

https://doi.org/10.11647/OBP.0078.08

Security was not absent from the independence debate, but nor was it prominent.[1] In Scotland, the highest profile security issue was Trident, although in policy and academic parlance this is a matter of 'defence' rather than 'security'.[2] The 670 page Scottish Government White Paper offered a chapter on international relations and defence and another containing six pages on security and intelligence. The latter offered proposals for an independent Scotland to work closely with current allies, create stronger constitutional limitations on war powers, and establish a single Scottish intelligence agency that would operate within a strong human rights framework.[3]

Measured by volume of material, the UK Government and UK Parliament produced more. This included the UK Government's 'Scotland Analysis' papers on defence and security. The latter is particularly interesting, representing an unprecedented accounting of every possible security-related agency in the UK, drawn very widely, from the intelligence services and their offshoots to specialised police agencies such as the Financial Intelligence Unit.[4] At the same time, parliament conducted inquiries into the defence, foreign policy, security, and intelligence implications of Scottish independence via its select committees.[5] The Foreign Affairs Committee evidence session

---

1   For more forensic examinations of the debate, see Chapters 6 and 7 in this volume.
2   For the Nationalists, demanding the removal of Trident from Scotland seemed more a matter of principle than national security as such. The SNP policy to remain in NATO — a nuclear defence alliance — suggested they did not wish to abandon the principle of nuclear deterrence entirely, or at least that their internal policy-making process had produced an ambiguity.
3   Scottish Government, *Scotland's Future: Your Guide to an Independent Scotland* (Edinburgh: Scottish Government, 2013), http://www.gov.scot/resource/0043/00 439021.pdf, pp. 232–51, 61–67.
4   HM Government, *Scotland Analysis: Cm. 8741: Security* (London: HMSO, 2013), https://www.gov.uk/government/uploads/system/uploads/attachment_data/ file/253500/Scotland_analysis_security.pdf
5   Scottish Affairs Committee, *The Referendum on Separation for Scotland: A Defence Force for Scotland-a Conspiracy of Optimism?* (London: House of Commons, 2012); Scottish Affairs Committee, *The Referendum on Separation for Scotland: How Would Separation Affect Jobs in the Scottish Defence Industry?, Eighth Report of Session 2012–13, Report, Together with Formal Minutes* (London: HMSO, 2013); Defence Committee, *The Defence Implications of Possible Scottish Independence. Sixth Report of Session 2013–14, Volume 1: Report, Together with an Appendix, Formal Minutes and Oral Evidence* (London: HMSO, 2013), https://books.google.co.uk/books?id=Ck76yDPw1r8C; Foreign Affairs Committee, 'Inquiry into Foreign Policy Implications of and for a Separate Scotland' (2012), http://www.parliament.uk/business/committees/committees-a-z/ commons-select/foreign-affairs-committee/inquiries1/parliament-2010/scotland/;

held in Edinburgh in January 2013 was significant because it seems to have changed SNP policy.[6] Nicola Sturgeon told the committee that her colleagues were consulting on the feasibility of a Scottish foreign intelligence service, a Scottish MI6 in effect. Committee member Rory Stewart MP made this look unrealistic through his questioning, pointing out the costs and the fact that only a handful of larger states had the capacity to maintain dedicated foreign intelligence services. The subsequent White Paper proposed that an independent Scotland would have only a single combined intelligence agency.

These documents and inquiries were discussed in the press by various protagonists and analysts, but they were not a feature of the headline public debate. More general security discussion was not extensive when compared with contentious issues such as the currency of an independent Scotland or the longevity of North Sea oil. In the televised debates, few questions asked were about national security or related issues such as terrorism. In one exception early on, Home Secretary Theresa May and Defence Secretary Philip Hammond made speeches claiming that an independent Scotland would be at greater risk of terrorist attack if it was deprived of the security umbrella and border controls of the UK.[7] Yet despite claims that the private name for the 'Better Together' campaign was 'Project Fear',[8] pro-Union campaigners did not repeat this type of security argument, which was easily dismissed by Nationalists as scaremongering.

Neither side made security a prominent feature of their campaigns. Instead, they repeated predictable and relatively uncontroversial lines. For the Nationalist, an independent Scotland would be secure outside

---

Foreign Affairs Committee (2013); Scottish Affairs Committee, *The Referendum on Separation for Scotland: Terminating Trident — Days or Decades?, Fourth Report of Session 2012–13, Report, Together with Formal Minutes* (London: HMSO, 2012).

6   N. Sturgeon evidence to the Foreign Affairs Committee, *Foreign Policy Considerations for the UK and Scotland in the Event of Scotland Becoming an Independent Country, Sixth Report of Session 2012–2013* (London: HMSO, 2013), http://www.publications. parliament.uk/pa/cm201213/cmselect/cmfaff/643/643.pdf, Ev 62.

7   [N.a.], 'Home Secretary Theresa May in Scots Immigration Warning', *BBC News*, 24 March 2012, http://www.bbc.co.uk/news/uk-scotland-scotland-politics-17498681; [N.a.], 'Scottish Independence: Warning over "Weakened Military"', *BBC News*, 2 June 2013, http://www.bbc.co.uk/news/uk-scotland-scotland-politics-21776602

8   Tom Gordon, 'I Admit It: The Man Who Coined the Project Fear Label', *Herald Scotland*, 21 December 2014, http://www.heraldscotland.com/news/13194407. I_admit_it__the_man_who_coined_Project_Fear_label/

the UK, and an independent Scottish government would act responsibly to make that so; for the Unionist, Scotland would be more secure within the UK, where it would continue to enjoy the protections of an extensive and well-established security and intelligence apparatus. Seen through the simplest interest-based political lens, Nationalists had an obvious stake in reassuring the public that Scotland did not face threats it could not manage alone or through anticipated partnerships with allies. Unionists had an obvious stake in stressing that an independent Scotland faced an uncertain world, and could no longer depend upon the UK security umbrella.

Arguably, there was an element of disingenuousness in both these positions, not because of their contestable assessment of threat, but because the future security partnerships of an independent Scotland were difficult to foresee. They would depend on the future goodwill of other states, particularly the remaining UK and US. The Nationalist and Unionist positions could be seen as performative, in that they attempted to describe a certain future in order to shape the politics of the present, and to 'perform' a particular reality. Neither side displayed an appetite to push security issues further. As such, security did not become as politicized as other issues.

Away from the campaigns, there were several attempts to provide independent expert assessments of the threats an independent Scotland might face. Examples included papers by the Royal United Services Institute (RUSI) and Chatham House, although these organisations are closely associated with the UK defence and intelligence community.[9] The reports of our ESRC seminar series, 'Security in Scotland, with or without Constitutional Change', offered a different perspective.[10] In particular, they pointed out that many important security-related questions that

---

9   Rebecca Johnson and others, *No Need to Be Afraid: An Assessment of Possible Threats to Scotland's Security and How They Should Be Addressed* (Biggar: The Jimmy Reid Foundation, 2012); Malcolm Chalmers, 'The End of an "Auld Sang"': Defence in an Independent Scotland', *RUSI Briefing Paper* (2012); Chatham House, 'Scotland's Independence Referendum', Chatham House (London   2013),   https://www.chathamhouse.org/research/regions/europe/UK/ scotlands-independence-referendum

10   Andrew W. Neal, Julie Kaarbo, and Charles Raab, 'ESRC Seminar Series: "Security in Scotland, with or without Constitutional Change"', Centre on Constitutional Change (Edinburgh 2013–2015), http://www.centreonconstitutionalchange.ac.uk/ tags/security-defence

a newly independent Scotland would face had not been discussed in public. These neglected issues included the democratic accountability of the UK security services in Scotland during the transition to independence and beyond, and the constitutional implications of any future security cooperation and intelligence sharing between Scotland and the remaining UK.[11] These expert reports received media coverage, but were not widely debated or politicised.[12]

With this summary in mind, the aim of this chapter is to consider the political implications of the security debate, or lack of. How should we judge the fact that security was not widely discussed? How much public debate on security would have been enough? To take the democratic position that more public debate is always better does not adequately consider the risks posed by security talk (see, for example, Chapter 7 in this volume). On the other hand, to take the 'securitarian' position that the threat always needs to be taken more seriously does not consider the extent to which security is a matter of intersubjective and manipulable collective fears, rather than merely cold hard realities (see, for example, Chapter 6 in this book). This chapter will argue that both security speech and security silence are implicated in the processes that shape and construct insecurities. This must be considered in light of the historic role that deference and recognition have played in the reproduction of state-based security authority.

The dilemma of speaking security

The idea that there is no simple way to 'measure' the reality of security threats has long been a cornerstone of the academic study of security.[13] This is because there is no neutral and objective Archimedean point from which to judge. Security threats are in the eye of the beholder. It is not that they are not real, but their perception and meaning is as much a part of their social and political 'reality' as any 'objective' aspect.

---

11 Andrew W. Neal, 'Fourth Report: Intelligence and Security Oversight in an Independent Scotland' (2014), http://www.centreonconstitutionalchange.ac.uk/sites/default/files/papers/Intelligence and security oversight in an independent scotland 4th REPORT FINAL.pdf

12 Although see the 'clash' prompted by our first report: [N.a.] (2013).

13 Barry Buzan, Ole Wæver, and Jaap de Wilde, *Security: A New Framework for Analysis* (Boulder and London: Lynne Rienner, 1998), p. 24.

This is to say nothing about the physical destructiveness or likelihood of explosions, storms, floods, etc. Rather, it is to highlight the role that fear, judgment, and subjectivity play in how governments and publics perceive threats.

Securitisation theory starts from this position. Its contribution is to offer an explanation of how insecurities are socially constructed through speech, and specifically through securitising speech acts that follow an established 'grammar' of threat, urgency, and exception.[14] This makes 'security' not a question of 'realities out there', but of political choices and responsibilities. Its founder Ole Waever argues:

> The securitization approach points to the inherently political nature of any designation of security issues and thus it puts an ethical question at the feet of analysts, decision-makers and activists alike: why do you call this a security issue? What are the implications of doing this — or of not doing it?[15]

Speaking security thus has constitutive effects on *insecurities*, and potentially in turn on security policy and practice. To talk about an issue in terms of 'security' — rather than in alternative terms such as 'social problem', 'political challenge' or 'economic opportunity' — adds to the security inflection of that issue. Such talk may help to justify draconian policies, make certain communities 'suspect', or persuade governments to remove issues from open deliberation in favour of closed executive decisions or other security 'black boxes' within the state. It may encourage a permissive atmosphere for violence and contribute to a general politics of fear. Whoever speaks security in public must be careful about the consequences. These concerns about responsibility have long been at the heart of securitisation theory.

The idea of a *dilemma* of speaking security comes from Jef Huysmans.[16] Huysmans teases out elements of securitisation theory to stress that processes of securitisation through speech do not occur

---

14 Buzan, Wæver, and de Wilde (1998), p. 32.

15 Ole Wæver, 'Securitizing Sectors?: Reply to Eriksson', *Cooperation and Conflict*, 34, 3 (1999), 334–40 (p. 334).

16 Jef Huysmans, 'Defining Social Constructivism in Security Studies: The Normative Dilemma of Writing Security', *Alternatives: Global, Local, Political*, 27, suppl. 1 (2002), 41–62. Huysmans (p. 62) uses the term 'writing security', in reference to David Campbell, *Writing Security: United States Foreign Policy and the Policies of Identity* (Manchester: Manchester University Press, 1992).

in a vacuum. 'Security' is historically and conceptually associated with an institutionalised set of security structures, expectations, and prerogatives, such as sovereign war powers and the military.[17] To talk about an issue in security terms may mean not only constructing it as a security issue, but mobilising existing security institutions and pathways.[18]

According to this view, the implications of security speech concern more than the immediate and instrumental political choice to construct a security issue or not. Security speech can tend towards extremes because 'security' is already historically structured as a discourse and practice of extremes. The legacy of 'security' is one of existential threats, operational secrecy, and exceptional security powers.[19] In any discussion of security there are already certain historical and institutionalised pathways that may end up being followed. Security speech — by potentially waking this sleeping giant of 'security' — can bring about consequences that reach 'beyond the intentions and control of the individual's practices of definition'.[20] Huysmans writes, 'speaking and writing about security is never innocent [...]. Security writings participate in a political field where social questions are already contested in terms of crisis, threats, and dangers'.[21]

To consider security and Scottish independence in terms of a dilemma of speaking security is to highlight the role of security speech in constituting insecurities and the perceived landscape of security threats faced by a country. In this light, the protagonists in the debate about Scottish independence did not simply face a political choice about how seriously to take 'real' security threats. Rather they faced a choice about how to speak about security in a volatile political situation that risked mobilising the historical grammar and institutional pathways of security. In the event, there was in fact little security talk in the Scottish independence debate, which largely avoided the risks of speaking

---

17 Huysmans (2002), pp. 42–43.
18 *Ibid.*
19 One problem with securitisation theory is that it, 'note[s] the sedimentation of a certain meaning of security, but transform[s] this observation into a conceptual axiom', as Felix Çiuta puts it in his 'Security and the Problem of Context: A Hermeneutical Critique of Securitisation Theory', *Review of International Studies*, 35, 02 (2009), 301–26 (p. 321).
20 Huysmans (2002), p. 42.
21 *Ibid.*, p. 43.

security. Nevertheless, this relative silence should not be considered innocent.

The dilemma of *not* speaking security

What did the referendum protagonists do by *not* speaking security? Waever implies in his quote above that there are implications and responsibilities in the choice *not* to securitise.[22] There is always the choice to talk down a perceived threat, to de-escalate a relationship of enmity, or to find alternative, non-securitarian terms of debate. This is to *desecuritise* an issue.[23]

Waever's ideas about securitisation and desecuritisation were inspired by the peace initiatives and East-West détente of the late 1980s. His theory established the idea that speech could construct issues as security issues, but that, in turn, speech could deconstruct them back into 'merely political' issues through desecuritisation.[24] Michael C. Williams argues that this two-way process offers hope from a democratic point of view: because securitisation is part of the discursive realm, 'security practices are thus susceptible to criticism and transformation'.[25] But this begs the question of security and silence: what if there is little security discourse in the first place?

Writing from a feminist perspective, Lene Hansen once mooted the possibility of a 'silent security dilemma'.[26] She pointed out the difficulty vulnerable individuals and groups may have in vocalising their insecurity. Examples include women facing domestic violence, or minorities persecuted in a repressive society. Hansen argued that this dilemma, 'occurs when insecurity cannot be voiced, when raising something as a security problem is impossible or might even aggravate

---

22   Wæver (1999), p. 334.

23   Ole Wæver, 'Securitization and Desecuritization', in *On Security*, ed. by Ronnie D. Lipschutz (New York and Chichester: Columbia University Press, 1995), pp. 46–86.

24   Buzan, Wæver, and de Wilde (1998), pp. 4–5; See also Lene Hansen, 'Reconstructing Desecuritisation: The Normative-Political in the Copenhagen School and Directions for How to Apply It', *Review of International Studies*, 38, 03 (2012), 525–46.

25   Michael C. Williams, 'Words, Images, Enemies: Securitization and International Politics', *International Studies Quarterly*, 47, 4 (2003), 511–31 (p. 512).

26   Lene Hansen, 'The Little Mermaid's Silent Security Dilemma and the Absence of Gender in the Copenhagen School', *Millennium-Journal of International Studies*, 29, 2 (2000), 285–306.

the threat being faced'.[27] Hansen is concerned about the occasions when the subject cannot speak, when they cannot vocalise what threatens them.

However, silence may not only be a sign of marginalisation or exclusion. French sociologist Pierre Bourdieu argued that silence may function as a form of power. It may confer legitimacy and recognition on those who *do* speak. Silence from a group, and 'the absence of any refutation', may imply that the one who is speaking speaks for them.[28] Silence may signify acquiescence, deference, or recognition. For Bourdieu, power depends on the conscious and unconscious choices of actors to go along with received wisdom and not to challenge recognised authorities. Such deference may be freely willed, but also coincide with subordinate positions in hierarchical power relationships, such as backbenchers toeing the party line. It may also reflect agreement, consensus, and shared outlooks on, for example, the nature of security threats and what should be done about them. As a former member of the Intelligence Security Committee explained to me on the committee's lack of internal divisions: 'It's not that it's not political, but that we all agree'.[29]

This calls for an extension of Huysmans' dilemma of speaking security. I argue that there is a political dilemma posed not only by the choice to speak security, but also by the choice *not* to speak security. Silence on security is not simply the absence of speech. In the context of security, silence has meanings and effects. In the simplest terms borrowed from securitisation theory, silence may denote 'audience acceptance' of an instance of securitisation.[30] Staying silent may be a responsible choice in some circumstances. It may be an irresponsible choice in others. It may mean abstaining from talking up threats and insecurities. It may mean not drawing attention to potential security risks, thereby encouraging complacency and leaving the public exposed to danger.[31] There are more subtle political implications too, as Hansen and Bourdieu suggest.

---

27 Hansen (2000), p. 287.
28 Pierre Bourdieu, *Language and Symbolic Power* (Cambridge: Polity, 1992), p. 190.
29 Anonymised interview with former ISC member.
30 Buzan, Wæver, and de Wilde (1998), p. 33.
31 On the distinction between threat and risk see M. V. Rasmussen, *The Risk Society at War: Terror, Technology and Strategy in the Twenty-First Century* (Cambridge: Cambridge University Press, 2006), pp. 1–2.

These do not relate to the judgment of specific instances of securitisation, but are structural and historically institutionalised. Silence may be the result of marginalisation and a lack of choice. And it may confer legitimacy on those who *do* speak security, especially if that means not challenging what they say or their authority to say it. As we will see, these points resonate with the history of British security politics and its structures of power, authority, and legitimacy.

Elite security discourse and silence

Discussion of security was not entirely absent in the Scottish independence debate. In expert circles there was extensive activity. Some of this was behind closed doors, but it led to the publication of several reports. This milieu of security expertise is a good representation of the exclusionary structure of security discourse. Chatham House, for example, has given the world its famous 'Chatham House rule', which allows sensitive matters to be discussed by people who hold sensitive positions under the agreement that it will not be attributed to them in public.

Expertise itself can be exclusionary, but particularly so on security when matters of secrecy and access are so important. The researchers at Chatham House and others such as RUSI often have the expertise, familiarity, access, and resources to offer authoritative analysis. One example is the RUSI report on the costs of relocating Trident.[32] These researchers can be considered security insiders, or at least close to security insiders. No such organisations exist in Scotland. Our ESRC seminar series partly fulfilled this role from a different perspective, but we too followed the exclusionary 'Chatham House rule', for it is often the only basis on which current and former members of the intelligence community, police, military, and civil service can and will speak.

In the context of the independence referendum, should security debate have extended further beyond this milieu of security experts? While their reports were met with media comment, and while there were private interactions between experts and government, there was

---

32 Hugh Chalmers and Malcolm Chalmers, 'Relocation, Relocation, Relocation: Could the UK's Nuclear Force Be Moved after Scottish Independence?', *RUSI Occasional Paper* (2014).

little interaction between this expert discourse and what might be called the 'political class' in Scotland. MSPs, for example, stayed well clear of security matters.

These circumstances call for a qualification of the meaning of security silence. The *de facto* alternative to public debate on security is not complete silence, but a relatively exclusive expert discourse, limited to closed seminars, specialist committees, insiders, and government officials. Not debating security in public means leaving it to the experts.

What does public and political silence on security mean in this context? Based on a reading of Bourdieu and an analysis of the history of British security politics, I argue that security silence confers recognition and legitimacy on those already authorised to speak security. As discussed, the security field is already structured to privilege certain actors: mainly the state, its representatives, and those close to them. Indeed, it is a fundamental feature of modern state sovereignty that the state claims the right and representative power to declare, define, and tackle security threats.

Silence, deference, and recognition in the history of British security politics

The historical conventions of British security politics show how this representative power has been reproduced through practices of exclusion, deference, and recognition. For example, historically, British MPs were actively prevented from asking parliamentary questions of the security services. The standing orders of Parliament ruled all such questions out of order.[33] Until the late 1980s, this exclusion was also manifest in the convention that that the intelligence services did not officially exist, and that by extension they would not subject be to parliamentary oversight as the rest of the executive was.[34]

There are different reasons that explain this tradition, and it still exerts a powerful legacy. It is not only that the state needs to keep hold of intelligence and operational secrets for fear of endangering agents,

---

33 H. Bochel, A. Defty, and J. Kirkpatrick, *Watching the Watchers: Parliament and the Intelligence Services* (Basingstoke: Palgrave Macmillan, 2014), p. 30.

34 Christopher Andrew, *The Defence of the Realm: The Authorized History of MI5* (London: Penguin Books Ltd, 2012).

.

giving away a tactical advantage to enemies, and sometimes hiding wrongdoing and preventing embarrassment. There has also been a general sense that national security is too important for grubby partisan politics. Politicians often repeat the principle that security is the first responsibility of the government. Many MPs remain silent on security, choosing not to speak. Historically, they rarely challenged the security prerogatives of the state (although this is changing). This deference, combined with exclusion through official secrecy and parliamentary rules and conventions, was the basis of the informal constitutional settlement on which the British security state rested, and to a large extent it remains so.

Generally speaking, one reason why MPs do not raise certain topics is a lack of expertise. Intelligence expertise is especially difficult to acquire unless one has been a security 'insider', such as a minister or ISC member. Such expertise cannot be gained overnight. Andrew Defty argues that once the first handful of parliamentarians started engaging in intelligence oversight through their ISC membership in 1994, it took many years of ISC member turnover for even a small number of MPs to feel qualified to speak on such matters.[35] Parliamentary debates on ISC reports remain sparsely attended to this day, with most speakers being current or former members of the ISC itself.[36] Not speaking because of a lack of expertise is not simply exclusion but *self*-exclusion. It is an extension and internalisation of silence; another aspect of the reproduction of existing structures of security authority.

Christopher Andrew, the official historian of MI5, considers that these conventions were recognised, supported, and upheld by Parliament.[37] In contrast, Bochel, Defty and Kirkpatrick show that there were many MPs who rejected this system of silence and tried to undermine it, particularly on the political left, but they were the exception rather than the norm.[38] Either way, these conventions and structures began to give way towards the end of the Cold War, beginning with the 'legalisation' of MI5 through the 1989 Security Service Act, and the creation of a

---

35 Andrew Defty, 'Educating Parliamentarians About Intelligence: The Role of the British Intelligence and Security Committee', *Parliamentary Affairs*, 61, 4 (2008), pp. 621–41 (p. 630).
36 Bochel, Defty, and Kirkpatrick (2014), pp. 93–97.
37 Andrew (2012), p. 753.
38 Bochel, Defty, and Kirkpatrick (2014), p. 33.

modicum of democratic intelligence oversight through the Intelligence and Security Committee in 1994.

The politics of intelligence oversight is only slowly changing, even after the Snowden revelations and recent ISC reform. But there have been challenges to the wider parliamentary convention of deference to security authorities since the 2003 Iraq war. Two broad developments are under way. First, fewer MPs are willing to trust the executive on security matters. Many current and former MPs now seriously regret the trust they placed in Tony Blair and the intelligence apparatus in 2003.[39] The repercussions of this are still playing out. The UK parliamentary vote against intervention in Syria in August 2013 was instructive not only because the Government lost (which can partly be explained by bad parliamentary timing and planning), but because of the type of questions and demands made by many MPs in the debate. The ghosts of Iraq haunted the chamber. Some MPs refused to accept the government's assessment of the intelligence on chemical weapons use in Syria. Some demanded to see raw intelligence material themselves in order to make their own assessments. This may also be an effect of greater availability of information and the rise of open source intelligence, which featured prominently in the debate. Amanda Gookins argues that this 'has led many policymakers to believe they can be their own analysts, rendering them sceptical of the value of intelligence products'.[40] This represents either a misunderstanding or a rejection of the way the intelligence assessment system — and specifically the Joint Intelligence Committee — works through caveats and not facts.[41]

The second development is that the meaning and scope of 'security' has expanded far beyond what it was in 1980s and 1990s. It is no longer limited to defence and intelligence, and hence no longer limited to defence and intelligence oversight. One effect is that it is no longer necessary for parliamentarians to engage directly with secretive intelligence policy in order to deal with 'security'. For example, parliamentary committees

---

39   Paul Flynn, *How to Be an MP* (London: Biteback, 2012), p. 211.

40   Amanda J. Gookins, 'The Role of Intelligence in Policy Making', *SAIS Review of International Affairs*, 28, 1 (2008), 65–74 (p. 68).

41   Lord Butler of Brockwell, *Review of Intelligence on Weapons of Mass Destruction* (London: HMSO, 2004), http://news.bbc.co.uk/nol/shared/bsp/hi/pdfs/14_07_04_butler.pdf

have in the last decade conducted inquiries into food security, energy security, cybersecurity, the meaning of national strategy, border control, surveillance, and communications data retention, to name a few. As a result, there is quantifiably more security speech at Westminster than in previous decades. Most of it does not follow the classic securitising 'grammar' of existential threat and exception.[42] It follows a general trend of security becoming less of an elite discourse, less exceptional and more normal. Parliament, the media, civil society, and the public are more willing to ask difficult questions and less willing to confer legitimacy on security authorities through silence.[43]

Security politics in Scotland by comparison

Holyrood seems isolated from these trends in British security politics. In addition to the general absence of security issues in the independence debate, there has been a lack of activity on anything security-related in the Scottish parliament and its committees. Neither have there been policy statements from the Scottish government or any of the Scottish political parties on contemporaneous scandals such as Snowden's revelations about GCHQ and NSA's surveillance capabilities. It is also difficult to find MSPs who have demonstrated an interest in security matters (one exception is former senior police officer and Labour MSP Graeme Pearson). This is strange given the long-standing politicisation of Trident in Scotland, the depth of anti-Iraq war feeling among the Scottish public (which may be a factor in the collapse of Scottish support for the Labour Party), and the security activism of SNP MPs at Westminster such as Angus Robertson.

The quietude of Holyrood on security might be explained by the fact that security is a 'reserved' matter: MSPs have not needed to engage with security. But it must also be remembered that if Scotland had voted Yes to independence, the Scottish Parliament would quickly have had

---

42   Ole Wæver, 'Politics, Security, Theory', *Security Dialogue*, 42, 4–5 (2011), 465–80 (p. 478).
43   See for example Andrew W. Neal, 'Normalization and Legislative Exceptionalism: Counterterrorist Lawmaking and the Changing Times of Security Emergencies', *International Political Sociology*, 6, 3 (2012), 260–76.

to engage with all hitherto 'reserved' matters, including security and intelligence oversight.

The implications of the silent security dilemma are significant in assessing the politics of security in the Scottish independence debate. The relative silence on the part of the protagonists could be judged as a responsible choice not to politicise security. But it is also an expression and reproduction of existing structures of power, expertise, and authority on security. Silence could reflect a form of marginalisation, specifically a lack of expertise on security amongst the Scottish political class. It is also possible that party leaders silenced discussion of security by their members because it was viewed as too politically risky. Yet although under devolution the Scottish political system has been structurally excluded from security matters, the decline of security deference at Westminster shows that these exclusionary structures are not set in stone. Their legitimacy and reproduction can be undermined by withdrawing the silence and passive deference on which they depend.

Scottish independence would not necessarily mean an end to a deferential security relationship with Whitehall. There would be a complicated and no doubt difficult transition. The Scottish Government White Paper all but accepted that it would take some time to build up independent intelligence and security capabilities, certainly longer than the 18 months between a Yes vote and the proposed independence day of 24 March 2016. It argued that there were precedents for the British state offering security assistance to newly independent states such as its former colonies.[44] The White Paper also suggested that it would be in the security interests of no one for a newly independent Scotland to be immediately ejected from the UK security umbrella and left to its own devices.[45] Instead, it proposed that an independent Scotland would continue to work closely with UK security agencies.[46] Between independence, transition, and continued UK assistance and cooperation, it is difficult to say whether this would have meant a withdrawal of UK intelligence and security capabilities from Scottish territory, such as MI5 field offices (of which are there are apparently two) and GCHQ surveillance capabilities, and what the timetable would have been.

---

44   Scottish Government (2013), p. 263.
45   *Ibid.*, pp. 264–65.
46   *Ibid.*, p. 263.

Conclusion

This chapter has explored the security content of the Scottish independence debate through the idea of a twin dilemma of speaking or not speaking security. It has argued that neither option can be seen as innocent. It has long been argued by the securitisation literature that security speech is constitutive of insecurities and, in turn, constitutive of security policies and practices. Security speech is not only a question of political choice, but also of unintended consequences, because speakers are not necessarily free to construct the meaning of security issues as they wish. They are always in danger of mobilising the legacy of security institutions, pathways, expectations, and meanings. In this sense, following Waever and Huysmans, the choice to speak security is political and comes with responsibilities. This is a good reason for political actors to exercise caution and stay quiet on security, as has been the case for much of the history of security politics in the UK.

The second part of the chapter argued that although security speech poses a dilemma, security silence does also. It not an innocent choice. Silence on security reinforces the authority of the state and to a lesser extent the associated milieu of security experts. Silence translates as deference. Deference confers recognition. Again, this has been the case in much of British political history. Today, despite signs of change at Westminster, security remains an elite discourse. Silence is central to the institutional authority and power of 'security'.

From this perspective, there are two ways to judge the lack of security debate in the Scottish independence campaigns. On the one hand, the lack of debate could be judged positively if it avoided the risk of escalating security talk towards an extreme politics of securitisation. In this sense, protagonists in the independence debate could be judged as acting responsibly. On the other hand, silence on security is not politically neutral. It works as a silent recognition of existing structures of security authority, which reside predominantly with the UK Government. More generally, a lack of public debate on any subject goes against democratic instincts. This symbolic power imbalance on security is something for both sides to consider from the point of view of political strategy should any second Scottish independence referendum arise.

Explaining the reasons for the relative silence of the Scottish political class on security in the independence debate, particularly on the pro-independence side, would require further research. It may have been born out of political calculation and an attempt to triangulate with a cautious electorate. This could be explored in research interviews with referendum campaign strategists, if they were willing to pull back the curtain. The relative silence may also have been a function of the Holyrood's structural marginalisation on security in the devolution settlement and a lack of security expertise among the Scottish political class. The latter is already evident from the CVs of MSPs, almost none of whom have security-related experience. Given existing research on the attitudes of Westminster MPs towards security engagement, it would not be a surprise if research interviews with MSPs revealed a reluctance to engage with security topics.[47] However, this should be offset against the demonstrable security and defence activism of SNP MPs Angus Robertson and Alex Salmond at Westminster (which was true for Robertson even before he became a 'security insider' by joining the ISC in 2015).

The historical example of Westminster illustrates how difficult it is for parliaments to engage with security issues, due to barriers of secrecy, lack of expertise, and conventions of responsibility and caution. Even when parliament has gained new avenues for security scrutiny and oversight, such as the creation and then recent reform of the ISC, it has taken decades for parliament to accrue security expertise, which does not seem to proliferate effectively beyond those directly involved.[48] Yet recent developments show that these hindrances may not be permanent obstacles to greater democratic engagement with security. Westminster offers a lesson, or perhaps an uncertain experiment, on what it means to challenge the historical and constitutional settlement between democracy and security. Parliament has won concessions from the Government by pressing for more intelligence oversight, tabling difficult questions, launching committee inquiries in emerging new areas of security, and staging rebellious votes. Change has happened piecemeal and is largely uncoordinated. As a process it is by no means complete. Its final destination and constitutional implications remain unclear. Increased parliamentary engagement with security is more democratic than silence, but can also be unpredictable, as the 2013 vote

---

47   See Bochel, Defty, and Kirkpatrick (2014).
48   See Defty (2008).

on Syria showed. There is a delicate political path to tread between, on the one hand, speaking out and damaging the conventions of caution and responsibility than can restrain the escalation of security discourse, and, on the other, remaining silent and reinforcing the existing structures of security power and authority.

References

[N.a.], 'Home Secretary Theresa May in Scots Immigration Warning', *BBC News*, 24 March 2012, http://www.bbc.co.uk/news/uk-scotland-scotland-politics-17498681

—, 'Scottish Independence: Warning over "Weakened Military"', *BBC News*, 2 June 2013, http://www.bbc.co.uk/news/uk-scotland-scotland-politics-21776602

—, 'Former Senior Police Officers Clash on Independence Security Report', *STV News*, 26 October 2013, http://stv.tv/news/politics/245660-graeme-pearson-and-allan-burnett-clash-on-independence-security-report/

Andrew, Christopher, *The Defence of the Realm: The Authorized History of MI5* (London: Penguin Books 2012).

Bochel, H., Defty, A., and Kirkpatrick, J., *Watching the Watchers: Parliament and the Intelligence Services* (Basingstoke: Palgrave Macmillan, 2014).

Bourdieu, Pierre, *Language and Symbolic Power*, ed. by John B. Thompson (Cambridge: Polity, 1992).

Buzan, Barry, Wæver, Ole, and de Wilde, Jaap, *Security: A New Framework for Analysis* (Boulder and London: Lynne Rienner, 1998).

Campbell, David, *Writing Security: United States Foreign Policy and the Policies of Identity* (Manchester: Manchester University Press, 1992).

Chalmers, Hugh and Chalmers, Malcolm, 'Relocation, Relocation, Relocation: Could the UK's Nuclear Force Be Moved after Scottish Independence?', *RUSI Occasional Paper* (2014), https://rusi.org/sites/default/files/201408_op_relocation_relocation_relocation.pdf

Chalmers, Malcolm, 'The End of an "Auld Sang": Defence in an Independent Scotland', *RUSI Briefing Paper* (2012).

Chatham House, *Scotland's Independence Referendum* (London: Chatham House, 2013), https://www.chathamhouse.org/research/regions/europe/UK/scotlands-independence-referendum

Ciută, Felix, 'Security and the Problem of Context: A Hermeneutical Critique of Securitisation Theory', *Review of International Studies*, 35 (2009), 301–26, http://dx.doi.org/10.1017/S0260210509008535

Defence Committee, *The Defence Implications of Possible Scottish Independence. Sixth Report of Session 2013–14, Volume 1: Report, Together with an Appendix, Formal Minutes and Oral Evidence* (London: HMSO, 2013), https://books.google.co.uk/books?id=Ck76yDPw1r8C

Defty, Andrew, 'Educating Parliamentarians About Intelligence: The Role of the British Intelligence and Security Committee', *Parliamentary Affairs*, 61 (2008), 621–41, http://dx.doi.org/10.1093/pa/gsn024

Flynn, Paul, *How to Be an MP* (London: Biteback, 2012).

Foreign Affairs Committee, 'Inquiry into Foreign Policy Implications of and for a Separate Scotland' (2012), http://www.parliament.uk/business/committees/committees-a-z/commons-select/foreign-affairs-committee/inquiries1/parliament-2010/scotland

—, *Foreign Policy Considerations for the UK and Scotland in the Event of Scotland Becoming an Independent Country, Sixth Report of Session 2012–2013* (London: HMSO, 2013), http://www.publications.parliament.uk/pa/cm201213/cm select/cmfaff/643/643.pdf

Gookins, Amanda J., 'The Role of Intelligence in Policy Making', *SAIS Review of International Affairs*, 28 (2008), 65–74, https://muse.jhu.edu/article/233086

Gordon, Tom, 'I Admit It: The Man Who Coined the Project Fear Label', *Herald Scotland*, 21 December 2014, http://www.heraldscotland.com/news/13194407.I_admit_it__the_man_who_coined_Project_Fear_label/

Hansen, Lene, 'The Little Mermaid's Silent Security Dilemma and the Absence of Gender in the Copenhagen School', *Millennium-Journal of International Studies*, 29 (2000), 285–306, http://dx.doi.org/10.1177/03058298000290020501

—, 'Reconstructing Desecuritisation: The Normative-Political in the Copenhagen School and Directions for How to Apply It', *Review of International Studies*, 38 (2012), 525–46, http://dx.doi.org/10.1017/S0260210511000581

HM Government, *Scotland Analysis: Cm. 8741: Security* (London: HMSO, 2013), https://www.gov.uk/government/uploads/system/uploads/attachment_data/file/253500/Scotland_analysis_security.pdf

Huysmans, Jef, 'Defining Social Constructivism in Security Studies: The Normative Dilemma of Writing Security', *Alternatives: Global, Local, Political*, 27 (2002), 41–62, http://dx.doi.org/10.1177/03043754020270s104

Johnson, Rebecca, Paterson, Bill, Rogers, Paul, and Walker, William, *No Need to Be Afraid: An Assessment of Possible Threats to Scotland's Security and How They Should Be Addressed* (Biggar: The Jimmy Reid Foundation, 2012).

Lord Butler of Brockwell, *Review of Intelligence on Weapons of Mass Destruction* (London: HMSO, 2004), http://news.bbc.co.uk/nol/shared/bsp/hi/pdfs/14_07_04_butler.pdf

Neal, Andrew W., 'Normalization and Legislative Exceptionalism: Counterterrorist Lawmaking and the Changing Times of Security Emergencies', *International Political Sociology*, 6 (2012), 260–76, http://dx.doi.org/10.1111/j.1749-5687.2012.00163.x

—, 'Fourth Report: Intelligence and Security Oversight in an Independent Scotland' (2014), http://www.centreonconstitutionalchange.ac.uk/sites/default/files/papers/Intelligence and security oversight in an independent scotland 4th REPORT FINAL.pdf

Neal, Andrew W., Kaarbo, Julie, and Raab, Charles, 'ESRC Seminar Series: "Security in Scotland, with or without Constitutional Change"', Centre on Constitutional Change (Edinburgh, 2013–2015), http://www.centre onconstitutionalchange.ac.uk/tags/security-defence

Rasmussen, M. V., *The Risk Society at War: Terror, Technology and Strategy in the Twenty-First Century* (Cambridge: Cambridge University Press, 2006).

Scottish Affairs Committee, *The Referendum on Separation for Scotland: A Defence Force for Scotland-a Conspiracy of Optimism?* (London: House of Commons, 2012).

—, *The Referendum on Separation for Scotland: Terminating Trident — Days or Decades?, Fourth Report of Session 2012–13, Report, Together with Formal Minutes* (London: HMSO, 2012).

—, *The Referendum on Separation for Scotland: How Would Separation Affect Jobs in the Scottish Defence Industry?, Eighth Report of Session 2012–13, Report, Together with Formal Minutes* (London: HMSO, 2013).

Scottish Government, *Scotland's Future: Your Guide to an Independent Scotland* (Edinburgh: Scottish Government, 2013), http://www.gov.scot/resource/0043/00439021.pdf

Wæver, Ole, 'Securitization and Desecuritization', in *On Security*, ed. by Ronnie D. Lipschutz (New York and Chichester: Columbia University Press, 1995), pp. 46–86.

—, 'Securitizing Sectors?: Reply to Eriksson', *Cooperation and Conflict*, 34 (1999), 334–40, http://dx.doi.org/10.1177/00108369921961906

—, 'Politics, Security, Theory', *Security Dialogue*, 42 (2011), 465–80, http://dx.doi.org/10.1177/0967010611418718

Williams, Michael C., 'Words, Images, Enemies: Securitization and International Politics', *International Studies Quarterly*, 47 (2003), 511–31, http://dx.doi.org/10.1046/j.0020-8833.2003.00277.x

Concluding Remarks: The Narrative of Security and Pathways of Transition

Thierry Balzacq

This contribution stands as a conclusion to the book, arguing that both the tone and the content of debates over security during the Scottish referendum were mainly underwritten by narratives which sought to harness the ambiguity of security. It postulates that ambiguity yields different outcomes and empowers different actors. In a context of deep uncertainty, such as that of a referendum over independence, the ambiguous nature of security would tend to impose exacting commitments on the revisionist side, since it has to show that the devil we don't know is better than the devil we know. Hence, perhaps, the hesitancy of the Yes side to prioritise security topics.

https://doi.org/10.11647/OBP.0078.09

If nothing else, debates over independence share one ineradicable trait: they are set in oppositional terms, as a struggle between the status quo and change. But the exact contents and contours of the discussion are often disrupted by the confusion — deliberate or not — between diagnosis and conviction. That is, a referendum over independence is as much about describing the situation now and after (depending of course on the outcome) as it is about defending firmly held beliefs. The reason, I argue, is that any discourse that attempts to make sense of the stakes brought about by the prospects of independence is primarily a 'narrative'. Contributors to this volume show that within the context of a referendum, politics is primarily about the competing narratives that describe a nation's future, vying for prominence. However, because narratives often need to accommodate various demands, they are communicated using ambiguous terms. The result is a blurring effect on the message, which may or may not be desirable but is certainly not without consequences for how people weigh opposing arguments.

Narratives, we know, are designed, not natural, entities. According to Molly Patterson and Kristen Renwick Monroe, a narrative is a 'sequence of events arranged around a problem and designed to restore equilibrium'.[1] Such narratives draw on different 'facts', and, when the facts seem to be the same, they endow them with different meanings, as if meaning depended on how the 'facts' are interpreted. Above all, the primary concern is how best to sideline the opposing argument. Further, while a referendum on independence seeks closure over the destiny of a country, the inherent ambiguity of 'security' does not easily lend itself to serene discussions.[2] This explains, at least partly, why, in times of transition, security discussion often stretches between two heightened narratives: continuity or change.

In this conclusion, my aim is to chart the importance of narratives in understanding the twists and turns undergone by 'security' during the Scottish referendum. I argue that the relatively low profile of this issue during the campaign might have had less to do with its lack of

1   Molly Patterson and Kristen Renwick Monroe, 'Narrative in Political Science', *Annual Review of Political Science*, 1, 1 (1998), 315–31 (p. 324); see also S. R. Shenhav, 'Political Narratives and Political Reality', *International Political Science Review / Revue internationale de science politique*, 27, 3 (2006), 245–62, http://dx.doi.org/10.1146/annurev.polisci.1.1.315
2   Arnold Wolfers, '"National Security" as an Ambiguous Symbol', *Political Science Quarterly*, 67, 4 (1952), 481–502, http://dx.doi.org/10.2307/2145138

political clout than with the difficulty of acknowledging and handling its ambiguous nature. This made it difficult for a single side to enter, let alone dominate, the technicalities of the security field. This conclusion therefore explores three interrelated themes raised by the Scottish referendum as they relate to security: narratives, politics, and ambiguity. In a sense, security expresses a way in which a community weaves different aspects of the present reality into a narrative in order to give meaning to its life.

Narratives

Referenda are always directed toward a goal. That goal divides; its nature varies. Stakeholders can speculate endlessly about the implications of their favourite outcome, but they seldom question the reality of their perspective. In a referendum, opposite sides must put forward their own accounts of what is at stake, what their preferred outcome would be and, more importantly, why it matters. Indeed, 'the chief characteristic of a narrative is that it renders understanding only by connecting (however unstably) parts of a constructed configuration or a social network (however incoherent or unrealizable) composed of symbolic, institutional, and material practices'.[3] Typically, such narratives order events by situating the community in the plot.[4] They are not a mere reporting of facts, though narrators pretend to draw on what is; rather, narratives aim to explain and justify why events should be assembled and organised in a particular way. It is in this sense that Patterson and Monroe argue that 'all narratives are essentially normative'.[5]

The chapters brought together in this book feature one main narrative, that is, 'smallness'. From this narrative, two heated dualities arise: first, strong versus weak Scotland; second, isolated versus integrated Scotland. There is not enough evidence to weigh the power of each component of these two pairs of dualities, but Juliet Kaarbo

---

3   M. R. Somers and G. D. Gibson, 'Reclaiming the Epistemological "Other": Narrative and the Social Constitution of Identity', in *Social Theory and the Politics of Identity*, ed. by Craig Calhoun (Cambridge, MA and Oxford: Wiley, 1994), pp. 37–99.

4   See Wallace Martin, *Recent Theories of Narrative* (Ithaca, NY and London: Cornell University Press, 1986); Robert Coles, *The Call of Stories: Teaching and the Moral Imagination* (Boston: Houghton Mifflin, 1989); Ronald R. Krebs, *Narrative and the Making of US National Security* (Cambridge: Cambridge University Press, 2015).

5   Patterson and Monroe (1998), p. 321.

and Daniel Keneally, on the one hand, and Baldur Thorhallsson and
Alysson J. K. Bailes, on the other, consistently document the invocation
of smallness during the Scottish referendum. The Yes and the No wings
saw in smallness two radically different types of future for Scotland. In
particular, the Yes side interpreted independence as an opportunity to
build a state that would be more sensitive to international rules, while
pursuing an ethical diplomacy of sorts. The No side, by contrast, saw
in smallness a vital vulnerability for Scotland. Overall, the discussion
boiled down to whether smallness was a strength, a risk, or a natural
weakness. For instance, Sandy Hardie's chapter holds that Scottish
independence would have diminished Scotland's ability to protect
its citizens, in particular abroad. It is not feasible here to bring all the
different aspects of this argument into sharper relief, but I can sketch
a possible counter-approach that may diminish its force. Part of
the difficulty with this view is that it depends upon an independent
Scotland pursuing the same goals and foreign policies as the UK, which
make UK citizens one of the prized targets for some violent groups the
world over. But Hardie implicitly captures an important element that
undergirds any debate over a referendum, namely the issue of time. In
fact, referenda show in a particularly acute form how it is tricky to know
what will happen once a state is independent. It might be that all really
rests with the capacity of the political elite to adapt swiftly to the new
environment, but adaptation is harder when the elite lacks expertise
in the domain at stake or is unprepared. Matters might even be worse
if the former 'shelter' decides to punish the newly independent entity.
That said, given the range of shared interests, it remains uncertain as to
whether the UK would have taken an aggressive stance with a newly
independent Scotland. In times of global interdependence, resentment
does not necessarily result in revenge.

Debates on small states have waxed and waned, but they generally
involve matters of resources, visibility, and influence. The now
voluminous literature on small states teaches us, among other things, that
the success or failure of small states in the international arena depends
on a host of factors for which size alone cannot account.[6] Perhaps this

---

6   For a start, see *inter alia*, C. Clarke and T. Payne, *Politics. Security and Development
     in Small States* (London: Allen & Unwin, 1987); Tom Crowards, 'Defining the
     Category of "Small States"', *Journal of International Development*, 14, 2 (2002), 143–

is why, as Thorhallsson and Bailes argue, in addition to interesting similarities with Nordic states, Scotland's case stirred up challenges which had less to do with its smallness than with the newness of the situation its independence would have created both for itself and for the international system. A dominant feature of international systems is that they abhor uncertainty. In this sense, the primary challenge that a narrative which supports independence confronts is to relieve the uncertainty that any change of such a magnitude creates. So whereas the No side could safely draw on the uncertainty sparked by what an independent Scotland would have to struggle against, the Yes side could only emphasise the view that the No wing occluded the long-term benefits of independence. This involves different ways — with respect to security — of: defining the problem, characterising choices, prioritising options, justifying strategies, assessing capacities (e.g., expertise and institutional robustness), and outlining solutions. The struggles around these challenges contribute to defining the politics of the referendum.

Politics

A second conversation that the book opens concerns the — relatively little — space afforded to security during the campaign. Though some chapters dig into the reasons for this marginalisation, they also note that the referendum did not entirely confirm the theoretical tendency within security studies to draw a line between normal politics and security politics.[7] This does not mean security and politics always enter

---

79, http://dx.doi.org/10.1002/jid.860; Peter J. Katzenstein, 'Small States and Small States Revisited', *New Political Economy*, 8, 1 (2003), 9–30, https://doi.org/10.1080/1 356346032000078705; Olav F. Knudsen, 'Small States, Latent and Extant: Towards a General Perspective', *Journal of International relations and Development*, 5, 2 (2002), 182–98, http://ams.hi.is/wp-content/uploads/2014/03/Small_States_Latent_Extant. pdf; Keohane (1969).

7   This can mainly be found in the Copenhagen School's version of securitisation theory. See, *inter alia*, Buzan, Wæver, and de Wilde (1998). For an extensive review of the different strands of securitisation theory and their treatment of the relations between security and politics, see: T. Balzacq and others, 'What Kind of Theory — If Any — Is Securitization?', *International Relations*, 29, 1 (2014), 96–136, http://dx.doi.org/10.1177/0047117814526606; T. Balzacq, S. Leonard, and J. Ruzicka, '"Securitization" Revisited: Theory and Cases', *International Relations*, 30, 4 (2015), pp. 494–531, http://dx.doi.org/10.1177/0047117815596590

into each other's orbit. Instead, it points to the view that the referendum was an intriguing case to study, as it challenged some of the premises students and scholars have about security. Andrew Neal, for instance, 'compares the quietude of security politics in Scotland with the history and transformation of politics at Westminster'. He points out that, of the 670 pages of the Scottish Government's White Paper, only 6 were devoted to security and intelligence. Of course, quantity is hardly the only reliable testimony of importance or priority, but it provides us with clues as to why security was not as widely debated as could have been expected. Perhaps the referendum sheds light on the undefined *work* of security rather than on the politics of security as such. It may in fact be argued that security's powerful ability to alter the mood and terms of the debate was profitably mobilised neither by the Yes nor by the No wing. Instead, security rode the tension between Yes and No, but did not tilt the balance in favour of either of the two sides.

Neal assesses the lack of security discourse in two ways. One is an apparently responsible silence, which prevented the debate veering into securitisation as an exceptional kind of politics. The second, he says, might have been a strategy of avoiding discussions of security at length, because they would have potentially disclosed the superior expertise of Westminster on the issue. In my view, the second part of the argument has more leverage. In many ways, this is confirmed by Colin Atkinson, Nick Brooke and Brian Harris' analysis of the Scottish Government's proposals on intelligence accountability.[8] But what are we to conclude from the apparently insufficient expertise of the Scottish political elite? Not that it could not live up to the challenges brought by potential security issues. Even those countries most learned about security do not always perform at the level expected. Nor that Scotland would have been more insecure out of the UK. The truth is, nobody knows. Pathways either to security or insecurity are numerous and not always predictable. Yet, what we know is that the Yes proposals on security exhibited several shortcomings. For instance, they did not sufficiently depart from the existing mechanisms of the current UK political settlement. This means, in other words, that the Yes side

---

8   See also Chapter 6 of this volume.

proclaimed the demise of processes to which it aimed to contribute. It wanted to sever ties with one specific shelter, but could only do so by acknowledging that a shelter was needed, the nature of which was to be negotiated after the referendum. The No side, on the other hand, relied on mechanisms over which it had little control. It wanted to remain inside the UK, but had to acknowledge that this meant a lack of security agency on the Scottish side, that is, a position of security dependence *vis-à-vis* London. Between the Yes and the No sides, then, sit different possibilities of how Scottish agency could have operated on security. A notable benefit of this book is to help us understand in what ways specific security narratives are able to produce Scotland as either an object or a subject of security.

Ambiguity

In general, parties involved in referendum campaigns need to display sureness regarding the most uncertain of events. The problem, however, is that security discussions only happen when there are questions about the current state of a polity, that is, when there is a form of uncertainty. Moreover, in the context of a referendum regarding a nation's independence, security might quickly become a point of contention for the different stakeholders. Because of its emotional weight, most actors would presumably make whatever effort they could to tap into security's power to catch people's attention. Be that as it may, in the Scottish case, the Yes side had to bear most of the burden of proof, because it had to convince people that Scotland would be better off without what the No side described as the 'UK shelter'.[9] The problem, however, is that it is difficult to assess the extent to which the future will be better than the present, under contingent circumstances.[10] In this light, the familiar security discourse maintained by the No side appeared more comforting, if not reassuring, than the leap into the unknown demanded by the Yes campaign. A referendum does not only happen in a given cultural and historical context, but it also creates its own context, in particular by betting on the future of the nation. In

9   See Chapter 2 in this volume.
10   A point well made by Hugh Bochel and Andrew Defty in Chapter 4 of this book.

this light, recourse to security talk appears a risky strategy, because of the evolving conditions of the discussion. While the Yes side required people to be open to a different, new, and unpredictable order, the No campaign held that order and security derived from remaining under an institutional blanket whose strengths (and flaws) had been tested. This is to say, the Yes side was unable to cut short the ambiguities inherent in security and close the gaps.[11]

Whether we like it or not, security arguments with a higher chance to succeed are usually those which offer a predetermined course, disqualify 'abstract principles', and privilege 'finite relations'.[12] The most important point is that securitisation, to this way of thinking, serves to close options and minimise political contingency. During the debates surrounding the Scottish referendum, for instance, the No side began with the presumptive reliability of the UK polity and drew upon uncertainty in order to securitise independence, whereas the Yes campaign, by proposing to revise previously established relations, had the indirect effect of opening the Scottish political community to unpredictability, making it harder to stimulate a broader public commitment.

The politics of independence, then, through which the Yes and the No sides represented their views, may be looked upon as a politics of dealing with ambiguity in security. In any case, the debate between Yes and No was a matter of degree. The more uncertainty was portrayed as a problem, the more a position leaned towards No. The greater the predominance of new, though indeterminate relations, the more the approach leaned towards Yes. Thus, in trying to intuit why security was dealt with or not addressed in the way it was, we need explicitly to engage the management of ambiguity by each side, since the difficulty of 'speaking security' owes something to the ambiguity that always looms in the background of security talks.

---

11   See Charles Raab's contribution in Chapter 3 of this volume.
12   Willem de Lint and Sirpa Virta, 'Security in Ambiguity Towards a Radical Security Politics', *Theoretical Criminology*, 8, 4 (2004), 465–89 (p. 474), http://dx.doi.org/10.1177/1362480604046660

Conclusion

My focus in these concluding remarks has been to identify the main lines that might enable us to connect the dots between the chapters assembled in this book. I would now like to raise a point which I think could constitute a next step in the discussion, because it matters beyond the Scottish case: the ethics of independence. I know the issue is slippery, but would it not be productive to ask: under what conditions is independence ethically defensible? Or, put differently, are all the claims made about or against secession 'right'? Is there a just secession, of sorts? What does secession teach us about the moral standing of group agents? These are not the same as whether independence from a polity in order to set up a new state is materially warranted or not. Though they are separate questions, the second — i.e. whether secession is practically feasible — is somewhat nested in the first group of questions. With various entities across Europe aspiring to independence, scholars would be well advised to develop more robust works on the ethics of independence.[13] This is even more urgent for those who claim to be working within critical approaches to security, wherein issues of emancipation and agency are so central. In this sense, the chapters brought together here constitute a viable first step towards such a task, for without a fine grained analysis of the meaning of different arguments, it is much more difficult to assess the ethical issues they generate.

---

13 A nice introduction can be found here: Allen Buchanan, *Secession: The Morality of Political Divorce from Fort Sumter to Lithuania and Quebec* (Boulder: Westview Press, 1991). Some advanced works are: Cass R. Sunstein, 'Constitutionalism and Secession', *The University of Chicago Law Review*, 58, 2 (1991), 633–70, http://dx.doi.org/10.2307/1599969; Avishai Margalit and Joseph Raz, 'National Self-Determination', *The Journal of Philosophy*, 87, 9 (1990), 439–61, http://dx.doi.org/10.2307/2026968; Daniel Weinstock, 'Constitutionalizing the Right to Secede', *Journal of Political Philosophy*, 9, 2 (2001), 182–203, http://dx.doi.org/10.1111/1467-9760.00124

References

Balzacq, T., Guzzini, S., Williams, M. C., Waever, O., and Patomaki, H., 'What Kind of Theory — If Any — Is Securitization?', *International Relations*, 29 (2014), 96–136, http://dx.doi.org/10.1177/0047117814526606

—, Leonard, S., and Ruzicka, J., '"Securitization" Revisited: Theory and Cases', *International Relations*, 30 (2015), pp. 494–531, http://dx.doi.org/10.1177/0047117815596590

Buchanan, Allen, *Secession: The Morality of Political Divorce from Fort Sumter to Lithuania and Quebec* (Boulder: Westview Press, 1991).

Buzan, Barry, Wæver, Ole, and de Wilde, Jaap, *Security: A New Framework for Analysis* (Boulder and London: Lynne Rienner, 1998).

Clarke, C. and Payne, T., eds., *Politics. Security and Development in Small States* (London: Allen and Unwin, 1987).

Coles, Robert, *The Call of Stories: Teaching and the Moral Imagination* (Boston: Houghton Mifflin, 1989).

Crowards, Tom, 'Defining the Category of "Small States"', *Journal of International Development*, 14 (2002), 143–79, http://dx.doi.org/10.1002/jid.860

Katzenstein, Peter J., 'Small States and Small States Revisited', *New Political Economy*, 8 (2003), 9–30, http://doi.org/10.1080/1356346032000078705

Keohane, Robert O., 'Lilliputians' Dilemmas: Small States in International Politics', *International Organization*, 23 (1969), 291–310, https://doi.org/10.1017/S002081830003160X

Knudsen, Olav F., 'Small States, Latent and Extant: Towards a General Perspective', *Journal of International Relations and Development*, 5 (2002), 182–98, http://ams.hi.is/wp-content/uploads/2014/03/Small_States_Latent_Extant.pdf

Krebs, Ronald R., *Narrative and the Making of US National Security* (Cambridge: Cambridge University Press, 2015), http://dx.doi.org/10.1017/cbo9781316218969.015

Lint, Willem de and Virta, Sirpa, 'Security in Ambiguity Towards a Radical Security Politics', *Theoretical Criminology*, 8 (2004), 465–89, http://dx.doi.org/10.1177/1362480604046660

Margalit, Avishai and Raz, Joseph, 'National Self-Determination', *The Journal of Philosophy*, 87 (1990), 439–61, http://dx.doi.org/10.2307/2026968

Martin, Wallace, *Recent Theories of Narrative* (Ithaca, NY and London: Cornell University Press, 1986).

Patterson, Molly and Monroe, Kristen Renwick, 'Narrative in Political Science', *Annual Review of Political Science*, 1 (1998), 315–31, http://dx.doi.org/10.1146/annurev.polisci.1.1.315

Shenhav, S. R., 'Political Narratives and Political Reality', *International Political Science Review / Revue internationale de science politique*, 27 (2006), 245–62, http://dx.doi.org/10.1177/0192512106064474

Somers, M. R. and Gibson, G. D., 'Reclaiming the Epistemological 'Other': Narrative and the Social Constitution of Identity', in *Social Theory and the Politics of Identity*, ed. by Craig Calhoun (Cambridge, MA and Oxford: Wiley, 1994), pp. 37–99.

Sunstein, Cass R., 'Constitutionalism and Secession', *The University of Chicago Law Review*, 58 (1991), 633–70, http://dx.doi.org/10.2307/1599969

Weinstock, Daniel, 'Constitutionalizing the Right to Secede', *Journal of Political Philosophy*, 9 (2001), 182–203, http://dx.doi.org/10.1111/1467-9760.00124

Wolfers, Arnold, '"National Security" as an Ambiguous Symbol', *Political Science Quarterly*, 67 (1952), 481–502, http://dx.doi.org/10.2307/2145138

This book need not end here…

At Open Book Publishers, we are changing the nature of the traditional academic book. The title you have just read will not be left on a library shelf, but will be accessed online by hundreds of readers each month across the globe. OBP publishes only the best academic work: each title passes through a rigorous peer-review process. We make all our books free to read online so that students, researchers and members of the public who can't afford a printed edition will have access to the same ideas.
This book and additional content is available at:
https://www.openbookpublishers.com/product/524

Customize

Personalize your copy of this book or design new books using OBP and third-party material. Take chapters or whole books from our published list and make a special edition, a new anthology or an illuminating coursepack. Each customized edition will be produced as a paperback and a downloadable PDF. Find out more at:
https://www.openbookpublishers.com/section/59/1

Donate

If you enjoyed this book, and feel that research like this should be available to all readers, regardless of their income, please think about donating to us. We do not operate for profit and all donations, as with all other revenue we generate, will be used to finance new Open Access publications.
https://www.openbookpublishers.com/section/13/1/support-us

Like Open Book Publishers [f]

Follow @OpenBookPublish

Read more at the Open Book Publishers **BLOG**

You may also be interested in:

The Infrastructure Finance Challenge
Edited by Ingo Walter

https://www.openbookpublishers.com/product/544

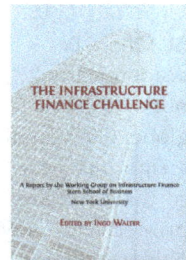

**The Universal Declaration of Human Rights
in the 21st Century**
Edited by Gordon Brown

https://www.openbookpublishers.com/product/467

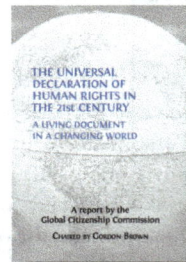

**Democracy and Power
The Delhi Lectures**
Noam Chomsky. Introduction by Jean Drèze

https://www.openbookpublishers.com/product/300

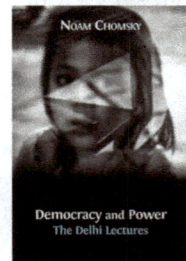

Peace and Democratic Society
Edited by Amartya Sen

http://www.openbookpublishers.com/product/78

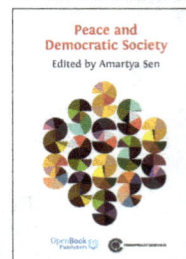

www.ingramcontent.com/pod-product-compliance
Lightning Source LLC
Chambersburg PA
CBHW070400270326
41926CB00014B/2638